W9-BNA-300

WILLIAM SHAKESPEARE was born in Stratford-upon-Avon in April, 1564, and his birth is traditionally celebrated on April 23. The facts of his life, known from surviving documents, are sparse. He was one of eight children born to John Shakespeare, a merchant of some standing in his community. William probably went to the King's New School in Stratford, but he had no university education. In November 1582, at the age of eighteen, he married Anne Hathaway, eight years his senior, who was pregnant with their first child, Susanna. She was born on May 26, 1583. Twins, a boy, Hamnet (who would die at age eleven), and a girl, Judith, were born in 1585. By 1592 Shakespeare had gone to London, working as an actor and already known as a playwright. A rival dramatist, Robert Greene, referred to him as "an upstart crow, beautified with our feathers." Shakespeare became a principal shareholder and playwright of the successful acting troupe the Lord Chamberlain's men (later, under James I, called the King's men). In 1599 the Lord Chamberlain's men built and occupied the Globe Theatre in Southwark near the Thames River. Here many of Shakespeare's plays were performed by the most famous actors of his time, including Richard Burbage, Will Kempe, and Robert Armin. In addition to his 37 plays, Shakespeare had a hand in others, including *Sir Thomas More* and *The Two Noble Kinsmen*, and he wrote poems, including *Venus and Adonis* and *The Rape of Lucrece*. His 154 sonnets were published, probably without his authorization, in 1609. In 1611 or 1612 he gave up his lodgings in London and devoted more and more of his time to retirement in Stratford, though he continued writing such plays as *The Tempest* and *Henry VIII* until about 1613. He died on April 23, 1616, and was buried in Holy Trinity Church, Stratford. No collected edition of his plays was published during his lifetime, but in 1623 two members of his acting company, John Heminges and Henry Condell, published the great collection now called the First Folio.

**Bantam Shakespeare
The Complete Works—29 Volumes
Edited by David Bevington
With forewords by Joseph Papp on the plays**

The Poems: Venus and Adonis, The Rape of Lucrece, The
Phoenix and Turtle, A Lover's Complaint,
the Sonnets

Antony and Cleopatra	*The Merchant of Venice*
As You Like It	*A Midsummer Night's Dream*
The Comedy of Errors	*Much Ado about Nothing*
Hamlet	*Othello*
Henry IV, Part One	*Richard II*
Henry IV, Part Two	*Richard III*
Henry V	*Romeo and Juliet*
Julius Caesar	*The Taming of the Shrew*
King Lear	*The Tempest*
Macbeth	*Twelfth Night*

Together in one volume:

Henry VI, Parts One, Two, and Three
King John and Henry VIII
*Measure for Measure, All's Well that Ends Well, and
Troilus and Cressida*
Three Early Comedies: Love's Labor's Lost, The Two
Gentlemen of Verona, The Merry
Wives of Windsor
Three Classical Tragedies: Titus Andronicus, Timon
of Athens, Coriolanus
The Late Romances: Pericles, Cymbeline, The Winter's
Tale, The Tempest

Two collections:

Four Comedies: The Taming of the Shrew, A Midsummer
Night's Dream, The Merchant of Venice,
Twelfth Night
Four Tragedies: Hamlet, Othello, King Lear, Macbeth

William Shakespeare

KING LEAR

Edited by
David Bevington

David Scott Kastan,
James Hammersmith,
and Robert Kean Turner,
Associate Editors

With a Foreword by
Joseph Papp

BANTAM BOOKS
NEW YORK·TORONTO·LONDON·SYDNEY·AUCKLAND

KING LEAR

A Bantam Book | published by arrangement
with Scott, Foresman and Company

PRINTING HISTORY
Scott, Foresman edition published | January 1980
Bantam edition, with newly edited text and substantially revised,
edited, and amplified notes, introductions, and other
materials, published | February 1988
Valuable advice on staging matters has been
provided by Richard Hosley
Collations checked by Eric Rasmussen
Additional editorial assistance by Claire McEachern

All rights reserved.
Copyright © 1980, 1973, 1961, 1951 by Scott, Foresman and Company.
Foreword copyright © 1988 by New York Shakespeare Festival.
Cover art copyright © 1988 by Mark English.
This edition copyright © 1988 by Bantam Books.
Revisions and annotations to Shakespeare text and its footnotes and
textual notes, Shakespeare's Sources essay and notes for the source,
and the play introduction copyright © 1988 by David Bevington.
The Playhouse text copyright © 1988 by David Bevington.
Performance history copyright © 1988
by David Bevington and David Scott Kastan.
Annotated bibliography copyright © 1988 by
David Scott Kastan and James Shapiro.
Memorable Lines copyright © 1988 by Bantam Books.
Library of Congress Catalog Card Number: 87-24093.
No part of this book may be reproduced or transmitted
in any form or by any means, electronic or mechanical,
including photocopying, recording, or by any information
storage and retrieval system, without permission
in writing from the publisher.
For information address: Bantam Books.

If you purchased this book without a cover you should be aware that this book is stolen
property. It was reported as "unsold and destroyed" to the publisher and neither the
author nor the publisher has received any payment for this "stripped book."

ISBN 0-553-21297-4
Published simultaneously in the United States and Canada

Bantam Books are published by Bantam Books, a division of Bantam Doubleday Dell Publishing
Group, Inc. Its trademark, consisting of the words "Bantam Books" and the portrayal of a
rooster, is Registered in U.S. Patent and Trademark Office and in other countries. Marca
Registrada. Bantam Books, 666 Fifth Avenue, New York, New York 10103.

PRINTED IN THE UNITED STATES OF AMERICA

OPM   15 14 13 12 11 10 9 8 7 6 5

Contents

Foreword

It's hard to imagine, but Shakespeare wrote all of his plays with a quill pen, a goose feather whose hard end had to be sharpened frequently. How many times did he scrape the dull end to a point with his knife, dip it into the inkwell, and bring up, dripping wet, those wonderful words and ideas that are known all over the world?

In the age of word processors, typewriters, and ballpoint pens, we have almost forgotten the meaning of the word "blot." Yet when I went to school, in the 1930s, my classmates and I knew all too well what an inkblot from the metal-tipped pens we used would do to a nice clean page of a test paper, and we groaned whenever a splotch fell across the sheet. Most of us finished the school day with ink-stained fingers; those who were less careful also went home with ink-stained shirts, which were almost impossible to get clean.

When I think about how long it took me to write the simplest composition with a metal-tipped pen and ink, I can only marvel at how many plays Shakespeare scratched out with his goose-feather quill pen, year after year. Imagine him walking down one of the narrow cobblestoned streets of London, or perhaps drinking a pint of beer in his local alehouse. Suddenly his mind catches fire with an idea, or a sentence, or a previously elusive phrase. He is burning with impatience to write it down—but because he doesn't have a ballpoint pen or even a pencil in his pocket, he has to keep the idea in his head until he can get to his quill and parchment.

He rushes back to his lodgings on Silver Street, ignoring the vendors hawking brooms, the coaches clattering by, the piteous wails of beggars and prisoners. Bounding up the stairs, he snatches his quill and starts to write furiously, not even bothering to light a candle against the dusk. "To be, or not to be," he scrawls, "that is the—." But the quill point has gone dull, the letters have fattened out illegibly, and in the middle of writing one of the most famous passages in the history of dramatic literature, Shakespeare has to stop to sharpen his pen.

Taking a deep breath, he lights a candle now that it's dark, sits down, and begins again. By the time the candle has burned out and the noisy apprentices of his French Huguenot landlord have quieted down, Shakespeare has finished Act 3 of *Hamlet* with scarcely a blot.

Early the next morning, he hurries through the fog of a London summer morning to the rooms of his colleague Richard Burbage, the actor for whom the role of Hamlet is being written. He finds Burbage asleep and snoring loudly, sprawled across his straw mattress. Not only had the actor performed in *Henry V* the previous afternoon, but he had then gone out carousing all night with some friends who had come to the performance.

Shakespeare shakes his friend awake, until, bleary-eyed, Burbage sits up in his bed. "Dammit, Will," he grumbles, "can't you let an honest man sleep?" But the playwright, his eyes shining and the words tumbling out of his mouth, says, "Shut up and listen—tell me what you think of *this*!"

He begins to read to the still half-asleep Burbage, pacing around the room as he speaks. ". . . Whether 'tis nobler in the mind to suffer the slings and arrows of outrageous fortune—"

Burbage interrupts, suddenly wide awake, "That's excellent, very good, 'the slings and arrows of outrageous fortune,' yes, I think it will work quite well. . . ." He takes the parchment from Shakespeare and murmurs the lines to himself, slowly at first but with growing excitement.

The sun is just coming up, and the words of one of Shakespeare's most famous soliloquies are being uttered for the first time by the first actor ever to bring Hamlet to life. It must have been an exhilarating moment.

Shakespeare wrote most of his plays to be performed live by the actor Richard Burbage and the rest of the Lord Chamberlain's men (later the King's men). Today, however, our first encounter with the plays is usually in the form of the printed word. And there is no question that reading Shakespeare for the first time isn't easy. His plays aren't comic books or magazines or the dime-store detective novels I read when I was young. A lot of his sentences are complex. Many of his words are no longer used in our everyday speech. His profound thoughts are often condensed into poetry, which is not as straightforward as prose.

Yet when you hear the words spoken aloud, a lot of the language may strike you as unexpectedly modern. For Shakespeare's plays, like any dramatic work, weren't really meant to be read; they were meant to be spoken, seen, and performed. It's amazing how lines that are so troublesome in print can flow so naturally and easily when spoken.

I think it was precisely this music that first fascinated me. When I was growing up, Shakespeare was a stranger to me. I had no particular interest in him, for I was from a different cultural tradition. It never occurred to me that his plays might be more than just something to "get through" in school, like science or math or the physical education requirement we had to fulfill. My passions then were movies, radio, and vaudeville—certainly not Elizabethan drama.

I was, however, fascinated by words and language. Because I grew up in a home where Yiddish was spoken, and English was only a second language, I was acutely sensitive to the musical sounds of different languages and had an ear for lilt and cadence and rhythm in the spoken word. And so I loved reciting poems and speeches even as a very young child. In first grade I learned lots of short nature verses—"Who has seen the wind?," one of them began. My first foray into drama was playing the role of Scrooge in Charles Dickens's *A Christmas Carol* when I was eight years old. I liked summoning all the scorn and coldness I possessed and putting them into the words, "Bah, humbug!"

From there I moved on to longer and more famous poems and other works by writers of the 1930s. Then, in junior high school, I made my first acquaintance with Shakespeare through his play *Julius Caesar*. Our teacher, Miss McKay, assigned the class a passage to memorize from the opening scene of the play, the one that begins "Wherefore rejoice? What conquest brings he home?" The passage seemed so wonderfully theatrical and alive to me, and the experience of memorizing and reciting it was so much fun, that I went on to memorize another speech from the play on my own.

I chose Mark Antony's address to the crowd in Act 3,

scene 2, which struck me then as incredibly high drama.
Even today, when I speak the words, I feel the same thrill I
did that first time. There is the strong and athletic Antony
descending from the raised pulpit where he has been speaking, right into the midst of a crowded Roman square. Holding the torn and bloody cloak of the murdered Julius
Caesar in his hand, he begins to speak to the people of
Rome:

> If you have tears, prepare to shed them now.
> You all do know this mantle. I remember
> The first time ever Caesar put it on;
> 'Twas on a summer's evening in his tent,
> That day he overcame the Nervii.
> Look, in this place ran Cassius' dagger through.
> See what a rent the envious Casca made.
> Through this the well-belovèd Brutus stabbed,
> And as he plucked his cursèd steel away,
> Mark how the blood of Caesar followed it,
> As rushing out of doors to be resolved
> If Brutus so unkindly knocked or no;
> For Brutus, as you know, was Caesar's angel.
> Judge, O you gods, how dearly Caesar loved him!
> This was the most unkindest cut of all . . .

I'm not sure now that I even knew Shakespeare had written a lot of other plays, or that he was considered "time-
less," "universal," or "classic"—but I knew a good speech
when I heard one, and I found the splendid rhythms of
Antony's rhetoric as exciting as anything I'd ever come
across.

Fifty years later, I still feel that way. Hearing good actors
speak Shakespeare gracefully and naturally is a wonderful
experience, unlike any other I know. There's a satisfying
fullness to the spoken word that the printed page just can't
convey. This is why seeing the plays of Shakespeare performed live in a theater is the best way to appreciate them.
If you can't do that, listening to sound recordings or watch-
ing film versions of the plays is the next best thing.

But if you do start with the printed word, use the play as a
script. Be an actor yourself and say the lines out loud. Don't
worry too much at first about words you don't immediately
understand. Look them up in the footnotes or a dictionary,

but don't spend too much time on this. It is more profitable (and fun) to get the sense of a passage and sing it out. Speak naturally, almost as if you were talking to a friend, but be sure to enunciate the words properly. You'll be surprised at how much you understand simply by speaking the speech "trippingly on the tongue," as Hamlet advises the Players.

You might start, as I once did, with a speech from *Julius Caesar*, in which the tribune (city official) Marullus scolds the commoners for transferring their loyalties so quickly from the defeated and murdered general Pompey to the newly victorious Julius Caesar:

> Wherefore rejoice? What conquest brings he home?
> What tributaries follow him to Rome
> To grace in captive bonds his chariot wheels?
> You blocks, you stones, you worse than senseless
>   things!
> O you hard hearts, you cruel men of Rome,
> Knew you not Pompey? Many a time and oft
> Have you climbed up to walls and battlements,
> To towers and windows, yea, to chimney tops,
> Your infants in your arms, and there have sat
> The livelong day, with patient expectation,
> To see great Pompey pass the streets of Rome.

With the exception of one or two words like "wherefore" (which means "why," not "where"), "tributaries" (which means "captives"), and "patient expectation" (which means patient waiting), the meaning and emotions of this speech can be easily understood.

From here you can go on to dialogues or other more challenging scenes. Although you may stumble over unaccustomed phrases or unfamiliar words at first, and even fall flat when you're crossing some particularly rocky passages, pick yourself up and stay with it. Remember that it takes time to feel at home with anything new. Soon you'll come to recognize Shakespeare's unique sense of humor and way of saying things as easily as you recognize a friend's laughter.

And then it will just be a matter of choosing which one of Shakespeare's plays you want to tackle next. As a true fan of his, you'll find that you're constantly learning from his plays. It's a journey of discovery that you can continue for the rest of your life. For no matter how many times you read or see a particular play, there will always be something new there that you won't have noticed before.

Why do so many thousands of people get hooked on Shakespeare and develop a habit that lasts a lifetime? What can he really say to us today, in a world filled with inventions and problems he never could have imagined? And how do you get past his special language and difficult sentence structure to understand him?

The best way to answer these questions is to go see a live production. You might not know much about Shakespeare, or much about the theater, but when you watch actors performing one of his plays on the stage, it will soon become clear to you why people get so excited about a playwright who lived hundreds of years ago.

For the story—what's happening in the play—is the most accessible part of Shakespeare. In *A Midsummer Night's Dream*, for example, you can immediately understand the situation: a girl is chasing a guy who's chasing a girl who's chasing another guy. No wonder *A Midsummer Night's Dream* is one of the most popular of Shakespeare's plays: it's about one of the world's most popular pastimes—falling in love.

But the course of true love never did run smooth, as the young suitor Lysander says. Often in Shakespeare's comedies the girl whom the guy loves doesn't love him back, or she loves him but he loves someone else. In *The Two Gentlemen of Verona*, Julia loves Proteus, Proteus loves Sylvia, and Sylvia loves Valentine, who is Proteus's best friend. In the end, of course, true love prevails, but not without lots of complications along the way.

For in all of his plays—comedies, histories, and tragedies—Shakespeare is showing you human nature. His characters act and react in the most extraordinary ways—and sometimes in the most incomprehensible ways. People are always trying to find motivations for what a character does. They ask, "Why does Iago want to destroy Othello?"

The answer, to me, is very simple—because that's the way Iago is. That's just his nature. Shakespeare doesn't explain his characters; he sets them in motion—and away they go. He doesn't worry about whether they're likable or not. He's interested in interesting people, and his most fascinating characters are those who are unpredictable. If you lean back in your chair early on in one of his plays, thinking you've figured out what Iago or Shylock (in *The Merchant of Venice*) is up to, don't be too sure—because that great judge of human nature, Shakespeare, will surprise you every time.

He is just as wily in the way he structures a play. In *Macbeth*, a comic scene is suddenly introduced just after the bloodiest and most treacherous slaughter imaginable, of a guest and king by his host and subject, when in comes a drunk porter who has to go to the bathroom. Shakespeare is tickling your emotions by bringing a stand-up comic on-stage right on the heels of a savage murder.

It has taken me thirty years to understand even some of these things, and so I'm not suggesting that Shakespeare is immediately understandable. I've gotten to know him not through theory but through practice, the practice of the *living* Shakespeare—the playwright of the theater.

Of course the plays are a great achievement of dramatic literature, and they should be studied and analyzed in schools and universities. But you must always remember, when reading all the words *about* the playwright and his plays, that *Shakespeare's* words came first and that in the end there is nothing greater than a single actor on the stage speaking the lines of Shakespeare.

Everything important that I know about Shakespeare comes from the practical business of producing and directing his plays in the theater. The task of classifying, criticizing, and editing Shakespeare's printed works I happily leave to others. For me, his plays really do live on the stage, not on the page. That is what he wrote them for and that is how they are best appreciated.

Although Shakespeare lived and wrote hundreds of years ago, his name rolls off my tongue as if he were my brother. As a producer and director, I feel that there is a professional relationship between us that spans the centuries. As a human being, I feel that Shakespeare has enriched my understanding of life immeasurably. I hope you'll let him do the same for you.

❖

Once it gets past the hurdle of the opening scene, *King Lear* moves quickly and inexorably to "the promised end." But the first scene poses a real problem, because everything in it seems so arbitrary. Why has Lear decided to divide his kingdom? Why are his daughters Goneril and Regan playing up to him? Why is the youngest, Cordelia, so stiff-necked? We watch perplexed as this super-egotist of a king disowns his youngest daughter, banishes his most loyal supporter, Kent, and stomps around the stage in a childish rage that no one can appease. We feel a sense of imminent doom as we see Lear so consumed with the sense of his own power that he fails to realize the terrible consequences of giving it away.

Blinded by his anger, he can't see properly and so proceeds headlong on his disastrous course. Aside from his inability to judge his daughters accurately, Lear is also not wise enough to know that once he's abdicated his power, he can never get it back. For him to imagine that he can hold on to the trappings of power—his one hundred knights, for example—after he has given away its substance is terribly naive and unworldly. Shakespeare gives Lear the Fool to remind him constantly of the terrible mistake he made in giving everything away. "Dost thou call me fool, boy?" Lear asks; "All thy other titles thou hast given away; that thou wast born with," the Fool replies. Indeed, as the Fool observes, Lear is the real fool of the play.

King Lear is a play about the problem of getting older but not wiser. Lear is obviously a poor judge of character. He has had a life of luxury, protected from poverty and unaware of the injustice in the world. The play charts his journey from the heights of wealth and power to the point where he has neither and is set naked against nature, an old man stripped of everything but his shaky wits and his aging body.

An important part of Lear's fantastic journey is his learning firsthand about the world he has never known, the world of hunger and corruption. I am reminded of an improvisation I created at Florida State University around a concept of Lear that introduced the King as a jovial fat man. As this improvisation progressed, it became clear to me that *Lear* is essentially a play about hunger, old age, madness, and dying. In the scene where Lear meets the blinded Gloucester on the heath (4.6), the unseeing lord begs to kiss Lear's hand. Lear replies, "Let me wipe it first; it smells of mortality." In fact, the entire play smells of mortality; it is the quintessential play about old age and death.

JOSEPH PAPP

JOSEPH PAPP GRATEFULLY ACKNOWLEDGES THE HELP OF ELIZABETH KIRKLAND IN PREPARING THIS FOREWORD.

Introduction

In *King Lear*, Shakespeare pushes to its limit the hypothesis of a malign or at least indifferent universe in which man's life is meaningless and brutal. Few plays other than *Hamlet* and *Macbeth* approach *King Lear* in evoking the wretchedness of human existence, and even they cannot match the devastating spectacle of Gloucester blinded or Cordelia dead in Lear's arms. The responses of the chief characters are correspondingly searing. "Is man no more than this?" rages Lear. "Unaccommodated man is no more but such a poor, bare, forked animal as thou art" (3.4.101–107). Life he calls a "great stage of fools," an endless torment: "the first time that we smell the air / We wawl and cry" (4.6.183, 179–180). Gloucester's despair takes the form of accusing the gods of gleeful malice toward humanity: "As flies to wanton boys are we to the gods; / They kill us for their sport" (4.1.36–37). Gloucester's ministering son Edgar can offer him no greater consolation than stoic resolve: "Men must endure / Their going hence, even as their coming hither; / Ripeness is all" (5.2.9–11). These statements need not be read as choric expressions of meaning for the play as a whole, but they do attest to the depth of suffering. In no other Shakespearean play does injustice appear to triumph so ferociously, for so long, and with such impunity. Will the heavens countenance this reign of injustice on earth? Retribution is late in coming and is not certainly the work of the heavens themselves. For, at the last, we must confront the wanton death of the innocent Cordelia, a death no longer willed even by the villain who arranged her execution. "Is this the promised end?" (5.3.268), asks Kent, stressing the unparalleled horror of the catastrophe.

Throughout its earlier history, the ancient story of King Lear had always ended happily. In the popular folktale of Cinderella, to which the legend of Lear's daughters bears a significant resemblance, the youngest and virtuous daughter triumphs over her two older wicked sisters and is married to her princely wooer. Geoffrey of Monmouth's *Historia Regum Britanniae* (c. 1136), the earliest known version of the Lear story, records that after Lear is overthrown by his sons-in-law (more than by his daughters), he is restored to his throne by the intervention of the French King and is allowed to enjoy his kingdom and Cordelia's love until his natural death. (Cordelia, as his successor, is later dethroned and murdered by her wicked nephews, but that is another story.) Sixteenth-century Tudor versions of the Lear story with which Shakespeare was familiar—John Higgins's account in *The First Part of the Mirror for Magistrates* (1574), Raphael Holinshed's *Chronicles* (1587), Edmund Spenser's *The Faerie Queene*, 2.10.27–32, and a play called *The True Chronicle History of King Leir* (by 1594, published 1605)—all retain the happy ending. The tragic pattern may have been suggested instead by Shakespeare's probable source for the Gloucester-Edgar-Edmund plot, Sir Philip Sidney's *Arcadia*, 2.10, in which the Paphlagonian King is the victim of filial ingratitude and deceit.

Yet even Shakespeare's authority was not sufficient to put down the craving for a happy resolution. Nahum Tate's adaptation (1681), which banished the Fool as indecorous for a tragedy and united Edgar and Cordelia in marriage, placing Lear once again on his throne, held the English stage for about 150 years. One of Shakespeare's editors, Dr. Samuel Johnson, evidently spoke for most eighteenth-century audiences when he confessed that he could not bring himself to read Shakespeare's text. Cordelia's slaughter violated that age's longing for "poetic justice." Her death implied a wanton universe and so counseled philosophic despair. Today, Shakespeare's relentless honesty and refusal to accept easy answers convince us that he was right to defy the conventions of his source, though no doubt we too distort the play to conform with our supposed toughness of vision.

Shakespeare evidently wrote *King Lear* some time before it was performed at court in December of 1606, probably in 1605 and certainly no earlier than 1603–1604; Edgar's speeches as Tom o' Bedlam contain references to Samuel Harsnett's *Declaration of Egregious Popish Impostures*, which was registered for publication in March of 1603. Thus *King Lear* was probably written between *Othello* (c. 1603–1604) and *Macbeth* (c. 1606–1607), when Shakespeare was at the height of his tragic power.

When we look at the play in formal terms, we are apt to be

struck first by its complex double plot. Nowhere else in
Shakespearean tragedy do we find anything approaching
the rich orchestration of the double plotting in *King Lear*.
The links and parallels between the two plots are estab-
lished on a narrative level early in the play and continue to
the end. King Lear misjudges his children and disinherits
his loving daughter Cordelia in favor of her duplicitous sisters, whereas Gloucester falls prey to Edmund's deceptions
and disinherits his loyal son Edgar; Lear is turned out into
the storm by his false daughters, while Gloucester is
branded as a traitor by Edmund and deprived of his eyesight; Lear in his madness realizes his fault against Cordelia, while the blind Gloucester "sees" at last the truth
about Edgar; both fathers are cared for by their loving children and are belatedly reconciled to them, but die broken-
hearted. As recent criticism has noted, these narrative
parallels are not especially significant in themselves; we
are moved not by the mere repetition of event but by the
enlargement of tragic vision that results from the counter-
pointing of two such actions. When we see juxtaposed to
each other two scenes of trial, Lear's mad arraignment of
the absent Goneril and Regan and then the cruel imposition
of the mere "form of justice" on the pinioned Gloucester
(3.6 and 3.7), we begin to measure the extent to which justice and injustice are inverted by cruelty. When at last the
two old men come together, during the storm scenes and
especially at Dover, the sad comfort they derive from shar-
ing the wreckage of their lives calls forth piercing eloquence against the stench of mortality. The sight is "most
pitiful in the meanest wretch, / Past speaking of in a king"
(4.6.204–205).

The play's double structure suggests another duality central to *King Lear*, an opposition of parable and realism, in
which "divided and distinguished worlds" are bound together for instructive contrast. (These terms are Maynard
Mack's, in his *King Lear in Our Time*, 1965.) To a remarkable degree, this play derives its story from folklore and
legend, with many of the wondrous and implausible
circumstances of popular romance. A prose rendition
might almost begin, "Once upon a time there was a king
who had three daughters. . . ." Yet Shakespeare arouses romantic expectation only to crush it by aborting the conven-

tional happy ending, setting up a dramatic tension between an idealized world of make-believe and the actual world of disappointed hopes. We are aware of artifice and convention and yet are deeply moved by the "truth" of suffering, love, and hatred. The characters pull us two ways at once; we regard them as types with universalized characteristics, a king and father, his cruel daughters, his loving daughter, and the like, and yet we scrutinize them for psychological motivation because they seem so real and individual.

This duality appears in both the central and the secondary characters. The King of France is in part a hero out of romance, one who makes selfless choices and rescues the heroine Cordelia from her distress; yet his motive must also be appraised in the context of a bitter struggle for power. Why does he leave the English court "in choler," and why does he return to England with an army? Is it only to aid his wife and her beleaguered father, or is he negotiating for military advantage? Certainly a French invasion of England on behalf of Lear complicates the issue of loyalty for the well-meaning Duke of Albany (and perhaps as well for an English Renaissance audience, with its habitual mistrust of the French). The dual focus of the play invites conflicting interpretation. Similarly, Edgar is presented to us on the one hand as the traduced victim in a starkly pessimistic story, dominated by his rationalistic brother, Edmund, who scoffs at religion and undertakes to manipulate those around him for personal gain; on the other hand, Edgar's story grows increasingly improbable as he undertakes a series of disguises and emerges finally as an anonymous champion of chivalry, challenging his brother in the lists like a knight-errant out of Arthurian romance. Edgar's motives are hard to follow. Is he the hero of a fabulous story whose disguises and contriving of illusions for his father are simply part of that storytelling tradition, or is he, in more realistic terms, a man whose disguises are a defensive mask and whose elaborate contrivances defeat themselves? Edmund, his brother, is no less complex. Onstage today he is usually interpreted as smooth and plausible, well motivated by his father's condescending attitude and by the arbitrariness of the law that has excluded him from legitimacy and inheritance. Yet parable elevates Edmund into something monstrous. He becomes an embodiment of glee-

ful villainy, like Iago in *Othello*, malignantly evil simply because the evil that is in the universe must find a human
form through which to express itself. Edmund's belated attempt to do some good adds to our difficulties in appraising
his character, but the restless power of the dual conception
supplies a vitality not to be found in pure fable or in realistic literature.

What we see then in Edmund and in others is the union of
the universal and the particular, making *King Lear* at once
parable and compellingly real. The parable or folktale element is prominent at the beginning of the play and focuses
attention on the archetypal situations with which the story
is concerned: rivalry between siblings, fear of parental rejection, and, at the same time, parental fear of children's
callousness. The "unrealistic" contrast between Cordelia
and her wicked sisters, or between Edgar and Edmund, is
something we accept as a convention of storytelling because it expresses vividly the psychic truth of rivalry between brothers and sisters. We identify with Cordelia and
Edgar as virtuous children whose worth is misjudged and
who are losing to wicked siblings the contest for parental
approval. (In folklore the rejecting parent is usually a step-
parent, which signifies our conviction that he or she is not a
true parent at all.) Similarly, we accept as a meaningful
convention of storytelling the equally "unrealistic" device
by which Lear tests the love of his daughters. Like any parent, he wishes to be loved and appreciated in response to
the kindnesses he has performed. The tension between
fathers and their marriageable daughters is a recurrent
pattern in Shakespeare's late plays, as in *Othello* (where
Brabantio accuses Desdemona of deceiving and deserting
him), in *Pericles, Cymbeline,* and *The Winter's Tale,* and in
The Tempest, where the pattern is best resolved. In *King
Lear*, Shakespeare explores the inherently explosive situation of an imperious father, who, having provided for his
children and grown old, assumes he has a right to expect
that those children will express their love and gratitude by
looking after him.

The difficulty is that the parable of Lear and his children
presents two contrasting viewpoints, that of the unappreci-
ated child and that of the unwanted aging parent. Tragic
misunderstanding is inevitable, and it outweighs the ques-

tion of assessing blame. From Lear's point of view, Cordelia's silence is a truculent scanting of obedience. What he has devised is, after all, only a prearranged formality, with Cordelia to receive the richest third of England. Cannot such a ceremony be answered with the conventional hyperbole of courtly language, to which the King's ear is attuned? Don't parents have a right to be verbally reassured of their children's love? How can children be so laconic about such a precious matter? For her part, however, Cordelia senses that Lear is demanding love as payment for his parental kindliness, quid pro quo. Genuine love ought rather to be selfless, as the King of France tells Burgundy: "Love's not love / When it is mingled with regards that stands / Aloof from th' entire point" (1.1.242–244). Is Cordelia being asked to prefer Lear before her own husband-to-be? Is this the price she must pay for her upbringing? Lear's ego seems fully capable of demanding this sacrifice from his daughters, especially from his favorite, Cordelia; he has given them his whole kingdom, now let them care for him as befits his royal rank and patriarchal role. The "second childishness" of his old age brings with it a self-centered longing to monopolize the lives of his children and to be a child again. Besides, as king, Lear has long grown accustomed to flattery and absolute obedience. Goneril and Regan are content to flatter and promise obedience, knowing they will turn him out once he has relinquished his authority. Cordelia refuses to lie in this fashion, but she also will not yield to Lear's implicit request for her undivided affection. Part of her must be loyal to her own husband and her children, in the natural cycle of the generations. "Haply, when I shall wed, / That lord whose hand must take my plight shall carry / Half my love with him, half my care and duty" (1.1.100–102). Marriage will not prevent her from obeying, loving and honoring her father as is fit, but will establish a new priority. To Lear, as to other fathers contemplating a daughter's marriage in late Shakespearean plays, this savors of desertion.

Lear is sadly deficient in self-knowledge. As Regan dryly observes, "he hath ever but slenderly known himself" (1.1.296–297), and has grown ever more changeable and imperious with age. By dividing his kingdom in three, ostensibly so that "future strife / May be prevented now" (ll. 44–45), he instead sets in motion a civil war and French invasion. His intention of putting aside his regal authority while still retaining "The name and all th' addition to a king" (l. 136) perhaps betrays a lack of comprehension of the realities of power, although Lear may also have plausible political reasons for what he does, in view of the restive ambitions of Cornwall, Albany, and Burgundy. In any case, he welcomes poisoned flattery but interprets well-intended criticism, whether from Cordelia or Kent, as treason. These failures in no sense justify what Lear's ungrateful children do to him; as he later says, just before going mad, "I am a man / More sinned against than sinning" (3.2.59–60). His failures are, however, tokens of his worldly insolence for which he must fall. The process is a painful one, but since it brings self-discovery it is not without its compensations. Indeed a central paradox of the play is that by no other way could Lear have learned what human suffering and need are all about.

Lear's Fool is instrumental in elucidating this paradox. The Fool offers Lear advice in palatable form as mere foolery or entertainment, and thus obtains a hearing when Kent and Cordelia have been angrily dismissed. Beneath his seemingly innocent jibes, however, are plain warnings of the looming disaster Lear blindly refuses to acknowledge. The Fool knows, as indeed any fool could tell, that Goneril and Regan are remorseless and unnatural. The real fool, therefore, is Lear himself, for having placed himself in their power. In a paradox familiar to Renaissance audiences—as in Erasmus's *In Praise of Folly*, Cervantes's *Don Quixote*, and Shakespeare's own earlier *As You Like It* and *Twelfth Night*—folly and wisdom exchange places. By a similar inversion of logic, the Fool offers his coxcomb to Kent for siding with Lear in his exile, "For taking one's part that's out of favor" (1.4.97). Worldly wisdom suggests that we serve those whose fortunes are on the rise, as the obsequious and servile Oswald does. Indeed, the sinister progress of the first half of the play seems to confirm the Fool's contention that kindness and love are a sure way to exile and poverty. "Let go thy hold when a great wheel runs down a hill lest it break thy neck with following; but the great one that goes upward, let him draw thee after" (2.4.70–73). Yet the Fool resolves to ignore his own cynical advice; "I would have none but knaves follow it, since a fool gives it" (ll. 74–75). Beneath his mocking, the Fool expresses the deeper truth that it is better to be a "fool" and suffer than to win on the cynical world's terms. The greatest fools truly are those who prosper through cruelty and become hardened in sin. As the Fool puts it, deriving a seemingly contrary lesson from Lear's rejection of Cordelia: "Why, this fellow has banished two on 's daughters and did the third a blessing against his will" (1.4.99–101).

These inversions find a parallel in Christian teaching, although the play is nominally pagan in setting. (The lack of explicit Christian reference may be in part the result of a recent parliamentary order banning references to "God" onstage as blasphemous.) Christianity does not hold a monopoly on the idea that one must lose the world in order to win a better world, but its expressions of that idea were plentifully available to Shakespeare: "Blessed are the meek, for they shall inherit the earth" (the Sermon on the Mount); "Go and sell that thou hast, and give to the poor, and thou shalt have treasure in heaven" (Matthew 19:21); "He hath put down the mighty from their seats, and exalted them of low degree" (Luke 1:52). Cordelia's vision of genuine love is of this exalted spiritual order. She is, as the King of France extols her, "most rich being poor, / Most choice, forsaken, and most loved, despised" (1.1.254–255). This is the sense in which Lear has bestowed on her an unintended blessing, by exiling her from a worldly prosperity that is inherently pernicious. Now, with poetic fitness, Lear must learn the same lesson himself. He does so, paradoxically, at the very moment he goes mad, parting ways with the conventional truths of the corrupted world. "My wits begin to turn" (3.2.67), he says, and then speaks his first kind words to the Fool, who is his companion in the storm. Lear senses companionship with a fellow mortal who is cold and outcast as he is. In his madness he perceives both the worth of this insight and the need for suffering to attain it: "The art of our necessities is strange, / And can make vile things precious" (ll. 70–71). Misery teaches Lear things he never could know as king about other "Poor naked wretches" who "bide the pelting of this pitiless storm." How are such poor persons to be fed and clothed? "O, I have ta'en / Too little care of this! Take physic, pomp; / Expose thyself to feel what wretches feel, / That thou mayst shake the superflux to them / And show the heavens more just" (3.4.28–36). This vision of perfect justice is visionary and utopian, utterly mad in fact, but it is also spiritual wisdom dearly bought.

Gloucester learns a similar truth and expresses it in much the same way. Like Lear he has driven into exile a virtuous child and has placed himself in the power of the wicked. Enlightenment comes only through suffering. Just as Lear achieves spiritual wisdom when he goes mad, Gloucester achieves spiritual vision when he is physically blinded. His eyes having been ground out by the heel of Cornwall's boot, Gloucester asks for Edmund only to learn that Edmund has betrayed him in return for siding with Lear in the approaching civil war. Gloucester's response, however, is not to accuse Edmund of treachery but to beg forgiveness of the wronged Edgar. No longer does Gloucester need eyes to see this truth; "I stumbled when I saw." Although the discovery is shattering, Gloucester perceives, as does Lear, that adversity is paradoxically of some benefit, since prosperity had previously caused him to be so spiritually blind. "Full oft 'tis seen / Our means secure us, and our mere defects / Prove our commodities" (4.1.19–21). And this realization leads him, as it does Lear, to express a longing for utopian social justice in which arrogant men will be humbled and the poor raised up by redistributed wealth. "Heavens, deal so still! / Let the superfluous and lust-dieted man, / That slaves your ordinance, that will not see / Because he does not feel, feel your pow'r quickly! / So distribution should undo excess / And each man have enough" (ll. 65–70).

To say that Lear and Gloucester learn something precious is not, however, to deny that they are also devastated and broken by their savage humiliation. Indeed, Gloucester is driven to a despairing attempt at suicide, and Lear remains obsessed with the rotten stench of his own mortality, "bound / Upon a wheel of fire" (4.7.47–48). Every decent value that we like to associate with civilization is grotesquely inverted during the storm scenes. Justice, for example, is portrayed in two sharply contrasting scenes: the mere "form of justice" (3.7.26), by which Cornwall condemns Gloucester for treason, and the earnestly playacted trial by which the mad Lear arraigns Goneril and Regan of filial ingratitude (3.6). The appearance and the reality of justice have exchanged places, as have folly and wisdom or blindness and seeing. The trial of Gloucester is outwardly correct, for Cornwall possesses the legal authority to try his subjects, and at least goes through the motions of interrogating his prisoner. The outcome is, however, cruelly predetermined. In the playacting trial concurrently taking place in a wretched hovel, the outward appearance of justice is pathetically absurd. Here justice on earth is personified by a madman (Lear), Edgar disguised as another madman (Tom o' Bedlam), and a Fool, the latter two addressed by Lear as "Thou robèd man of justice" and "thou, his yokefellow of equity" (ll. 36–37). They are caught up in a pastime of illusion, using a footstool to represent Lear's ungrateful daughters. Yet true justice is here and not inside the manor house.

Similar contrasts invert the values of loyalty, obedience, and family bonds. Edmund becomes, in the language of the villains, the "loyal" son whose loyalty is demonstrated by turning on his own "traitorous" father. Cornwall becomes a new father to Edmund ("thou shalt find a dearer father in my love," 3.5.25–26). Conversely, a servant who tries to restrain Cornwall from blinding Gloucester is, in Regan's eyes, monstrously insubordinate. "A peasant stand up thus?" (3.7.83). Personal and sexual relationships betray signs of the universal malaise. The explicitly sexual ties in the play, notably those of Goneril, Regan, and Edmund, are grossly carnal and lead to jealousy and murder, while in Cordelia's wifely role the sensual is underplayed. The relationships we cherish—those of Cordelia, Kent, the Fool, and Gloucester to King Lear, and Edgar to Gloucester—are filial or are characterized by loyal service, both pointedly nonsexual. Nowhere do we find an embodiment of love that is both sensual and spiritual, as in Desdemona in *Othello* or Hermione in *The Winter's Tale*. The Fool's and Tom o' Bedlam's (i.e., Edgar's) gibes about codpieces and plackets (3.2.27–40, 3.4.96) anticipate Lear's towering indictment of carnality, in which his fear of woman's insatiable appetite and his revulsion at what she resembles "Down from the waist" ("there is the sulfurous pit, burning, scalding, stench, consumption. Fie, fie, fie! Pah, pah!") combine with a destructive self-hatred (4.6.124–130).

All these inversions and polarizations are subsumed in the inversion of the word "natural." Edmund is the "natural" son of Gloucester, meaning literally that he is illegitimate. Figuratively he therefore represents a violation of traditional moral order. In appearance he is smooth and plausible, but in reality he is an archdeceiver like the Vice in a morality play, a superb actor who boasts to the audience in soliloquy of his protean villainy. "Nature" is Edmund's goddess, and by this he means something like a naturalistic universe in which the race goes to the swiftest and in which conscience, morality, and religion are empty myths. Whereas Lear invokes Nature as a goddess who will punish ungrateful daughters and defend rejected fathers (1.4.274–288), and whereas Gloucester believes in a cosmic correspondence between eclipses of the moon or sun and mutinous discords among men (1.2.106–117), Edmund scoffs at all such metaphysical speculations. He spurns, in other words, the Boethian conception of a divine harmony uniting the cosmos and man, with man at the center of the universe. As a rationalist, Edmund echoes Jacobean disruptions of the older world order in politics and religion as well as in science. He is a Machiavellian, atheist, Epicurean, everything inimical to traditional Elizabethan ideals of order. To him, "natural" means precisely what Lear and Gloucester call "unnatural."

His creed provides the play with its supreme test. Which definition of "natural" is true? Does heaven exist, and will it let Edmund and the other villainous persons get away with their evil? The question is frequently asked, but the answers are ambiguous. "If you do love old men," Lear implores the gods, "if your sweet sway / Allow obedience, if you yourselves are old, / Make it your cause" (2.4.191–193). His exhortations mount into frenzied rant, until finally the heavens do send down a terrible storm—on Lear himself. Witnesses agree that the absence of divine order in the universe would have the gravest consequences. "If that the heavens do not their visible spirits / Send quickly down to tame these vile offenses," says Albany of Lear's ordeal, "It will come, / Humanity must perforce prey on itself, / Like monsters of the deep" (4.2.47–51). And Cornwall's servants have perceived earlier the dire implications of their masters' evil deeds. "I'll never care what wickedness I do, / If this man come to good," says one, and his fellow agrees: "If she [Regan] live long, / And in the end meet the old course of death, / Women will all turn monsters" (3.7.102–105; quarto text only). Yet these servants do in fact obey their own best instincts, turning on Cornwall and ministering to Gloucester despite danger to themselves. Similarly, Albany abandons his mild attempts to conciliate his domineering wife and instead uses his power for good. The crimes of the villains are punished, and Albany sees divine cause in this. Just as plausibly, however, one can postulate an innate decency in humankind that has at last asserted itself, horrified by what it has seen. In part, too, villainy destroys itself, for Edmund's insatiable ambition extends past Cornwall to the English throne, and Goneril and Regan would each willingly kill the other to be Edmund's queen. Even in Cordelia's capture and death we can find affirmation of the human spirit, in her ability to forgive and cherish her father; and Edgar's comparable ministering to Gloucester gives the lie to Edmund's "natural" or amoral view of humanity. Certain it is that whatever force oversees the restoration of at least some semblance of justice cannot or will not prevent the death of Cordelia. The last tableau is a vision of doomsday, with Cordelia strangled, Lear dying of heartbreak, and the "gored state" (5.3.326) in such disarray that we cannot be sure what restoration can occur. Indeed, the political question of order is dwarfed by the enormity of Lear's disaster. No one wishes longer life for the King: "He hates him / That would upon the rack of this tough world / Stretch him out longer." He is dead; "The wonder is he hath endured so long" (ll. 319–322). Lear's view of life's terrible corruption, pronounced in his madness, seems confirmed in his end, but so is his greatness of heart confirmed. Overwhelmed as we are by the testimonial before us of mankind's vicious capacity for self-destruction, we are stirred too by the ability of some men and women to confront their fearful destiny with probity, adhering to what they believe to be good. The power of love, though learned too late to avert catastrophe, is at last discovered in its very defeat.

King Lear
in Performance

The history of *King Lear* onstage amply confirms a view of the play as almost unbearably distressing. It was acted during Shakespeare's lifetime at the Globe Theatre, before King James at the palace at Whitehall on December 26, 1606, in Yorkshire in 1610 by a group of strolling players, and probably on other occasions; at least two revivals took place during the 1660s and 1670s, with Thomas Betterton as Lear. When Nahum Tate introduced a happily ending *History of King Lear* at the theater at Dorset Garden, London, in 1681, however, the appeal of his sentimentalized adaptation was so powerful that Shakespeare's play simply disappeared from the theater for a century and a half. Tate was, after all, restoring the reunion of Lear and Cordelia contained in all the accounts of the historical Lear (or Leir) before Shakespeare: in Geoffrey of Monmouth's twelfth-century *Historia Regum Britanniae*, in *The First Part of the Mirror for Magistrates* (1574 edition), in the anonymous play called *The True Chronicle History of King Leir* (c. 1588–1594), and others. Shakespeare's vision of an unrelenting tragedy in which injustice is not always righted had to await a modern and disillusioned world in order to be adequately comprehended.

Tate was responding to the same discomfort later felt by Samuel Johnson, who confessed that he found *Lear* so unendurably painful that he could read Shakespeare's text only in the line of duty as an editor. Ideas of poetic justice demanded that, as Tate put it in his concluding lines, "Truth and virtue shall at last succeed." "Regularity" and "probability," thought to be lacking in Shakespeare's plot, were needed in order to confirm that the gods were beneficent providers for human destiny. The slaughter of Cordelia, which seemed to imply a wanton universe and to counsel philosophical despair, could not be allowed to stand. Accordingly, Tate not only reunited father and daughter at the play's end, but also provided a love interest throughout between Edgar and Cordelia (leaving out

France and Burgundy entirely). The love story gave the play a much-desired romantic titillation. It also, in Tate's view, gave a better motivation for Edgar: his disguise was no longer merely "a poor shift to save his life" but rather a "generous design" to aid Cordelia. Tate also eliminated the Fool, motivated presumably by a desire to fulfill neoclassical standards of decorum that eschewed low comedy in a tragedy. Tate's revisions had a political point to make as well: by eliminating the King of France and the French invasion of England, he transformed the military conflict in *Lear* into one of horrifying civil war and joyful reestablishment of royal authority—an object lesson not easily missed by Restoration audiences with vivid memories of their own civil war.

Tate's *Lear* enjoyed a remarkable success. It was acted in all but nine of the years in the eighteenth century. Thomas Betterton played Tate's Lear every year until his death in 1710 and was succeeded by (among others) Barton Booth, James Quin, and, beginning in 1742, David Garrick. Anne Bracegirdle, Peg Woffington, Susannah Cibber, and George Anne Bellamy were notable Cordelias of the century. There were, to be sure, some attempts to resist the awesome popularity of Tate's version. Garrick restored a good deal of Shakespeare's language in 1756, especially at the start of the play, fitting Edmund's soliloquy in its usual place (1.2) instead of at the beginning and presenting most of Lear's scene of the division of the kingdom; nevertheless, Garrick still omitted the King of France and the Fool and retained the love of Edgar and Cordelia, leading up to the happy ending. George Colman the elder suffered a serious failure in 1768 at the Theatre Royal, Covent Garden, when he dared to remove the love story, even though he retained the happy reunion of father and daughter, arranged matters so that Gloucester was blinded offstage, and prevented Gloucester's too-improbable suicide by the timely arrival of Lear.

John Philip Kemble (with his sister, Sarah Siddons, as Cordelia, and later his brother Charles as Edmund and then as Edgar) began with Garrick's *Lear* in 1788 but reverted to a slightly restored version of Tate in 1792. This version still had Gloucester speak from offstage during his blinding and brought on Lear in time to forestall the unpalatable "fall" of Gloucester from Dover cliff. Edmund Kean, after doing well with Tate's *Lear* (or something close to it) in a production in 1820 that emphasized spectacular scenic effects, summoned up the courage to restore the tragic ending at the Theatre Royal, Drury Lane, in 1823 and in subsequent productions until his retirement. Yet even Kean retained the love story of Edgar and Cordelia and banished the Fool. Literary critics such as Joseph Addison, William Hazlitt, and Charles Lamb, long dissatisfied with the stage *Lear*, were not mollified; Hazlitt in particular was disappointed with Kean's halfhearted attempts at restoration. *Lear* had become, in the view of many nineteenth-century readers, a play incapable of being staged adequately; it existed most powerfully on the page and in the imagination.

William Charles Macready first acted Lear at Swansea in 1833, still in Tate's version. Prompted, however, by a newspaper article by John Forster urging the return of the Shakespeare play to the stage, he successfully presented a cut version of Shakespeare's text at Covent Garden in 1834, though he still excluded the Fool. Even when Macready finally restored the Fool, in 1838 at Covent Garden, he did so only after great hesitation and then assigning the part to a young actress, Priscilla Horton—the first of many actresses to play the role. Macready also eliminated the blinding of Gloucester, even when spoken from the wings, and the imaginary fall from Dover cliff. So too did Samuel Phelps at the Sadler's Wells Theatre in 1845 and afterward. Although *Bell's Weekly Messenger* rejoiced that Phelps "produced the entire play as it came from the mind of its immortal author," in fact the production made many of the same cuts as had Macready's. Later in the century, at the Lyceum Theatre in 1892, Henry Irving eliminated Gloucester's blinding and nine other scenes, leaving the play "considerably reduced," though for the most part, according to *The Times*, "in the condition in which it left the author's hand."

All these actor-managers cut extensively, though preserving in the main the ordering of Shakespeare's scenes, and provided instead a spectacular array of storm effects and monumental scenery. (Anyone who has seen Albert Finney and Tom Courtenay in the film *The Dresser* has taken a hilarious, albeit exaggerated, backstage tour of the contraptions needed to generate wind, rain, thunder, and lightning for a proscenium-arch performance, with Lear onstage doing his best to be heard over the din.) Macready's *Lear* concentrated visually on solid, warlike castles, processions, marches, druid circles on the heath, and lightning flashes that alternately lit up the stage and left it in darkness while the winds howled. Phelps sumptuously decorated his stage in the idiom of Saxon Britain. Irving set the play at the end of the Roman occupation of Britain, providing period costumes and historically accurate architectural details. Though Irving did not bestow the scenic effort on this play he had just given to *Henry VIII* (1892), he impressively produced for the storm scene a desolate heath, swept, as *The Times* reviewer wrote, "by furious blasts and beating rain, and illumined by coruscating lightning as dazzling in its brilliancy as the rolling thunder that accompanies it is terrifying." Through such effects, which took precedence over the text, nineteenth-century theater managers attempted to play up the tragic grandeur of Lear, while still ducking such apparently intractable material as the blinding of Gloucester.

The twentieth century has embraced the bitterness of *Lear* as if discovering in it a way of newly comprehending a world filled with wanton evil and uncertain justice. Restoration of the text to a virtual whole (in fact to a conflation of Folio and quarto texts that was probably never staged in Shakespeare's day) has enabled audiences to see the distressing scenes that had so long remained unknown in the theater. Harcourt Williams's production at the Old Vic in 1931, with John Gielgud as Lear and Ralph Richardson as Kent, and another by Lewis Casson and Harley Granville-Barker at the Old Vic in 1940, did much to let the play be seen as it was written, preserving its unity and rhythm. Unlocalized setting, employed for example by Nugent Monck in 1926 at the Maddermarket Theatre in Norwich and by Theodore Komisarjevsky in 1936 at Stratford-upon-Avon, permitted a new kind of fluidity in staging that recaptured some hitherto lost staging effects of Shakespeare's original.

Donald Wolfit acted Lear powerfully at London's Scala Theatre in 1944, a performance that James Agate proclaimed "the greatest piece of Shakespearean acting I have seen since I have been privileged to write for the *Sunday*

Times." Laurence Olivier directed and starred in the play at London's New Theatre in 1946, describing his Lear as "bad tempered arrogance with a crown perched on top." With Olivier's selfish and inconsiderate Lear and Alec Guinness's wry and vindictive Fool, the production emphasized the damage Lear inflicts as much as what he suffers. With greater emphasis upon the pathos of Lear's suffering, Gielgud returned to the role in 1950 and 1955, first at Stratford-upon-Avon in a production he directed with Anthony Quayle, and then at London's Palace Theatre, directed by George Devine.

One modern tendency has been to see the play in as bleak and unforgiving terms as possible. The Polish critic Jan Kott's distorted but compelling view of the play as speaking to our existential gloom (published in English in 1964 as "King Lear, or Endgame," in *Shakespeare Our Contemporary*) influenced what has been perhaps the most important twentieth-century interpretation of the play, Peter Brook's production at Stratford-upon-Avon in 1962 and the subsequent film (1970), with Paul Scofield as Lear. In this version Cordelia's role is reduced and devastatingly offset by the horrors of what Lear and Gloucester must suffer. The setting is wintry throughout. Lear's followers, crowding into Goneril's hall in Scotland, are rowdy enough to give plausibility to Goneril's impatience with her father. Cuts and rearrangement of some speeches are calculated to add to rather than relieve the horror. Lear and Gloucester, together on the beach at Dover in Act 4, scene 6, splendidly invoke a spectacle of ruin as these two old men cling together and behold their world crumble around them. Brook sees little reason to believe that Lear and Gloucester have learned much from their suffering beyond what suffering is like.

The uncompromisingly tragic vision of Brook's *Lear*, derived as much from Jan Kott, Bertolt Brecht, and Samuel Beckett as from Shakespeare, gained much of its shocking power of relevance from the disillusionment of the 1960s and 1970s. Other directors have continued to explore and at the same time qualify Brook's nihilism in ways that are sometimes more complex and less sensational in their view of the play's emotional dynamics. Trevor Nunn lessened the radical pessimism of Brook's version in his production on a virtually bare stage in 1968 at Stratford-upon-Avon, capturing the agony of Lear's experience and allowing an audience to share his suffering. In New York in 1973, Edwin Sherin directed James Earl Jones in a production at the Delacorte Theater, in which Lear, for all his arrogance, was, according to *The New York Times*, the victim of "a compassionless society, in which everything is usurped by the young." Donald Sinden's Lear, in a production directed by Nunn in collaboration with John Barton and Barry Kyle at Stratford-upon-Avon in 1976, displayed the cruelty and self-indulgence of a spoiled child, and, if the performance lacked the tragic dignity that earlier generations associated with the role, it effectively revealed the dangers of unchecked power. David Hare's production of *King Lear* at London's National Theatre in 1986 starred Anthony Hopkins as a man helpless before the brutality his own actions have released.

On film *King Lear* shows the richness and variety of perspective from which the play can be understood in our time. Brook's movie version is bleakly pessimistic. A brilliant *Lear* directed by Grigori Kozintsev (1970) sees the story from a Russian perspective, one in which individuals are caught up in larger forces of history. Peasants wordlessly behold the goings-on of their social masters and wait for deliverance; massive armies determine the outcome of battle. Yuri Yarvet's Lear is small and frail, at once pathetic and heroic as he stands defenseless against loneliness and brutality. The visual effects in this black-and-white film are, as in Brook's version, stark and uncompromising, but, unlike Brook, Kozintsev has tried, as he has said, "to strengthen the voice of Good, even in those instances when it has no words to speak." Most recently, the Japanese director Akira Kurosawa has adapted the *Lear* story in his film *Ran* (1985). Set in feudal Japan against a background of grass-covered hills, fallen castles, and a sky whose swirling clouds testify to the elemental powers that have been unleashed, Kurosawa's *Ran* ("chaos") reworks *King Lear* into the story of Lord Hidetora, the aging patriarch of the Ichimonja clan, who desperately tries to contain the passions of his family and the legacy of his own brutality.

Perhaps Laurence Olivier's television *King Lear* (1983) best sums up what the twentieth century has been able to contribute to the interpretation of this play in performance. Olivier's Lear is very frail and old—indeed, like Olivier himself when he shot this film. He is seen at first as deeply fond of Cordelia, but also accustomed to mastery of his kingdom and susceptible to the flattery plentifully bestowed upon him by his courtiers. He is thus understandably outraged at what he takes to be a betrayal of him by Cordelia and Kent. Goneril and Regan (Dorothy Tutin and Diana Rigg) are suave in their flattery, outwardly attractive, plausibly motivated, yet vicious. Edmund (Robert Lindsay) betrays his villainy with his restless and glistening eyes, well caught by the camera in close-ups. The Fool (John Hurt) is solicitous, distressed beneath his clowning, aware of the disaster to come. Gloucester (Leo McKern) is a fleshy and gullible but well-meaning old man whose ordeal of blinding and attempted suicide leaves him broken, knowing too late his folly. Lear's restoration to Cordelia is touchingly tender, all the more so because of its certain brevity. The contrast between vicious and virtuous behavior is unbridgeable; the victimization of Lear and Cordelia is heartbreaking. Olivier presents us with a *Lear* that causes pain and offers no false hopes, and yet makes the case for some kind of survival of human dignity and compassion. Olivier confronts human brutality in its full extent but provides a meaningfully tragic response as well.

On Shakespeare's stage, the effect of certain scenes in *Lear* must have been particularly suited to the theater for which they were designed. For example, the unlocalized setting enabled Shakespeare to place Kent in the stocks in the course of Act 2, scene 2, and leave him there until scene 4 when Lear arrives in Gloucestershire to find him still enfettered; in the interim, scene 3, Kent has slumbered while Edgar comes onstage in a presumably different though nearby location. Visual conventions encourage this kind of theatrical juxtaposition: Edgar ponders the danger of his being arrested and resolves to disguise himself, while simultaneously onstage another disguised outcast sleeps or meditates on his ruined fortune. The two figures are not "literally" a part of the same scene; staging flexibility in the absence of scenery makes possible such a visual pairing.

Later (4.6), Gloucester's attempted suicide makes simi-

larly imaginative use of stage space. He and the disguised
Edgar are on the bare platform stage of the Elizabethan
playhouse (or at King James's court). In this theatrical envi-
ronment, Edgar then conjures up for his blind father a
scene of cliffs, vast heights, and a ship far below bobbing on
the waves like a toy boat. What is the audience to believe?
This sort of verbal scene-setting is the way Elizabethan actors regularly establish a sense of place around them onstage. Only when Gloucester falls forward and is not killed
after all can the audience be sure that Edgar is playing a
role, acting as director or dramatist, making up a little play
for his father that is supposed to cure his despair. Edgar's
theatricality, his changes of costume and voice, his com-
menting in soliloquy on his own performance, are only a
few of the ways in which *King Lear* is fitted to the theater
where it was originally performed, a theater in which the
play's unsurpassed power can be fully experienced.

The Playhouse

UTRECHT UNIVERSITY LIBRARY

This early copy of a drawing by Johannes de Witt of the Swan Theatre in London (c. 1596), made by his friend Arend van Buchell, is the only surviving contemporary sketch of the interior of a public theater in the 1590s.

From other contemporary evidence, including the stage directions and dialogue of Elizabethan plays, we can surmise that the various public theaters where Shakespeare's plays were produced (the Theatre, the Curtain, the Globe) resembled the Swan in many important particulars, though there must have been some variations as well. The public playhouses were essentially round, or polygonal, and open to the sky, forming an acting arena approximately 70 feet in diameter; they did not have a large curtain with which to open and close a scene, such as we see today in opera and some traditional theater. A platform measuring approximately 43 feet across and 27 feet deep, referred to in the de Witt drawing as the *proscaenium*, projected into the yard, *planities sive arena*. The roof, *tectum*, above the stage and supported by two pillars, could contain machinery for ascents and descents, as were required in several of Shakespeare's late plays. Above this roof was a hut, shown in the drawing with a flag flying atop it and a trumpeter at its door announcing the performance of a play. The underside of the stage roof, called the heavens, was usually richly decorated with symbolic figures of the sun, the moon, and the constellations. The platform stage stood at a height of 5½ feet or so above the yard, providing room under the stage for underworldly effects. A trapdoor, which is not visible in this drawing, gave access to the space below.

The structure at the back of the platform (labeled *mimorum aedes*), known as the tiring-house because it was the actors' attiring (dressing) space, featured at least two doors, as shown here. Some theaters seem to have also had a discovery space, or curtained recessed alcove, perhaps between the two doors—in which Falstaff could have hidden from the sheriff (*1 Henry IV,* 2.4) or Polonius could have eavesdropped on Hamlet and his mother (*Hamlet,* 3.4). This discovery space probably gave the actors a means of access to and from the tiring-house. Curtains may also have been hung in front of the stage doors on occasion. The de Witt drawing shows a gallery above the doors that extends across the back and evidently contains spectators. On occasions when action "above" demanded the use of this space, as when Juliet appears at her "window" (*Romeo and Juliet,* 2.2 and 3.5), the gallery seems to have been used by the actors, but large scenes there were impractical.

The three-tiered auditorium is perhaps best described by Thomas Platter, a visitor to London in 1599 who saw on that occasion Shakespeare's *Julius Caesar* performed at the Globe:

> The playhouses are so constructed that they play on a raised platform, so that everyone has a good view. There are different galleries and places [*orchestra, sedilia, porticus*], however, where the seating is better and more comfortable and therefore more expensive. For whoever cares to stand below only pays one English penny, but if he wishes to sit, he enters by another door [*ingressus*] and pays another penny, while if he desires to sit in the most comfortable seats, which are cushioned, where he not only sees everything well but can also be seen, then he pays yet another English penny at another door. And during the performance food and drink are carried round the audience, so that for what one cares to pay one may also have refreshment.

Scenery was not used, though the theater building itself was handsome enough to invoke a feeling of order and hierarchy that lent itself to the splendor and pageantry onstage. Portable properties, such as thrones, stools, tables, and beds, could be carried or thrust on as needed. In the scene pictured here by de Witt, a lady on a bench, attended perhaps by her waiting-gentlewoman, receives the address of a male figure. If Shakespeare had written *Twelfth Night* by 1596 for performance at the Swan, we could imagine Malvolio appearing like this as he bows before the Countess Olivia and her gentlewoman, Maria.

KING LEAR

[*Dramatis Personae*

KING LEAR
GONERIL,
REGAN, } *Lear's daughters*
CORDELIA,
DUKE OF ALBANY, *Goneril's husband*
DUKE OF CORNWALL, *Regan's husband*
KING OF FRANCE, *Cordelia's suitor and husband*
DUKE OF BURGUNDY, *suitor to Cordelia*

EARL OF KENT, *later disguised as Caius*
EARL OF GLOUCESTER
EDGAR, *Gloucester's son and heir, later disguised as poor Tom*
EDMUND, *Gloucester's bastard son*

OSWALD, *Goneril's steward*
A KNIGHT *serving King Lear*
Lear's FOOL
CURAN, *in Gloucester's household*
GENTLEMEN
Three SERVANTS
OLD MAN, *a tenant of Gloucester*
Three MESSENGERS
DOCTOR *attending Cordelia*
Two CAPTAINS
HERALD

*Knights, Gentlemen, Attendants, Servants, Officers, Soldiers,
   Trumpeters*

SCENE: *Britain*]

1.1 *Enter Kent, Gloucester, and Edmund.*

KENT I thought the King had more affected the Duke of 1
Albany than Cornwall. 2

GLOUCESTER It did always seem so to us; but now in
the division of the kingdom it appears not which of
the dukes he values most, for equalities are so weighed 5
that curiosity in neither can make choice of either's 6
moiety. 7

KENT Is not this your son, my lord?

GLOUCESTER His breeding, sir, hath been at my charge. 9
I have so often blushed to acknowledge him that now
I am brazed to 't. 11

KENT I cannot conceive you. 12

GLOUCESTER Sir, this young fellow's mother could;
whereupon she grew round-wombed and had indeed, sir, a son for her cradle ere she had a husband
for her bed. Do you smell a fault? 16

KENT I cannot wish the fault undone, the issue of it 17
being so proper. 18

GLOUCESTER But I have a son, sir, by order of law, some 19
year elder than this, who yet is no dearer in my ac- 20
count. Though this knave came something saucily to 21
the world before he was sent for, yet was his mother
fair, there was good sport at his making, and the
whoreson must be acknowledged.—Do you know this 24
noble gentleman, Edmund?

EDMUND No, my lord.

GLOUCESTER My lord of Kent. Remember him hereafter
as my honorable friend.

EDMUND My services to your lordship. 29

1.1. Location: King Lear's palace.
1 more affected better liked **2 Albany** i.e., Scotland **5–7 equalities . . .
moiety** the shares balance so equally that close scrutiny cannot find
advantage in either's portion **9 breeding** raising, care. **charge** expense **11 brazed** hardened **12 conceive** understand. (But Gloucester
puns in the sense of "become pregnant.") **16 fault** (1) sin (2) loss of
scent by the hounds **17 issue** (1) result (2) offspring **18 proper**
(1) excellent (2) handsome **19 by order of law** legitimate **19–20 some
year** about a year **20–21 account** estimation **21 knave** young fellow
(not said disapprovingly, though the word is ironic). **something** somewhat **24 whoreson** low fellow; suggesting bastardy, but (like *knave*
above) used with affectionate condescension **29 services** duty

KENT   I must love you, and sue to know you better.   30
EDMUND   Sir, I shall study deserving.   31
GLOUCESTER   He hath been out nine years, and away he   32
  shall again. The King is coming.   33

> *Sennet. Enter [one bearing a coronet, then] King*
> *Lear, Cornwall, Albany, Goneril, Regan, Cordelia,*
> *and attendants.*

LEAR
  Attend the lords of France and Burgundy, Gloucester.   34
GLOUCESTER   I shall, my liege.   *Exit.*
LEAR
  Meantime we shall express our darker purpose.   36
  Give me the map there. [*He takes a map.*] Know that
    we have divided
  In three our kingdom; and 'tis our fast intent   38
  To shake all cares and business from our age,
  Conferring them on younger strengths while we
  Unburdened crawl toward death. Our son of Cornwall,
  And you, our no less loving son of Albany,
  We have this hour a constant will to publish   43
  Our daughters' several dowers, that future strife   44
  May be prevented now. The princes, France and
    Burgundy,   45
  Great rivals in our youngest daughter's love,
  Long in our court have made their amorous sojourn
  And here are to be answered. Tell me, my daughters—
  Since now we will divest us both of rule,
  Interest of territory, cares of state—   50
  Which of you shall we say doth love us most,
  That we our largest bounty may extend
  Where nature doth with merit challenge? Goneril,   53

30 sue petition, beg   **31 study deserving** strive to be worthy (of your
esteem)   **32 out** i.e., abroad, absent   **33 s.d. Sennet** trumpet signal
heralding a procession.   **one . . . then** (This direction is from the
quarto. The *coronet* is perhaps intended for Cordelia or her betrothed.
A coronet signifies nobility below the rank of king.)   **34 Attend** i.e., wait
on them ceremonially, usher them into our presence   **36 we, our** (The
royal plural; also in ll. 37–44, etc.)   **darker purpose** undeclared intention   **38 fast** firm   **43 constant . . . publish** firm resolve to proclaim
44 several individual   **45 prevented** forestalled   **50 Interest** possession   **53 Where . . . challenge** where both natural affection and merit
claim it as due

Our eldest born, speak first.

GONERIL

Sir, I love you more than words can wield the matter,
Dearer than eyesight, space, and liberty,   56
Beyond what can be valued, rich or rare,   57
No less than life, with grace, health, beauty, honor;
As much as child e'er loved, or father found;   59
A love that makes breath poor and speech unable.   60
Beyond all manner of so much I love you.

CORDELIA [*Aside*]

What shall Cordelia speak? Love and be silent.

LEAR [*Indicating on map*]

Of all these bounds, even from this line to this,
With shadowy forests and with champains riched,   64
With plenteous rivers and wide-skirted meads,   65
We make thee lady. To thine and Albany's issue
Be this perpetual.—What says our second daughter,
Our dearest Regan, wife of Cornwall? Speak.

REGAN

I am made of that self mettle as my sister,   69
And prize me at her worth. In my true heart   70
I find she names my very deed of love;   71
Only she comes too short, that I profess   72
Myself an enemy to all other joys
Which the most precious square of sense possesses,   74
And find I am alone felicitate   75
In your dear Highness' love.

CORDELIA [*Aside*]   Then poor Cordelia!

And yet not so, since I am sure my love's
More ponderous than my tongue.   78

LEAR

To thee and thine hereditary ever

---

56 space freedom from confinement.   **liberty** freedom of action
57 valued estimated   **59 found** i.e., found himself to be loved
60 breath voice, speech.   **unable** incompetent, inadequate   **64 shadowy**
shady.   **champains riched** fertile plains   **65 wide-skirted meads** exten-
sive, spread out meadows   **69 self** same.   **mettle** spirit, temperament.
(But with the meaning also of *metal*, substance, continued in the meta-
phor of *prize* and *worth,* l. 70.)   **70 prize . . . worth** value myself as her
equal (in love for you). (*Prize* suggests "price.")   **71 names . . . love**
describes my love in very deed   **72 that** in that   **74 most . . . possesses**
most delicate test of my sensibility, most delicately sensitive part of my
nature, can enjoy   **75 felicitate** made happy   **78 ponderous** weighty

Remain this ample third of our fair kingdom,
No less in space, validity, and pleasure   81
Than that conferred on Goneril.—Now, our joy,
Although our last and least, to whose young love   83
The vines of France and milk of Burgundy   84
Strive to be interested, what can you say to draw   85
A third more opulent than your sisters'? Speak.

CORDELIA   Nothing, my lord. —7HiGH MiNDED

LEAR   Nothing?

CORDELIA   Nothing.

LEAR
Nothing will come of nothing. Speak again.

CORDELIA
Unhappy that I am, I cannot heave
My heart into my mouth. I love Your Majesty
According to my bond, no more nor less.   93

LEAR
How, how, Cordelia? Mend your speech a little,
Lest you may mar your fortunes.

CORDELIA   Good my lord,
You have begot me, bred me, loved me. I
Return those duties back as are right fit,   97
Obey you, love you, and most honor you.
Why have my sisters husbands if they say
They love you all? Haply, when I shall wed,   100
That lord whose hand must take my plight shall carry   101
Half my love with him, half my care and duty.
Sure I shall never marry like my sisters,
To love my father all.

LEAR
But goes thy heart with this?

CORDELIA   Ay, my good lord.

LEAR   So young, and so untender?

CORDELIA   So young, my lord, and true.

LEAR
Let it be so! Thy truth then be thy dower!

---

81 validity value.   **pleasure** pleasing features   **83 least** youngest
84 vines vineyards.   **milk** pastures (?)   **85 be interessed** be affiliated,
establish a claim, be admitted as to a privilege.   **draw** win   **93 bond**
filial obligation   **97 right fit** proper and fitting   **100 all** exclusively, and
with all of themselves.   **Haply** perhaps   **101 plight** troth-plight, pledge

For, by the sacred radiance of the sun,
The mysteries of Hecate and the night,   110
By all the operation of the orbs   111
From whom we do exist and cease to be,   112
Here I disclaim all my paternal care,
Propinquity, and property of blood,   114
And as a stranger to my heart and me
Hold thee from this forever. The barbarous Scythian,   116
Or he that makes his generation messes   117
To gorge his appetite, shall to my bosom
Be as well neighbored, pitied, and relieved
As thou my sometime daughter.
KENT   Good my liege—   120
LEAR   Peace, Kent!
Come not between the dragon and his wrath.
I loved her most, and thought to set my rest   123
On her kind nursery. [*To Cordelia.*] Hence, and avoid my
   sight!—   124
So be my grave my peace, as here I give   125
Her father's heart from her! Call France. Who stirs?   126
Call Burgundy. [*Exit one.*] Cornwall and Albany,
With my two daughters' dowers digest the third.   128
Let pride, which she calls plainness, marry her.   129
I do invest you jointly with my power,
Preeminence, and all the large effects   131
That troop with majesty. Ourself by monthly course,   132
With reservation of an hundred knights   133
By you to be sustained, shall our abode
Make with you by due turns. Only we shall retain

110 mysteries secret rites.   **Hecate** goddess of witchcraft and the
moon   **111 operation** influence.   **orbs** heavenly bodies   **112 From
whom** under whose influence   **114 Propinquity . . . blood** intimacy and
close kinship   **116 this** this time forth.   **Scythian** (Scythians were
famous in antiquity for savagery.)   **117 makes . . . messes** makes meals
of his children or parents   **120 sometime** former   **123 set my rest**
repose myself. (A phrase from a game of cards meaning "to stake
all.")   **124 nursery** nursing, care.   **avoid** leave   **125 So . . . peace, as** as
I hope to rest peacefully in my grave   **126 Who stirs?** i.e., somebody do
something; don't just stand there   **128 digest** assimilate, incorporate
129 Let . . . her let her pride be her dowry and get her a husband
131 effects outward shows   **132 troop with** accompany, serve.   **Ourself**
(The royal "we.")   **133 With reservation of** reserving to myself the right
to be attended by

The name and all th' addition to a king.   136
The sway, revenue, execution of the rest,
Belovèd sons, be yours, which to confirm,
This coronet part between you.

KENT   Royal Lear,   139
Whom I have ever honored as my king,
Loved as my father, as my master followed,
As my great patron thought on in my prayers—

LEAR
The bow is bent and drawn. Make from the shaft.   143

KENT
Let it fall rather, though the fork invade   144
The region of my heart. Be Kent unmannerly   145
When Lear is mad. What wouldst thou do, old man?   146
Think'st thou that duty shall have dread to speak
When power to flattery bows?
To plainness honor's bound   149
When majesty falls to folly. Reserve thy state,   150
And in thy best consideration check   151
This hideous rashness. Answer my life my judgment,   152
Thy youngest daughter does not love thee least,
Nor are those emptyhearted whose low sounds
Reverb no hollowness.

LEAR   Kent, on thy life, no more.   155

KENT
My life I never held but as a pawn   156
To wage against thine enemies, nor fear to lose it,   157
Thy safety being motive.

LEAR   Out of my sight!   158

---

136 addition honors and prerogatives   **139 coronet** (Perhaps Lear
gestures toward this coronet that was to have symbolized Cordelia's
dowry and marriage, or hands it to his sons-in-law, or actually attempts
to divide it.)   **143 Make from** get out of the way of   **144 fall** strike.
fork barbed head of an arrow   **145–146 Be . . . mad** i.e., I must be
unmannerly when you behave so madly   **149 To . . . bound** allegiance
demands frankness   **150 Reserve thy state** retain your royal authority
151 in . . . consideration with wise deliberation.   **check** restrain, with-
hold   **152 Answer . . . judgment** I wager my life on my judgment that
155 Reverb no hollowness i.e., do not reverberate like a hollow drum,
insincerely   **156 held** regarded.   **pawn** stake, chess piece   **157 wage**
wager, hazard in warfare   **158 motive** that which prompts me to act

KENT
  See better, Lear, and let me still remain   159
  The true blank of thine eye.   160
LEAR   Now, by Apollo—
KENT   Now, by Apollo, King,
  Thou swear'st thy gods in vain.
LEAR   O, vassal! Miscreant!   164
                 [*Laying his hand on his sword.*]
ALBANY, CORNWALL   Dear sir, forbear.
KENT
  Kill thy physician, and the fee bestow
  Upon the foul disease. Revoke thy gift,
  Or whilst I can vent clamor from my throat
  I'll tell thee thou dost evil.
LEAR
  Hear me, recreant, on thine allegiance hear me!   170
  That thou hast sought to make us break our vows,   171
  Which we durst never yet, and with strained pride   172
  To come betwixt our sentence and our power,   173
  Which nor our nature nor our place can bear,   174
  Our potency made good, take thy reward.   175
  Five days we do allot thee for provision
  To shield thee from disasters of the world,   177
  And on the sixth to turn thy hated back
  Upon our kingdom. If on the tenth day following
  Thy banished trunk be found in our dominions,   180
  The moment is thy death. Away! By Jupiter,
  This shall not be revoked.
KENT
  Fare thee well, King. Sith thus thou wilt appear,   183
  Freedom lives hence and banishment is here.

---

159 still always   **160 The true . . . eye** i.e., the means to enable you to
see better. (*Blank* means the white center of the target, or, more probably, the true direct aim, as in "point-blank," traveling in a straight
line.)   **164 vassal** i.e., wretch.   **Miscreant** (Literally, infidel; hence, villain, rascal.)   **170 recreant** traitor   **171 That** in that, since   **172 strained**
excessive   **173 To . . . power** i.e., to block my power to give sentence
174 Which . . . place which neither my temperament nor my office as
king   **175 Our . . . good** my potency now being validated, to show that
I am not merely threatening   **177 disasters** misfortunes   **180 trunk**
body   **183 Sith** since

[*To Cordelia.*] The gods to their dear shelter take thee,
   maid,
That justly think'st and hast most rightly said!
[*To Regan and Goneril.*] And your large speeches may
   your deeds approve,   187
That good effects may spring from words of love.
Thus Kent, O princes, bids you all adieu.
He'll shape his old course in a country new.   *Exit.* 190

   Flourish. Enter Gloucester, with France and
   Burgundy; attendants.

GLOUCESTER
Here's France and Burgundy, my noble lord.
LEAR   My lord of Burgundy,
   We first address toward you, who with this king   193
   Hath rivaled for our daughter. What in the least   194
   Will you require in present dower with her
   Or cease your quest of love?
BURGUNDY   Most royal Majesty,
   I crave no more than hath Your Highness offered,
   Nor will you tender less.
LEAR   Right noble Burgundy,   198
   When she was dear to us we did hold her so,   199
   But now her price is fallen. Sir, there she stands.
   If aught within that little-seeming substance,   201
   Or all of it, with our displeasure pieced,   202
   And nothing more, may fitly like Your Grace,   203
   She's there, and she is yours.
BURGUNDY   I know no answer.
LEAR
   Will you, with those infirmities she owes,   205
   Unfriended, new-adopted to our hate,
   Dowered with our curse and strangered with our oath, 207
   Take her, or leave her?

---

187 your . . . approve may your deeds confirm your speeches with their
vast claims   **190 shape . . . course** follow his traditional plainspoken
ways   **193 address** address myself   **194 rivaled** competed   **198 tender**
offer   **199 so** i.e., *dear*, beloved and valued at a high price   **201 little-
seeming substance** one who seems substantial but whose substance is
in fact little; or, one who refuses to flatter   **202 pieced** added, joined
203 like please   **205 owes** owns   **207 strangered with** made a
stranger by

BURGUNDY   Pardon me, royal sir.
Election makes not up in such conditions.   209

LEAR
Then leave her, sir, for by the power that made me,
I tell you all her wealth. [*To France*.] For you, great King, 211
I would not from your love make such a stray   212
To match you where I hate; therefore beseech you   213
T' avert your liking a more worthier way   214
Than on a wretch whom Nature is ashamed
Almost t' acknowledge hers.

FRANCE   This is most strange,
That she whom even but now was your best object,   217
The argument of your praise, balm of your age,   218
The best, the dearest, should in this trice of time
Commit a thing so monstrous to dismantle   220
So many folds of favor. Sure her offense
Must be of such unnatural degree
That monsters it, or your forevouched affection   223
Fall into taint, which to believe of her   224
Must be a faith that reason without miracle
Should never plant in me.   226

CORDELIA   I yet beseech Your Majesty—
If for I want that glib and oily art   228
To speak and purpose not, since what I well intend   229
I'll do 't before I speak—that you make known
It is no vicious blot, murder, or foulness,
No unchaste action or dishonored step
That hath deprived me of your grace and favor,
But even for want of that for which I am richer: 234
A still-soliciting eye and such a tongue   235

---

209 Election . . . conditions no choice is possible under such conditions   **211 tell you** (1) inform you of (2) enumerate for you.   **For** as
for   **212 make such a stray** stray so far   **213 To** as to.   **beseech** I
beseech   **214 avert your liking** turn your affections   **217 whom** who.
best object main object of love   **218 argument** theme   **220 to** as to
223 monsters it makes it monstrous   **223–224 or . . . taint** or else the
affection for her you have hitherto affirmed (*forevouched*) must fall into
suspicion (*taint*); or, before (ere, *or*) your hitherto-proclaimed affection
could have fallen into decay   **224 which** i.e., that her offense is monstrous   **226 Should** could   **228 for I want** because I lack   **229 purpose
not** not intend to do what I say   **234 for which** for want of which
235 still-soliciting ever-begging

That I am glad I have not, though not to have it
Hath lost me in your liking.

LEAR   Better thou
Hadst not been born than not t' have pleased me better.

FRANCE
Is it but this? A tardiness in nature
Which often leaves the history unspoke   240
That it intends to do? My lord of Burgundy,
What say you to the lady? Love's not love
When it is mingled with regards that stands   243
Aloof from th' entire point. Will you have her?   244
She is herself a dowry.

BURGUNDY   Royal King,
Give but that portion which yourself proposed,
And here I take Cordelia by the hand,
Duchess of Burgundy.

LEAR
Nothing. I have sworn. I am firm.

BURGUNDY [*To Cordelia*]
I am sorry, then, you have so lost a father
That you must lose a husband.

CORDELIA   Peace be with Burgundy!
Since that respects of fortune are his love,   252
I shall not be his wife.

FRANCE
Fairest Cordelia, that art most rich being poor,
Most choice, forsaken, and most loved, despised,
Thee and thy virtues here I seize upon,
Be it lawful I take up what's cast away.   257
                              [*He takes her hand.*]
Gods, gods! 'Tis strange that from their cold'st neglect 258
My love should kindle to inflamed respect.—   259
Thy dowerless daughter, King, thrown to my chance,   260
Is queen of us, of ours, and our fair France.
Not all the dukes of waterish Burgundy   262

---

240 leaves . . . unspoke does not speak aloud the action   **243–244 regards
. . . point** irrelevant considerations   **252 Since that** since. **respects of
fortune** concern for wealth and position   **257 Be it lawful** if it be lawful
that   **258 from . . . neglect** i.e., because the gods seem to have deserted
Cordelia   **259 inflamed respect** ardent affection   **260 chance** lot
262 waterish (1) well-watered with rivers (2) feeble, watery

Can buy this unprized precious maid of me.— 263
Bid them farewell, Cordelia, though unkind. 264
Thou losest here, a better where to find. 265

LEAR
Thou hast her, France. Let her be thine, for we
Have no such daughter, nor shall ever see
That face of hers again. Therefore begone 268
Without our grace, our love, our benison. 269
Come, noble Burgundy.

　　　　Flourish. Exeunt [all but France, Goneril,
　　　　　　　　　　　　Regan, and Cordelia].

FRANCE　Bid farewell to your sisters.

CORDELIA
The jewels of our father, with washed eyes 272
Cordelia leaves you. I know you what you are,
And like a sister am most loath to call 274
Your faults as they are named. Love well our father. 275
To your professèd bosoms I commit him. 276
But yet, alas, stood I within his grace,
I would prefer him to a better place. 278
So, farewell to you both.

REGAN
Prescribe not us our duty.

GONERIL　　　　　　　　Let your study
Be to content your lord, who hath received you
At Fortune's alms. You have obedience scanted, 282
And well are worth the want that you have wanted. 283

CORDELIA
Time shall unfold what plighted cunning hides; 284

---

263 unprized not appreciated (with perhaps a sense also of "price-less") **264 though unkind** though they have behaved unnaturally **265 here** this place. **where** place elsewhere **268–269 Therefore . . . benison** (Said perhaps to Cordelia and to the King of France.) **benison** blessing **272 The** you, the. **washed** tear-washed **274 like a sister** i.e., because I am your sister **275 as . . . named** by their true names **276 professèd bosoms** publicly avowed love **278 prefer** advance, recommend **282 At . . . alms** as a pittance or dole from Fortune. **scanted** stinted **283 well . . . wanted** well deserve the lack of affection which you yourself have shown. (*Want* may also refer to her dowry.) **284 plighted** pleated, enfolded

Who covers faults, at last shame them derides.   285
Well may you prosper!
FRANCE   Come, my fair Cordelia.
                 Exeunt France and Cordelia.
GONERIL   Sister, it is not little I have to say of what most
nearly appertains to us both. I think our father will
hence tonight.
REGAN   That's most certain, and with you; next month
with us.
GONERIL   You see how full of changes his age is; the
observation we have made of it hath not been little.
He always loved our sister most, and with what poor
judgment he hath now cast her off appears too grossly.   295
REGAN   'Tis the infirmity of his age. Yet he hath ever but
slenderly known himself.
GONERIL   The best and soundest of his time hath been   298
but rash. Then must we look from his age to receive   299
not alone the imperfections of long-ingraffed condi-   300
tion, but therewithal the unruly waywardness that in-   301
firm and choleric years bring with them.
REGAN   Such unconstant starts are we like to have from   303
him as this of Kent's banishment.
GONERIL   There is further compliment of leave-taking   305
between France and him. Pray you, let us hit together.   306
If our father carry authority with such disposition as
he bears, this last surrender of his will but offend us.   308
REGAN   We shall further think of it.
GONERIL   We must do something, and i' the heat.   310
                         Exeunt.

✤

285 Who . . . derides i.e., time, who may conceal faults for a while, at
last exposes and derides them shamefully   **295 grossly** obviously
298–299 The best . . . rash i.e., even in the prime of his life, he was
stormy and unpredictable   **300–301 long-ingraffed condition** long-
implanted habit   **301 therewithal** added thereto   **303 unconstant starts**
impulsive acts.   **like** likely   **305 compliment** ceremony   **306 hit**
agree   **308 last surrender** latest abdication.   **offend** harm, injure
310 i' the heat i.e., while the iron is hot

1.2 *Enter Bastard [Edmund, with a letter].*

EDMUND

Thou, Nature, art my goddess; to thy law　　　　　　1
My services are bound. Wherefore should I
Stand in the plague of custom and permit　　　　　　3
The curiosity of nations to deprive me,　　　　　　4
For that I am some twelve or fourteen moonshines　5
Lag of a brother? Why bastard? Wherefore base?　6
When my dimensions are as well compact,　　　　　　7
My mind as generous, and my shape as true,　　　　8
As honest madam's issue? Why brand they us　　　　9
With base? With baseness? Bastardy? Base, base?
Who in the lusty stealth of nature take　　　　　　11
More composition and fierce quality　　　　　　　　12
Than doth within a dull, stale, tirèd bed
Go to th' creating a whole tribe of fops　　　　　　14
Got 'tween asleep and wake? Well then,　　　　　　15
Legitimate Edgar, I must have your land.
Our father's love is to the bastard Edmund
As to th' legitimate. Fine word, "legitimate"!
Well, my legitimate, if this letter speed　　　　　　19
And my invention thrive, Edmund the base　　　　　20
Shall top th' legitimate. I grow, I prosper.
Now, gods, stand up for bastards!

　　Enter Gloucester.

GLOUCESTER

Kent banished thus? And France in choler parted?
And the King gone tonight? Prescribed his power,　24
Confined to exhibition? All this done　　　　　　　25
Upon the gad? Edmund, how now? What news?　　26

1.2. Location: The Earl of Gloucester's house.
1 Nature i.e., the material world, governed solely by mechanistic amoral forces   **3 Stand . . . custom** submit to the vexatious injustice of convention   **4 curiosity** fastidious distinctions.   **nations** societies   **5 For that** because.   **moonshines** months   **6 Lag of** younger than   **7 compact** knit together, fitted   **8 generous** noble, refined   **9 honest** chaste   **11–12 take . . . quality** acquire greater completeness and energetic force   **14 fops** fools   **15 Got** begotten   **19 speed** succeed, prosper   **20 invention thrive** scheme prosper   **24 tonight** last night.   **Prescribed** limited   **25 exhibition** an allowance, pension   **26 Upon the gad** suddenly, as if pricked by a gad or spur

EDMUND   So please your lordship, none.
                              [*Putting up the letter.*]
GLOUCESTER   Why so earnestly seek you to put up that
    letter?
EDMUND   I know no news, my lord.
GLOUCESTER   What paper were you reading?
EDMUND   Nothing, my lord.
GLOUCESTER   No? What needed then that terrible dis- 33
    patch of it into your pocket? The quality of nothing 34
    hath not such need to hide itself. Let's see. Come, if it
    be nothing I shall not need spectacles.
EDMUND   I beseech you, sir, pardon me. It is a letter
    from my brother, that I have not all o'erread; and for
    so much as I have perused, I find it not fit for your
    o'erlooking.   40
GLOUCESTER   Give me the letter, sir.
EDMUND   I shall offend either to detain or give it. The
    contents, as in part I understand them, are to blame.   43
GLOUCESTER   Let's see, let's see.
                              [*Edmund gives the letter.*]
EDMUND   I hope for my brother's justification he wrote
    this but as an essay or taste of my virtue.   46
GLOUCESTER (*Reads*) "This policy and reverence of age 47
    makes the world bitter to the best of our times, keeps 48
    our fortunes from us till our oldness cannot relish
    them. I begin to find an idle and fond bondage in the   50
    oppression of aged tyranny, who sways not as it hath   51
    power but as it is suffered. Come to me, that of this I 52
    may speak more. If our father would sleep till I waked
    him, you should enjoy half his revenue forever and
    live the beloved of your brother,   Edgar."
    Hum! Conspiracy! "Sleep till I waked him, you
    should enjoy half his revenue." My son Edgar! Had he
    a hand to write this? A heart and brain to breed it

33–34 terrible dispatch fearful haste   40 o'erlooking perusal   43 to
blame (The Folio reading, *too blame*, "too blameworthy to be shown,"
may be correct.)   46 essay or taste i.e., assay, test   47 policy and reverence of i.e., policy of reverencing   48 the best . . . times the best years
of our lives, i.e., our youth   50 idle useless. fond foolish   51 who
sways which rules   52 suffered permitted (by the young, who could
seize power if they wished)

in? When came you to this? Who brought it?   59

EDMUND It was not brought me, my lord; there's the
cunning of it. I found it thrown in at the casement of   61
my closet.   62

GLOUCESTER You know the character to be your broth-   63
er's?

EDMUND If the matter were good, my lord, I drust   65
swear it were his; but in respect of that I would fain   66
think it were not.

GLOUCESTER It is his.

EDMUND It is his hand, my lord, but I hope his heart is
not in the contents.

GLOUCESTER Has he never before sounded you in this
business?

EDMUND Never, my lord. But I have heard him oft
maintain it to be fit that, sons at perfect age and fathers 74
declined, the father should be as ward to the son, and   75
the son manage his revenue.

GLOUCESTER O villain, villain! His very opinion in the   77
letter! Abhorred villain! Unnatural, detested, brutish   78
villain! Worse than brutish! Go, sirrah, seek him. I'll   79
apprehend him. Abominable villain! Where is he?

EDMUND I do not well know, my lord. If it shall please
you to suspend your indignation against my brother
till you can derive from him better testimony of his
intent, you should run a certain course; where, if you   84
violently proceed against him, mistaking his purpose,
it would make a great gap in your own honor and
shake in pieces the heart of his obedience. I dare pawn   87
down my life for him that he hath writ this to feel my   88
affection to your honor, and to no other pretense of   89
danger.   90

---

59 to this upon this (letter) **61 casement** window **62 closet** private
room **63 character** handwriting **65 matter** contents **66 in . . . that**
considering what the contents are. **fain** gladly **74 fit** fitting, appropriate. **perfect age** full maturity **75 declined** having become feeble
77 villain i.e., vile wretch, diabolical schemer **78 Abhorred** abhor-
rent. **detested** detestable **79 sirrah** (Form of address used to inferiors
or children.) **84 run a certain course** proceed with safety and cer-
tainty. **where** whereas **87–88 pawn down** stake **88 feel** feel out
89–90 pretense of danger dangerous purpose

GLOUCESTER Think you so?

EDMUND If your honor judge it meet, I will place you 92
where you shall hear us confer of this, and by an au-
ricular assurance have your satisfaction, and that without any further delay than this very evening.

GLOUCESTER He cannot be such a monster—

EDMUND Nor is not, sure.

GLOUCESTER To his father, that so tenderly and enfirely
loves him. Heaven and earth! Edmund, seek him out;
wind me into him, I pray you. Frame the business 100
after your own wisdom. I would unstate myself to be 101
in a due resolution. 102

EDMUND I will seek him, sir, presently, convey the 103
business as I shall find means, and acquaint you
withal. 105

GLOUCESTER These late eclipses in the sun and moon 106
portend no good to us. Though the wisdom of nature 107
can reason it thus and thus, yet nature finds itself
scourged by the sequent effects. Love cools, friendship 109
falls off, brothers divide; in cities, mutinies; in countries, discord; in palaces, treason; and the bond
cracked twixt son and father. This villain of mine
comes under the prediction; there's son against father.
The King falls from bias of nature; there's father 114
against child. We have seen the best of our time.
Machinations, hollowness, treachery, and all ruinous
disorders follow us disquietly to our graves. Find out
this villain, Edmund; it shall lose thee nothing. Do it
carefully. And the noble and truehearted Kent banished! His offense, honesty! 'Tis strange.   *Exit.*

EDMUND This is the excellent foppery of the world, that 121
when we are sick in fortune—often the surfeits of our
own behavior—we make guilty of our disasters the
sun, the moon, and stars, as if we were villains on 124
necessity, fools by heavenly compulsion, knaves,

92 meet fitting, proper   **100 wind me into him** insinuate yourself into
his confidence. (*Me* is used colloquially.)   **Frame** arrange   **101 after
your own wisdom** as you think best   **101–102 unstate . . . resolution** suffer loss of all to know the truth, have my doubts resolved
103 presently immediately.   **convey** manage   **105 withal** therewith
106 late recent   **107 the wisdom of nature** natural science   **109 sequent
effects** i.e., devastating consequences   **114 bias of nature** natural incli-
nation   **121 foppery** foolishness   **124 on** by

thieves, and treachers by spherical predominance, 126
drunkards, liars, and adulterers by an enforced obedience of planetary influence, and all that we are evil
in, by a divine thrusting on. An admirable evasion of 129
whoremaster man, to lay his goatish disposition on 130
the charge of a star! My father compounded with my 131
mother under the Dragon's tail and my nativity was 132
under Ursa Major, so that it follows I am rough and 133
lecherous. Fut, I should have been that I am, had the 134
maidenliest star in the firmament twinkled on my bas-
tardizing. Edgar—

    Enter Edgar.

and pat he comes like the catastrophe of the old com- 137
edy. My cue is villainous melancholy, with a sigh like
Tom o' Bedlam.—O, these eclipses do portend these 139
divisions! Fa, sol, la, mi.

EDGAR How now, brother Edmund, what serious con-
templation are you in?

EDMUND I am thinking, brother, of a prediction I read
this other day, what should follow these eclipses.   144

EDGAR Do you busy yourself with that?

EDMUND I promise you, the effects he writes of succeed 146
unhappily, as of unnaturalness between the child and 147
the parent, death, dearth, dissolutions of ancient ami-
ties, divisions in state, menaces and maledictions
against king and nobles, needless diffidences, banish- 150
ment of friends, dissipation of cohorts, nuptial 151
breaches, and I know not what.

EDGAR How long have you been a sectary astronom- 153
ical?   154

EDMUND Come, come, when saw you my father last?

---

126 treachers traitors. **spherical predominance** astrological determi-
nism; because a certain planet was ascendant at the hour of our birth
129 divine supernatural **130 goatish** lecherous **131–132 compounded
. . . Dragon's tail** had sex with my mother under the constellation
Draco **133 Ursa Major** the big bear **134 Fut** i.e., 'sfoot, by Christ's
foot. **that** what **137 catastrophe** conclusion, resolution (of a play)
139 Tom o' Bedlam a lunatic patient of Bethlehem Hospital in London
turned out to beg for his bread **144 this other day** the other day
146–147 succeed unhappily follow unluckily **150 needless diffidences**
groundless distrust of others **151 dissipation of cohorts** breaking up of
military companies, large-scale desertions **153–154 sectary astronomi-
cal** believer in astrology

EDGAR The night gone by.

EDMUND Spake you with him?

EDGAR Ay, two hours together.

EDMUND Parted you in good terms? Found you no displeasure in him by word nor countenance?   160

EDGAR None at all.

EDMUND Bethink yourself wherein you may have offended him, and at my entreaty forbear his presence 163
until some little time hath qualified the heat of his dis- 164
pleasure, which at this instant so rageth in him that
with the mischief of your person it would scarcely 166
allay.   167

EDGAR Some villain hath done me wrong.

EDMUND That's my fear. I pray you, have a continent 169
forbearance till the speed of his rage goes slower; and, 170
as I say, retire with me to my lodging, from whence I
will fitly bring you to hear my lord speak. Pray ye, go! 172
There's my key. [*He gives a key.*] If you do stir abroad,
go armed.

EDGAR Armed, brother?

EDMUND Brother, I advise you to the best. I am no honest man if there be any good meaning toward you. I 177
have told you what I have seen and heard, but faintly,
nothing like the image and horror of it. Pray you, 179
away.

EDGAR Shall I hear from you anon?

EDMUND

I do serve you in this business.   *Exit* [*Edgar*].
A credulous father and a brother noble,
Whose nature is so far from doing harms
That he suspects none; on whose foolish honesty
My practices ride easy. I see the business.   186
Let me, if not by birth, have lands by wit.   187
All with me's meet that I can fashion fit.   *Exit.* 188

❖

160 countenance demeanor   **163 forbear his presence** avoid meeting him
164 qualified moderated   **166 with . . . person** with the harmful effect of
your presence; or, even if there were injury done to you   **167 allay** be
allayed   **169–170 have . . . forbearance** keep a wary distance   **172 fitly** at a
fit time   **177 meaning** intention   **179 image and horror** horrid reality
186 practices plots.   **the business** i.e., how my plots should proceed
187 wit intelligence   **188 meet** justifiable.   **fit** i.e., to my purpose

1.3   *Enter Goneril, and [Oswald, her] steward.*

GONERIL   Did my father strike my gentleman for chid-
ing of his fool?
OSWALD   Ay, madam.
GONERIL
By day and night he wrongs me! Every hour
He flashes into one gross crime or other   5
That sets us all at odds. I'll not endure it.
His knights grow riotous, and himself upbraids us
On every trifle. When he returns from hunting
I will not speak with him. Say I am sick.
If you come slack of former services   10
You shall do well; the fault of it I'll answer.
                                        [*Horns within.*]
OSWALD   He's coming, madam. I hear him.
GONERIL
Put on what weary negligence you please,
You and your fellows. I'd have it come to question.   14
If he distaste it, let him to my sister,   15
Whose mind and mine, I know, in that are one,
Not to be overruled. Idle old man,   17
That still would manage those authorities   18
That he hath given away! Now, by my life,
Old fools are babes again, and must be used
With checks as flatteries, when they are seen abused.   21
Remember what I have said.
OSWALD   Well, madam.
GONERIL
And let his knights have colder looks among you.
What grows of it, no matter. Advise your fellows so.
I would breed from hence occasions, and I shall,   26
That I may speak. I'll write straight to my sister   27
To hold my very course. Prepare for dinner.   *Exeunt.*

1.3. Location: The Duke of Albany's palace.
5 crime offense   **10 come slack** fall short   **14 come to question** be
made an issue   **15 distaste** dislike   **17 Idle** foolish   **18 manage those
authorities** i.e., assert those prerogatives   **21 With . . . abused** with
rebukes instead of flattery, when they (old men) act unselfknowingly (as
Lear does)   **26–27 I would . . . speak** I wish to create from these inci-
dents the opportunity to speak out   **27 straight** immediately

1.4   *Enter Kent [disguised].*

KENT
  If but as well I other accents borrow   1
  That can my speech diffuse, my good intent   2
  May carry through itself to that full issue   3
  For which I rased my likeness. Now, banished Kent,   4
  If thou canst serve where thou dost stand condemned,
  So may it come thy master, whom thou lov'st,   6
  Shall find thee full of labors.

    *Horns within. Enter Lear, [Knights,] and
    attendants.*

LEAR   Let me not stay a jot for dinner. Go get it ready.   8
  [*Exit an Attendant.*] How now, what art thou?   9
KENT   A man, sir.
LEAR   What dost thou profess? What wouldst thou   11
  with us?
KENT   I do profess to be no less than I seem: to serve
  him truly that will put me in trust, to love him that is
  honest, to converse with him that is wise and says   15
  little, to fear judgment, to fight when I cannot choose,   16
  and to eat no fish.   17
LEAR   What art thou?
KENT   A very honest-hearted fellow, and as poor as the
  King.
LEAR   If thou be'st as poor for a subject as he's for a
  king, thou'rt poor enough. What wouldst thou?
KENT   Service.
LEAR   Who wouldst thou serve?
KENT   You.

**1.4. Location: The Duke of Albany's palace still. The sense of time is
virtually continuous.**
1 as well i.e., as well as I have disguised myself by means of costume
2 diffuse i.e., disguise   **3 carry . . . issue** succeed to that perfect result
4 rased my likeness erased my outward appearance (perhaps with a
sense also of having *razed* or scraped off his beard)   **6 come** come to
pass that   **8 stay** wait   **9 s.d. Attendant** (This attendant may be a
knight; certainly the one who speaks at l. 50 is a knight.)   **11 What . . .
profess** what is your special calling. (But Kent puns in his answer on
profess meaning to "claim.")   **15 honest** honorable.   **converse** associate   **16 judgment** i.e., God's judgment.   **choose** i.e., choose but to
fight   **17 eat no fish** i.e., eat a manly diet (?), be a good Protestant (?)

LEAR　Dost thou know me, fellow?

KENT　No, sir, but you have that in your countenance 27
which I would fain call master.

LEAR　What's that?

KENT　Authority.

LEAR　What services canst thou do?

KENT　I can keep honest counsel, ride, run, mar a curi- 32
ous tale in telling it, and deliver a plain message 33
bluntly. That which ordinary men are fit for I am
qualified in, and the best of me is diligence.

LEAR　How old art thou?

KENT　Not so young, sir, to love a woman for singing, 37
nor so old to dote on her for anything. I have years on
my back forty-eight.

LEAR　Follow me; thou shalt serve me. If I like thee no
worse after dinner, I will not part from thee yet. Dinner, ho, dinner! Where's my knave, my fool? Go you
and call my fool hither.　　　　　　　　　[Exit one.]

　　　Enter steward [Oswald].

You! You, sirrah, where's my daughter?

OSWALD　So please you—　　　　　　　　　　Exit.

LEAR　What says the fellow there? Call the clodpoll back. 46
[Exit a Knight.] Where's my fool, ho? I think the
world's asleep.

　　　[Enter Knight.]

How now? Where's that mongrel?

KNIGHT　He says, my lord, your daughter is not well.

LEAR　Why came not the slave back to me when I called
him?

KNIGHT　Sir, he answered me in the roundest manner, 53
he would not.

LEAR　He would not?

KNIGHT　My lord, I know not what the matter is, but to
my judgment Your Highness is not entertained with 57
that ceremonious affection as you were wont. There's
a great abatement of kindness appears as well in the

27 **countenance** face and bearing　32 **keep honest counsel** respect
confidences　32–33 **curious** ornate, elaborate　37 **to love** as to love
46 **clodpoll** blockhead　53 **roundest** bluntest　57 **entertained** treated

general dependents as in the Duke himself also and
your daughter.

LEAR Ha? Sayst thou so?

KNIGHT I beseech you, pardon me, my lord, if I be mis-
taken, for my duty cannot be silent when I think Your
Highness wronged.

LEAR Thou but rememberest me of mine own concep- 66
tion. I have perceived a most faint neglect of late, 67
which I have rather blamed as mine own jealous curi- 68
osity than as a very pretense and purpose of unkind- 69
ness. I will look further into 't. But where's my fool? I
have not seen him this two days. 71

KNIGHT Since my young lady's going into France, sir,
the Fool hath much pined away.

LEAR No more of that. I have noted it well. Go you and
tell my daughter I would speak with her. [*Exit one.*]
Go you call hither my fool. [*Exit one.*]

Enter steward [Oswald].

O, you, sir, you, come you hither, sir. Who am I, sir?

OSWALD My lady's father.

LEAR "My lady's father"? My lord's knave! You whoreson dog, you slave, you cur!

OSWALD I am none of these, my lord, I beseech your
pardon.

LEAR Do you bandy looks with me, you rascal? 83
[*He strikes Oswald.*]

OSWALD I'll not be strucken, my lord. 84

KENT Nor tripped neither, you base football player. 85
[*He trips up Oswald's heels.*]

LEAR I thank thee, fellow. Thou serv'st me, and I'll love
thee.

KENT Come, sir, arise, away! I'll teach you differences. 88

---

66 rememberest remind **66-67 conception** idea, thought **67 faint**
halfhearted **68-69 jealous curiosity** overscrupulous regard for matters
of etiquette **69 very pretense** true intention **71 this** these **83 bandy**
volley, exchange (as in tennis) **84 strucken** struck **85 football** (A
raucous street game played by the lower classes.) **88 differences**
distinctions in rank

Away, away! If you will measure your lubber's length   89
again, tarry; but away! Go to. Have you wisdom? So.   90
        [*He pushes Oswald out.*]

LEAR Now, my friendly knave, I thank thee. There's
earnest of thy service. [*He gives Kent money.*]   92

 Enter Fool.

FOOL Let me hire him too. Here's my coxcomb.   93
        [*Offering Kent his cap.*]
LEAR How now, my pretty knave, how dost thou?
FOOL [*To Kent*] Sirrah, you were best take my coxcomb.   95
KENT Why, Fool?
FOOL Why? For taking one's part that's out of favor.
Nay, an thou canst not smile as the wind sits, thou'lt   98
catch cold shortly. There, take my coxcomb. Why, this   99
fellow has banished two on 's daughters and did the   100
third a blessing against his will. If thou follow him, thou   101
must needs wear my coxcomb.—How now, nuncle?   102
Would I had two coxcombs and two daughters.
LEAR Why, my boy?
FOOL If I gave them all my living, I'd keep my cox-   105
combs myself. There's mine; beg another of thy
daughters.
LEAR Take heed, sirrah—the whip.
FOOL Truth's a dog must to kennel. He must be
whipped out, when the Lady Brach may stand by the   110
fire and stink.
LEAR A pestilent gall to me!   112
FOOL Sirrah, I'll teach thee a speech.
LEAR Do.
FOOL Mark it, nuncle:

89–90 If . . . again i.e., if you want to be laid out flat again, you clumsy
ox **90 Have you wisdom** i.e., are you smart enough to make a quick
retreat **92 earnest** partial advance payment **93 coxcomb** fool's cap,
crested with a red comb **95 you were best** you had better **98 an . . .
sits** i.e., if you can't play along with those in power **99 catch cold** i.e.,
find yourself out in the cold **100 banished** (i.e., paradoxically, by giving
Goneril and Regan his kingdom, Lear has lost them, given them power
over him). **on 's** of his **101 blessing** i.e., bestowing Cordelia on
France **102 nuncle** (Contraction of "mine uncle," the Fool's way of
addressing Lear.) **105 living** property **110 Brach** hound bitch (here
suggesting flattery) **112 gall** irritation

Have more than thou showest,
Speak less than thou knowest,
Lend less than thou owest,   118
Ride more than thou goest,   119
Learn more than thou trowest,   120
Set less than thou throwest;   121
Leave thy drink and thy whore,
And keep in-a-door,   123
And thou shalt have more   124
Than two tens to a score.   125

KENT This is nothing, Fool.

FOOL Then 'tis like the breath of an unfee'd lawyer; you   127
gave me nothing for 't. Can you make no use of nothing, nuncle?

LEAR Why, no, boy. Nothing can be made out of
nothing.

FOOL [*To Kent*] Prithee, tell him; so much the rent of his   132
land comes to. He will not believe a fool.

LEAR A bitter fool!   134

FOOL Dost thou know the difference, my boy, between
a bitter fool and a sweet one?

LEAR No, lad. Teach me.

FOOL

That lord that counseled thee
   To give away thy land,
Come place him here by me;
   Do thou for him stand.   141
The sweet and bitter fool
   Will presently appear: 143
The one in motley here,   144
   The other found out there.   145

LEAR Dost thou call me fool, boy?

---

118 owest own   **119 goest** i.e., on foot. (Travel prudently on horseback,
not afoot.)   **120 Learn** i.e., listen to.   **trowest** believe   **121 Set . . .
throwest** stake less at dice than you have a chance to throw, i.e., don't
bet all you can   **123 in-a-door** indoors, at home   **124–125 shalt . . .
score** i.e., will do better than break even (since a *score* equals two tens,
or 20)   **127 breath** speech, counsel   **132 rent** (Lear has no land, hence
no rent.)   **134 bitter** satirical   **141 for him stand** impersonate him
143 presently immediately   **144 motley** the particolored dress of the
professional fool. (The Fool identifies himself as the sweet fool, Lear as
the bitter fool who counseled himself to give away his kingdom.)
145 there (The Fool points at Lear.)

FOOL All thy other titles thou hast given away; that
thou wast born with.

KENT This is not altogether fool, my lord.

FOOL No, faith, lords and great men will not let me; if 150
I had a monopoly out, they would have part on 't. And 151
ladies too, they will not let me have all the fool to myself; they'll be snatching. Nuncle, give me an egg and 153
I'll give thee two crowns.

LEAR What two crowns shall they be?

FOOL Why, after I have cut the egg i' the middle and eat 156
up the meat, the two crowns of the egg. When thou 157
clovest thy crown i' the middle and gav'st away both
parts, thou bor'st thine ass on thy back o'er the dirt. 159
Thou hadst little wit in thy bald crown when thou
gav'st thy golden one away. If I speak like myself in 161
this, let him be whipped that first finds it so. 162
[Sings.] "Fools had ne'er less grace in a year, 163
          For wise men are grown foppish 164
        And know not how their wits to wear, 165
          Their manners are so apish."

LEAR When were you wont to be so full of songs,
sirrah?

FOOL I have used it, nuncle, e'er since thou mad'st thy 169
daughters thy mothers; for when thou gav'st them the
rod and putt'st down thine own breeches,
[Sings] "Then they for sudden joy did weep,
          And I for sorrow sung,
        That such a king should play bo-peep 174
          And go the fools among."
Prithee, nuncle, keep a schoolmaster that can teach thy
fool to lie. I would fain learn to lie.

---

150 No ... let me i.e., great persons at court will not let me monopolize
folly; I am not *altogether fool* in the sense of being "all the fool there
is"   **151 a monopoly out** a corner on the market. (The granting of
monopolies was a common abuse under King James and Queen Elizabeth.)   **on 't** of it   **153 snatching** i.e., at the Fool's phallic bauble
156 eat eaten, et   **157 the meat** the edible part   **159 bor'st ... dirt** i.e.,
bore the ass instead of letting the ass bear you   **161 like myself** i.e., like
a fool   **162 whipped** i.e., as a fool.   **finds it so** discovers from his
experience that it is true (as Lear is now discovering)   **163 Fools ...
year** fools have never enjoyed less favor; i.e., they are made obsolete by
the folly of supposed wise men   **164 foppish** foolish, vain   **165 wear**
use   **169 used** practiced   **174 bo-peep** a child's game

LEAR An you lie, sirrah, we'll have you whipped. 178

FOOL I marvel what kin thou and thy daughters are.
They'll have me whipped for speaking true, thou'lt
have me whipped for lying, and sometimes I am
whipped for holding my peace. I had rather be any
kind o' thing than a fool. And yet I would not be thee,
nuncle. Thou hast pared thy wit o' both sides and left
nothing i' the middle. Here comes one o' the parings.

Enter Goneril.

LEAR

How now, daughter? What makes that frontlet on? 186
You are too much of late i' the frown.

FOOL Thou wast a pretty fellow when thou hadst no
need to care for her frowning; now thou art an O with- 189
out a figure. I am better than thou art now; I am a fool, 190
thou art nothing. [*To Goneril.*] Yes, forsooth, I will
hold my tongue; so your face bids me, though you say
nothing.

Mum, mum,
He that keeps nor crust nor crumb, 195
Weary of all, shall want some. 196

[*Pointing to Lear.*] That's a shelled peascod. 197

GONERIL

Not only, sir, this your all-licensed fool, 198
But other of your insolent retinue
Do hourly carp and quarrel, breaking forth 200
In rank and not-to-be-endurèd riots. Sir, 201
I had thought by making this well known unto you
To have found a safe redress, but now grow fearful, 203
By what yourself too late have spoke and done, 204
That you protect this course and put it on 205
By your allowance; which if you should, the fault 206

(handwritten margin notes:) Rejects THE Fool B/C HE is TRUTHFUL, speaks THE TRUTH AB...Go...

---

178 An if **186 frontlet** a band worn on the forehead; here, frown
189–190 O without a figure cipher of no value unless preceded by a
digit **195–196 He . . . some** i.e., that person who gives away all his
possessions, having wearied of them, will find himself in need of
part of what is gone. **nor . . . nor** either . . . nor **196 want** lack
197 shelled peascod shelled pea pod, i.e., nothing, empty **198 all-
licensed** authorized to speak or act freely **200 carp** find fault
201 rank gross, excessive **203 safe** certain **204 too late** all too recently **205 put it on** encourage it **206 allowance** approval

Would not scape censure, nor the redresses sleep   207
Which in the tender of a wholesome weal   208
Might in their working do you that offense,
Which else were shame, that then necessity   210
Will call discreet proceeding.   211

FOOL   For you know, nuncle,

    "The hedge sparrow fed the cuckoo so long   213
    That it had its head bit off by its young."   214

So, out went the candle, and we were left darkling.   215

LEAR   Are you our daughter?

GONERIL

I would you would make use of your good wisdom,
Whereof I know you are fraught, and put away   218
These dispositions which of late transport you   219
From what you rightly are.

FOOL   May not an ass know when the cart draws the   221
horse? Whoop, Jug! I love thee.   222

LEAR

Docs any here know me? This is not Lear.
Does Lear walk thus, speak thus? Where are his eyes?
Either his notion weakens, his discernings   225
Are lethargied—Ha! Waking? 'Tis not so.   226
Who is it that can tell me who I am?

FOOL   Lear's shadow.

LEAR

I would learn that; for, by the marks of sovereignty, 229
Knowledge, and reason, I should be false persuaded   230
I had daughters.   231

---

207 redresses sleep punishments (for the riotous conduct of Lear's
attendants) lie dormant   **208 tender . . . weal** care for preservation of
the peace of the state   **210 else were** in other circumstances would be
regarded as.   **then necessity** the necessity of the times   **211 discreet**
prudent   **213 cuckoo** a bird that lays its eggs in other birds' nests
214 its young i.e., the young cuckoo   **215 darkling** in the dark
218 fraught freighted, laden   **219 dispositions** states of mind, moods
221–222 May . . . horse i.e., may not even a fool see that matters are
backwards when a daughter lectures her father   **222 Jug** i.e., Joan. (The
origin of this phrase is uncertain.)   **225 notion** intellectual power
225–226 discernings Are lethargied faculties are asleep   **226 Waking**
i.e., am I really awake   **229 that** i.e., who I am.   **marks of sovereignty**
outward and visible evidence of being king   **230–231 I should . . .
daughters** i.e., all these outward signs of sanity and status would seem
to suggest (falsely) that I am the king who had obedient daughters

FOOL Which they will make an obedient father.   232
LEAR Your name, fair gentlewoman?
GONERIL
  This admiration, sir, is much o' the savor   234
  Of other your new pranks. I do beseech you   235
  To understand my purposes aright.
  As you are old and reverend, should be wise.   237
  Here do you keep a hundred knights and squires,
  Men so disordered, so debauched and bold,   239
  That this our court, infected with their manners,
  Shows like a riotous inn. Epicurism and lust   241
  Makes it more like a tavern or a brothel
  Than a graced palace. The shame itself doth speak   243
  For instant remedy. Be then desired,   244
  By her that else will take the thing she begs,
  A little to disquantity your train,   246
  And the remainders that shall still depend   247
  To be such men as may besort your age,   248
  Which know themselves and you.
LEAR   Darkness and devils!
  Saddle my horses! Call my train together! [*Exit one.*]
  Degenerate bastard, I'll not trouble thee.
  Yet have I left a daughter.
GONERIL
  You strike my people, and your disordered rabble
  Make servants of their betters.

          Enter Albany.

LEAR
  Woe, that too late repents!—O, sir, are you come?   255
  Is it your will? Speak, sir.—Prepare my horses.
                                        [*Exit one.*]
  Ingratitude, thou marble-hearted fiend,
  More hideous when thou show'st thee in a child
  Than the sea monster!
ALBANY Pray, sir, be patient.

---

232 **Which** whom   234 **admiration** (guise of) wonderment   235 **other**
other of   237 **should** i.e., you should   239 **disordered** disorderly
241 **Shows** appears. **Epicurism** luxury   243 **graced** honorable
244 **desired** requested   246 **disquantity your train** diminish the number
of your attendants   247 **the remainders . . . depend** those who remain
to attend you   248 **besort** befit   255 **Woe, that** woe to the person who

LEAR [*To Goneril*]   Detested kite, thou liest!   261
  My train are men of choice and rarest parts,   262
  That all particulars of duty know
  And in the most exact regard support   264
  The worships of their name. O most small fault,   265
  How ugly didst thou in Cordelia show!
  Which, like an engine, wrenched my frame of nature   267
  From the fixed place, drew from my heart all love,
  And added to the gall. O Lear, Lear, Lear!
  Beat at this gate [*Striking his head*] that let thy folly in
  And thy dear judgment out! Go, go, my people.   271
                              [*Exeunt some.*]

ALBANY
  My lord, I am guiltless as I am ignorant
  Of what hath moved you.
LEAR   It may be so, my lord.
  Hear, Nature, hear! Dear goddess, hear!
  Suspend thy purpose if thou didst intend
  To make this creature fruitful!
  Into her womb convey sterility;
  Dry up in her the organs of increase,
  And from her derogate body never spring   279
  A babe to honor her! If she must teem,   280
  Create her child of spleen, that it may live   281
  And be a thwart disnatured torment to her!   282
  Let it stamp wrinkles in her brow of youth,
  With cadent tears fret channels in her cheeks,   284
  Turn all her mother's pains and benefits   285
  To laughter and contempt, that she may feel
  How sharper than a serpent's tooth it is
  To have a thankless child! Away, away!
                              Exit [*with Kent and the rest*
                                  of Lear's followers].

---

261 **kite** bird of prey   262 **parts** qualities   264 **in . . . regard** with
extreme care   265 **worships** honors, reputations   267 **engine** powerful
mechanical contrivance, able to wrench Lear's *frame of nature* or
natural self from his *fixed place* or foundation like a building being torn
from its foundation   271 **dear** precious   279 **derogate** debased
280 **teem** increase the species   281 **of spleen** consisting only of malice   282 **thwart disnatured** obstinate, perverse, and unnatural, unfil-
ial   284 **cadent** falling.   **fret** wear   285 **mother's** motherly.   **benefits**
kind offerings

ALBANY
  Now, gods that we adore, whereof comes this?
GONERIL
  Never afflict yourself to know more of it,
  But let his disposition have that scope   291
  As dotage gives it.   292

  Enter Lear.

LEAR
  What, fifty of my followers at a clap?
  Within a fortnight?
ALBANY   What's the matter, sir?
LEAR
  I'll tell thee. [*To Goneril.*] Life and death! I am ashamed
  That thou hast power to shake my manhood thus,
  That these hot tears, which break from me perforce,
  Should make thee worth them. Blasts and fogs upon
    thee!
  Th' untented woundings of a father's curse   299
  Pierce every sense about thee! Old fond eyes,   300
  Beweep this cause again, I'll pluck ye out   301
  And cast you, with the waters that you loose,   302
  To temper clay. Yea, is 't come to this?   303
  Ha! Let it be so. I have another daughter,
  Who, I am sure, is kind and comfortable.   305
  When she shall hear this of thee, with her nails
  She'll flay thy wolvish visage. Thou shalt find
  That I'll resume the shape which thou dost think
  I have cast off forever.   *Exit.*
GONERIL   Do you mark that?
ALBANY
  I cannot be so partial, Goneril,
  To the great love I bear you—   311
GONERIL
  Pray you, content.—What, Oswald, ho!
  [*To the Fool.*] You, sir, more knave than fool, after your
    master.

---

291 disposition humor, mood **292 As** which **299 untented** too deep to
be probed and cleansed **300 fond** foolish **301 Beweep** if you weep
for **302 loose** let loose **303 temper** soften **305 comfortable** willing to
comfort **311 To** because of

FOOL   Nuncle Lear, nuncle Lear! Tarry, take the Fool with 314
    thee.   315
  A fox, when one has caught her,
  And such a daughter
  Should sure to the slaughter,   318
  If my cap would buy a halter.
  So the Fool follows after.   *Exit.*

GONERIL
 This man hath had good counsel. A hundred knights?
 'Tis politic and safe to let him keep   322
 At point a hundred knights—yes, that on every dream, 323
 Each buzz, each fancy, each complaint, dislike,   324
 He may enguard his dotage with their powers
 And hold our lives in mercy.—Oswald, I say!   326
ALBANY   Well, you may fear too far.   327
GONERIL   Safer than trust too far.
 Let me still take away the harms I fear,   329
 Not fear still to be taken. I know his heart.   330
 What he hath uttered I have writ my sister.
 If she sustain him and his hundred knights
 When I have showed th' unfitness—

  Enter steward [Oswald].

        How now, Oswald?
 What, have you writ that letter to my sister?
OSWALD   Ay, madam.
GONERIL
 Take you some company and away to horse.
 Inform her full of my particular fear,
 And thereto add such reasons of your own
 As may compact it more. Get you gone,   339
 And hasten your return. [*Exit Oswald.*] No, no, my lord,
 This milky gentleness and course of yours   341
 Though I condemn not, yet, under pardon,   342

314–315 take . . . thee (1) take me with you (2) take the name "fool" with
you. (A stock phrase of taunting farewell.)   **318 Should sure** should
certainly be sent   **322 politic** prudent. (Said ironically.)   **323 At point**
under arms   **324 buzz** idle rumor   **326 in mercy** at his mercy   **327 fear
too far** overestimate the danger   **329 take away** remove   **329, 330 still**
always   **330 taken** overtaken (by the *harms*)   **339 compact** confirm
341 milky . . . course humane and gentle way   **342 under pardon** if
you'll excuse my saying so

You're much more attasked for want of wisdom   343
Than praised for harmful mildness.   344

ALBANY
How far your eyes may pierce I cannot tell.   345
Striving to better, oft we mar what's well.

GONERIL   Nay, then—
ALBANY   Well, well, th' event.   *Exeunt.* 348

❖

1.5   *Enter Lear, Kent [disguised as Caius], and Fool.*

LEAR [*Giving a letter to Kent*]   Go you before to Gloucester 1
   with these letters. Acquaint my daughter no further 2
   with anything you know than comes from her demand 3
   out of the letter. If your diligence be not speedy, I shall 4
   be there afore you.
KENT   I will not sleep, my lord, till I have delivered your
   letter.   *Exit.*
FOOL   If a man's brains were in 's heels, were 't not in
   danger of kibes?   9
LEAR   Ay, boy.
FOOL   Then, I prithee, be merry. Thy wit shall not go
   slipshod.   12
LEAR   Ha, ha, ha!
FOOL   Shalt see thy other daughter will use thee kindly, 14
   for though she's as like this as a crab's like an apple, 15
   yet I can tell what I can tell.
LEAR   What canst tell, boy?
FOOL   She will taste as like this as a crab does to a crab.
   Thou canst tell why one's nose stands i' the middle
   on 's face?   20

343 attasked taken to task for, blamed   **344 harmful mildness** mildness
that causes harm   **345 pierce** i.e., see into matters   **348 th' event** i.e.,
time will show

1.5. Location: Before Albany's palace.
1 Gloucester i.e., the place in Gloucestershire   **2 these letters** this
letter   **3 demand** inquiry   **4 out of** prompted by   **9 kibes** chilblains
12 slipshod in slippers, worn because of chilblains. (There are no
brains, thinks the Fool, in Lear's heels when they are on their way to
visit Regan.)   **14 Shalt** thou shalt.   **kindly** (1) according to filial nature.
(Said ironically.) (2) according to her own nature   **15 crab** crab apple
20 on 's of his

LEAR   No.

FOOL   Why, to keep one's eyes of either side 's nose,   22
that what a man cannot smell out he may spy into.

LEAR   I did her wrong.   24

FOOL   Canst tell how an oyster makes his shell?

LEAR   No.

FOOL   Nor I neither. But I can tell why a snail has a
house.

LEAR   Why?

FOOL   Why, to put 's head in, not to give it away to his
daughters and leave his horns without a case.   31

LEAR   I will forget my nature. So kind a father! — Be my   32
horses ready?

FOOL   Thy asses are gone about 'em. The reason why   34
the seven stars are no more than seven is a pretty   35
reason.

LEAR   Because they are not eight.

FOOL   Yes, indeed. Thou wouldst make a good fool.

LEAR   To take 't again perforce! Monster ingratitude!   39

FOOL   If thou wert my fool, nuncle, I'd have thee beaten
for being old before thy time.

LEAR   How's that?

FOOL   Thou shouldst not have been old till thou hadst
been wise.

LEAR

O, let me not be mad, not mad, sweet heaven!
Keep me in temper; I would not be mad!

[*Enter Gentleman.*]

How now, are the horses ready?

GENTLEMAN   Ready, my lord.

LEAR   Come, boy.   [*Exeunt all except the Fool.*]

---

22 of either side 's on either side of his   **24 her** i.e., Cordelia   **31 horns**
(Suggests cuckold's horns, as though Lear were figuratively not the
father of Goneril and Regan.)   **32 forget my nature** (Compare 1.4.227:
"Who is it that can tell me who I am?" Lear can no longer recognize
the kind, beloved father he thought himself to be.)   **34 Thy . . . 'em** i.e.,
your servants (who labor like asses) have gone about readying the
horses   **35 seven stars** Pleiades   **39 To take . . . perforce** i.e., to think
that Goneril would forcibly take back again the privileges guaranteed to
me. (Some editors suggest, less persuasively, that Lear is meditating an
armed restoration of his monarchy.)

FOOL

   She that's a maid now, and laughs at my departure,
   Shall not be a maid long, unless things be cut shorter. 51

                                             Exit.

❖

---

51 things i.e., penises.   **cut shorter** (A bawdy joke addressed to the audience.)

2.1 *Enter Bastard [Edmund] and Curan, severally.*

EDMUND Save thee, Curan. 1

CURAN And you, sir. I have been with your father and given him notice that the Duke of Cornwall and Regan his duchess will be here with him this night.

EDMUND How comes that?

CURAN Nay, I know not. You have heard of the news abroad—I mean the whispered ones, for they are yet 7 but ear-kissing arguments? 8

EDMUND Not I. Pray you, what are they?

CURAN Have you heard of no likely wars toward twixt 10 the Dukes of Cornwall and Albany?

EDMUND Not a word.

CURAN You may do, then, in time. Fare you well, sir.

Exit.

EDMUND

The Duke be here tonight? The better! Best! 14
This weaves itself perforce into my business.
My father hath set guard to take my brother,
And I have one thing, of a queasy question, 17
Which I must act. Briefness and fortune, work!— 18
Brother, a word. Descend. Brother, I say!

Enter Edgar.

My father watches. O sir, fly this place!
Intelligence is given where you are hid.
You have now the good advantage of the night.
Have you not spoken 'gainst the Duke of Cornwall?
He's coming hither, now, i' the night, i' the haste, 24
And Regan with him. Have you nothing said
Upon his party 'gainst the Duke of Albany? 26
Advise yourself.

EDGAR   I am sure on 't, not a word. 27

2.1. Location: The Earl of Gloucester's house.
s.d. severally separately **1 Save** God save **7 ones** i.e., the news, regarded as plural **8 ear-kissing arguments** lightly whispered topics **10 toward** impending **14 The better! Best** so much the better; in fact, the best that could happen **17 queasy question** hazardous or ticklish nature **18 Briefness and fortune** expeditious dispatch and good luck **24 i' the haste** in great haste **26 Upon his party 'gainst** i.e., on Cornwall's side, reflecting on his feud with **27 Advise yourself** think it over carefully. **on 't** of it

EDMUND
I hear my father coming. Pardon me;
In cunning I must draw my sword upon you.
Draw. Seem to defend yourself. Now, quit you well.—   30
                              [*They draw.*]
Yield! Come before my father!—Light, ho, here!—   31
Fly, brother.—Torches, torches!—So, farewell.   32
                              Exit Edgar.
Some blood drawn on me would beget opinion   33
Of my more fierce endeavor. I have seen drunkards   34
Do more than this in sport. [*He wounds himself in the
    arm.*] Father, Father!
Stop, stop! No help?

        Enter Gloucester, and servants with torches.

GLOUCESTER   Now, Edmund, where's the villain?
EDMUND
Here stood he in the dark, his sharp sword out,
Mumbling of wicked charms, conjuring the moon
To stand 's auspicious mistress.
GLOUCESTER   But where is he?   39
EDMUND
Look, sir, I bleed.
GLOUCESTER   Where is the villain, Edmund?
EDMUND
Fled this way, sir. When by no means he could—
GLOUCESTER
Pursue him, ho! Go after. [*Exeunt some servants.*] By
    no means what?
EDMUND
Persuade me to the murder of your lordship,
But that I told him the revenging gods   44
'Gainst parricides did all the thunder bend,   45
Spoke with how manifold and strong a bond
The child was bound to the father; sir, in fine,   47
Seeing how loathly opposite I stood   48

---

30 quit you defend, acquit yourself   **31–32 Yield . . . farewell** (Edmund
speaks loudly as though trying to arrest Edgar, calls for others to help,
and privately bids Edgar to flee.)   **33–34 beget . . . endeavor** create an
impression of my having fought fiercely   **39 stand 's** stand his, act as
his   **44 that** when   **45 bend** aim   **47 in fine** in conclusion   **48 loathly
opposite** loathingly opposed

To his unnatural purpose, in fell motion   49
With his preparèd sword he charges home   50
My unprovided body, latched mine arm;   51
And when he saw my best alarumed spirits,   52
Bold in the quarrel's right, roused to th' encounter,   53
Or whether gasted by the noise I made,   54
Full suddenly he fled.
GLOUCESTER   Let him fly far.   55
Not in this land shall he remain uncaught;
And found—dispatch. The noble Duke my master,   57
My worthy arch and patron, comes tonight.   58
By his authority I will proclaim it.
That he which finds him shall deserve our thanks,
Bringing the murderous coward to the stake;   61
He that conceals him, death.
EDMUND
When I dissuaded him from his intent
And found him pight to do it, with curst speech   64
I threatened to discover him. He replied,   65
"Thou unpossessing bastard, dost thou think,   66
If I would stand against thee, would the reposal   67
Of any trust, virtue, or worth in thee
Make thy words faithed? No. What I should deny—   69
As this I would, ay, though thou didst produce
My very character—I'd turn it all   71
To thy suggestion, plot, and damnèd practice;   72
And thou must make a dullard of the world   73
If they not thought the profits of my death   74
Were very pregnant and potential spirits   75
To make thee seek it."

---

49 fell motion deadly thrust   **50 preparèd** unsheathed and ready.
home to the very heart   **51 unprovided** unprotected.   **latched** nicked,
lanced   **52 best alarumed** thoroughly aroused to action as by a trumpet   **53 quarrel's right** justice of the cause   **54 gasted** frightened
55 Let him fly far i.e., any fleeing, no matter how far, will be in vain
57 dispatch i.e., that will be the end for him   **58 arch and patron** chief
patron   **61 to the stake** i.e., to reckoning   **64 pight** determined.   **curst**
angry   **65 discover** expose   **66 unpossessing** unable to inherit, beg-
garly   **67 reposal** placing   **69 faithed** believed   **71 character** written
testimony, handwriting   **72 suggestion** instigation.   **practice** plot
73 make . . . world think everyone idiotic   **74 not thought** did not
think.   **of my death** i.e., that Edmund would gain through Edgar's
death   **75 pregnant . . . spirits** fertile and potent tempters

GLOUCESTER   O strange and fastened villain!   76
  Would he deny his letter, said he?
  I never got him.   *Tucket within.*   78
  Hark, the Duke's trumpets! I know not why he comes.
  All ports I'll bar; the villain shall not scape.   80
  The Duke must grant me that. Besides, his picture
  I will send far and near, that all the kingdom
  May have due note of him; and of my land,
  Loyal and natural boy, I'll work the means   84
  To make thee capable.   85

Enter Cornwall, Regan, and attendants.

CORNWALL
  How now, my noble friend? Since I came hither,
  Which I can call but now, I have heard strange news.
REGAN
  If it be true, all vengeance comes too short
  Which can pursue th' offender. How dost, my lord?
GLOUCESTER
  O madam, my old heart is cracked, it's cracked!
REGAN
  What, did my father's godson seek your life?
  He whom my father named? Your Edgar?
GLOUCESTER
  O, lady, lady, shame would have it hid!
REGAN
  Was he not companion with the riotous knights
  That tended upon my father?
GLOUCESTER
  I know not, madam. 'Tis too bad, too bad.
EDMUND
  Yes, madam, he was of that consort.   97
REGAN
  No marvel, then, though he were ill affected.   98

---

76 strange unnatural. **fastened** hardened   **78 got** begot   **s.d. Tucket**
series of notes on the trumpet, here indicating Cornwall's arrival
80 ports seaports, or gateways   **84 natural** (1) prompted by natural
feelings of loyalty and affection (2) bastard   **85 capable** legally able to
become the inheritor   **97 consort** set, company   **98 though** if.   **ill
affected** ill disposed, disloyal

'Tis they have put him on the old man's death,   99
To have th' expense and waste of his revenues.   100
I have this present evening from my sister
Been well informed of them, and with such cautions
That if they come to sojourn at my house
I'll not be there.
CORNWALL   Nor I, assure thee, Regan.
Edmund, I hear that you have shown your father
A childlike office.
EDMUND   It was my duty, sir.   106
GLOUCESTER [*To Cornwall*]
He did bewray his practice, and received   107
This hurt you see striving to apprehend him.   108
CORNWALL   Is he pursued?
GLOUCESTER   Ay, my good lord.
CORNWALL
If he be taken, he shall never more
Be feared of doing harm. Make your own purpose,   112
How in my strength you please. For you, Edmund,   113
Whose virtue and obedience doth this instant
So much commend itself, you shall be ours.
Natures of such deep trust we shall much need;
You we first seize on.
EDMUND   I shall serve you, sir,
Truly, however else.   118
GLOUCESTER   For him I thank Your Grace.
CORNWALL.
You know not why we came to visit you—
REGAN
—Thus out of season, threading dark-eyed night:
Occasions, noble Gloucester, of some prize,   122
Wherein we must have use of your advice.
Our father he hath writ, so hath our sister,
Of differences, which I best thought it fit   125

---

99 put him on incited him to   **100 expense and waste** squandering
106 childlike filial   **107 bewray his practice** expose his (Edgar's) plot
108 apprehend arrest   **112–113 Make . . . please** form your plans,
making free use of my authority and resources   **113 For** as for
118 however else i.e., whether capably or not   **122 prize** significance
125 differences quarrels.   **which** i.e., Lear's and Goneril's letters

To answer from our home; the several messengers   126
From hence attend dispatch. Our good old friend,   127
Lay comforts to your bosom, and bestow
Your needful counsel to our businesses,   129
Which craves the instant use.
GLOUCESTER   I serve you, madam.   130
Your Graces are right welcome.

Flourish. Exeunt.

✤

2.2   *Enter Kent [disguised as Caius] and steward
        [Oswald], severally.*

OSWALD Good dawning to thee, friend. Art of this 1
    house?
KENT Ay.
OSWALD Where may we set our horses?
KENT I' the mire.
OSWALD Prithee, if thou lov'st me, tell me.   6
KENT I love thee not.
OSWALD Why then, I care not for thee.   8
KENT If I had thee in Lipsbury pinfold, I would make 9
    thee care for me.   10
OSWALD Why dost thou use me thus? I know thee not. 11
KENT Fellow, I know thee.   12
OSWALD What dost thou know me for?
KENT A knave, a rascal, an eater of broken meats; 14
    a base, proud, shallow, beggarly, three-suited, 15

126 from away from   **127 attend dispatch** wait to be dispatched
129 needful necessary   **130 the instant use** immediate attention

2.2. Location: Before Gloucester's house.
s.d. severally at separate doors   **1 dawning** (It is not yet day.)   **6 if thou
lov'st me** i.e., if you bear good will toward me. (But Kent deliberately
takes the phrase in its literal, not courtly, sense.)   **8–10 care not for . . .
care for** do not like . . . have an anxious regard for   **9 Lipsbury pinfold**
i.e., within the pinfold of the lips, between my teeth. (A *pinfold* is a
pound for stray animals.)   **11–12 know thee not . . . know thee** am
unacquainted with you . . . can see through you   **14 broken meats**
scraps of food (such as were passed out to the most lowly)   **15 three-
suited** (Three suits a year were allowed to servants.)

hundred-pound, filthy worsted-stocking knave; a 16
lily-livered, action-taking, whoreson, glass-gazing, 17
superserviceable, finical rogue; one-trunk-inheriting 18
slave; one that wouldst be a bawd in way of good ser- 19
vice, and art nothing but the composition of a knave, 20
beggar, coward, pander, and the son and heir of a
mongrel bitch; one whom I will beat into clamorous
whining if thou deny'st the least syllable of thy addi- 23
tion.   24

OSWALD Why, what a monstrous fellow art thou thus
to rail on one that is neither known of thee nor knows
thee!

KENT What a brazen-faced varlet art thou to deny thou
knowest me! Is it two days since I tripped up thy heels
and beat thee before the King? Draw, you rogue, for
though it be night, yet the moon shines. I'll make a
sop o' the moonshine of you, you whoreson cullionly 32
barbermonger. Draw!   [*He brandishes his sword.*] 33

OSWALD Away! I have nothing to do with thee.

KENT Draw, you rascal! You come with letters against
the King, and take Vanity the puppet's part against 36
the royalty of her father. Draw, you rogue, or I'll so
carbonado your shanks—draw, you rascal! Come your 38
ways.   39

OSWALD Help, ho! Murder! Help!

KENT Strike, you slave! Stand, rogue, stand, you neat 41
slave, strike!   [*He beats him.*]

---

16 hundred-pound (Possible allusion to the minimum property qualifica-
tion for the status of gentleman.) **worsted-stocking** i.e., too poor and
menial to wear silk stockings **17 lily-livered** cowardly (the liver being
pale through lack of blood). **action-taking** settling quarrels by resort to
law instead of arms, cowardly. **glass-gazing** fond of looking in the
mirror **18 superserviceable** officious. **finical** foppish, fastidious.
one-trunk-inheriting possessing effects sufficient for one trunk only
19–20 bawd . . . service i.e., pimp or pander as a way of providing good
service **20 composition** compound **23–24 addition** titles **32 sop o'
the moonshine** something so perforated that it will soak up moonshine
as a sop (floating piece of toast) soaks up liquor **32–33 cullionly
barbermonger** base frequenter of barber shops, fop. (*Cullion* originally
meant "testicle.") **36 Vanity . . . part** i.e., the part of Goneril (here
personified as a character in a morality play) **38 carbonado** cut cross-
wise like meat for broiling **38–39 Come your ways** come on **41 neat**
(1) foppish (2) calflike. (*Neat* means "horned cattle.")

OSWALD Help, ho! Murder! Murder!

Enter Bastard [Edmund, with his rapier drawn],
Cornwall, Regan, Gloucester, servants.

EDMUND How now, what's the matter? Part!   44
KENT With you, goodman boy, an you please! Come, I'll 45
flesh ye. Come on, young master.   46
GLOUCESTER Weapons? Arms? What's the matter here?
CORNWALL Keep peace, upon your lives! [*Kent and Os-*
wald are parted.] He dies that strikes again. What is
the matter?
REGAN The messengers from our sister and the King.
CORNWALL What's your difference? Speak.   52
OSWALD I am scarce in breath, my lord.
KENT No marvel, you have so bestirred your valor. You
cowardly rascal, nature disclaims in thee. A tailor 55
made thee.
CORNWALL Thou art a strange fellow. A tailor make
a man?
KENT A tailor, sir. A stonecutter or a painter could not
have made him so ill, though they had been but two
years o' the trade.
CORNWALL Speak yet, how grew your quarrel?
OSWALD This ancient ruffian, sir, whose life I have
spared at suit of his gray beard—
KENT Thou whoreson zed! Thou unnecessary letter!—My 65
lord, if you'll give me leave, I will tread this un- 66
bolted villain into mortar and daub the wall of a jakes 67
with him.—Spare my gray beard, you wagtail?   68
CORNWALL Peace, sirrah!
You beastly knave, know you no reverence?
KENT
Yes, sir, but anger hath a privilege.
CORNWALL Why art thou angry?

---

44 matter i.e., trouble. (But Kent takes the meaning "cause for quarrel.")
45 With you I'll fight with you; my quarrel is with you.   **goodman boy** (A
contemptuous epithet, a title of mock respect, addressed seemingly to
Edmund.)   **an** if   **46 flesh** initiate into combat   **52 difference** quarrel
55 disclaims in disowns   **65 zed** the letter z, regarded as unnecessary and
often not included in dictionaries of the time   **66–67 unbolted** unsifted;
hence, coarse   **67 daub** plaster.   **jakes** privy   **68 wagtail** i.e., bird wagging
its tail feathers in pert obsequiousness

KENT
   That such a slave as this should wear a sword,
   Who wears no honesty. Such smiling rogues as these,
   Like rats, oft bite the holy cords atwain   75
   Which are t' intrinse t' unloose; smooth every passion 76
   That in the natures of their lords rebel,
   Bring oil to fire, snow to their colder moods,   78
   Renege, affirm, and turn their halcyon beaks   79
   With every gale and vary of their masters,   80
   Knowing naught, like dogs, but following.—
   A plague upon your epileptic visage!   82
   Smile you my speeches, as I were a fool?   83
   Goose, an I had you upon Sarum plain,   84
   I'd drive ye cackling home to Camelot.   85
CORNWALL   What, art thou mad, old fellow?
GLOUCESTER   How fell you out? Say that.
KENT
   No contraries hold more antipathy
   Than I and such a knave.
CORNWALL
   Why dost thou call him knave? What is his fault?
KENT   His countenance likes me not.   91
CORNWALL
   No more, perchance, does mine, nor his, nor hers.
KENT
   Sir, 'tis my occupation to be plain:
   I have seen better faces in my time
   Than stands on any shoulder that I see
   Before me at this instant.
CORNWALL   This is some fellow
   Who, having been praised for bluntness, doth affect

75 holy cords sacred bonds of affection and order   **76 t' intrinse** too intrinsicate, tightly knotted.   **smooth** flatter, humor   **78 Bring oil to fire** i.e., flattering servants fuel the flame of their masters' angry passions   **79 Renege** deny   **halcyon beaks** (The halcyon or kingfisher, if hung up, would supposedly turn its beak against the wind.)   **80 gale and vary** variation in the wind   **82 epileptic** i.e., trembling and pale with fright and distorted with a grin   **83 Smile you** do you smile at. **as** as if   **84–85 Goose . . . Camelot** (The reference is obscure, but the general sense is that Kent scorns Oswald as a cackling goose.)   **an** if.   **Sarum** Salisbury.   **Camelot** legendary seat of King Arthur and his Round Table, said to have been at Cadbury and at Winchester and hence in the general vicinity of Salisbury and Gloucester   **91 likes** pleases

A saucy roughness, and constrains the garb   98
Quite from his nature. He cannot flatter, he;   99
An honest mind and plain, he must speak truth!
An they will take 't, so; if not, he's plain.   101
These kind of knaves I know, which in this plainness
Harbor more craft and more corrupter ends
Than twenty silly-ducking observants   104
That stretch their duties nicely.   105

KENT

Sir, in good faith, in sincere verity,   106
Under th' allowance of your great aspect,   107
Whose influence, like the wreath of radiant fire   108
On flickering Phoebus' front—

CORNWALL   What mean'st by this?   109

KENT   To go out of my dialect, which you discommend
so much. I know, sir, I am no flatterer. He that be-   111
guiled you in a plain accent was a plain knave, which   112
for my part I will not be, though I should win your   113
displeasure to entreat me to 't.   114

CORNWALL [*To Oswald*] What was th' offense you gave him?

OSWALD   I never gave him any.

It pleased the King his master very late   117
To strike at me, upon his misconstruction;   118
When he, compact, and flattering his displeasure,   119

98–99 constrains . . . nature i.e., distorts plainness to the point of carica-
ture, away from its true purpose   **101 An . . . plain** if people will take
his rudeness, fine; if not, his excuse is that he speaks plain truth
104 silly-ducking observants foolishly bowing, obsequious attendants
105 stretch . . . nicely exert themselves in their courtly duties punctiliously   **106 Sir, in good faith,** etc. (Kent assumes the wordy mannerisms
of courtly flattery.)   **107 allowance** approval.   **aspect** (1) countenance
(2) astrological position   **108 influence** astrological might   **109 Phoebus
front** i.e., the sun's forehead   **111–112 He . . . accent** i.e., the man who
used plain speech to you craftily (see ll. 102–105) and thereby taught
you to suspect plain speakers of deceit   **112–114 which . . . me to 't** i.e.,
I will no longer use plain speech, despite the incentive of incurring your
displeasure by doing so. (Kent prefers to displease Cornwall, since Cornwall is pleased only by flatterers, and Kent has assumed until now that
plain speech was the best way to offend; but he now argues mockingly
that he can no longer speak plainly, since his honest utterance will be
interpreted as duplicity.)   **117 late** recently   **118 upon his misconstruction** as a result of the King's misunderstanding (me)   **119 he** i.e.,
Kent.   **compact** joined, united with the King.   **flattering his displeasure** gratifying the King's anger (at me)

Tripped me behind; being down, insulted, railed,   120
And put upon him such a deal of man   121
That worthied him, got praises of the King   122
For him attempting who was self-subdued;   123
And, in the fleshment of this dread exploit,   124
Drew on me here again.

KENT   None of these rogues and cowards   126
But Ajax is their fool.

CORNWALL   Fetch forth the stocks!   127
You stubborn ancient knave, you reverend braggart,   128
We'll teach you.

KENT   Sir, I am too old to learn.
Call not your stocks for me. I serve the King,
On whose employment I was sent to you.
You shall do small respect, show too bold malice
Against the grace and person of my master,   133
Stocking his messenger.

CORNWALL
Fetch forth the stocks! As I have life and honor,
There shall he sit till noon.

REGAN
Till noon? Till night, my lord, and all night too.

KENT
Why, madam, if I were your father's dog
You should not use me so.   139

REGAN   Sir, being his knave, I will.   140

CORNWALL
This is a fellow of the selfsame color   141
Our sister speaks of.—Come, bring away the stocks!   142
                    Stocks brought out.

GLOUCESTER
Let me beseech Your Grace not to do so.
His fault is much, and the good King his master

---

120 being down, insulted i.e., when I was down, he exulted over me
121 put . . . man acted like such a hero   **122 worthied** won reputation
for   **123 For . . . self-subdued** for assailing one (i.e., myself) who chose
not to resist   **124 fleshment** excitement resulting from a first success.
dread exploit (Said ironically.)   **126–127 None . . . fool** i.e., you never
find any rogues and cowards of this sort who do not outdo the bluster-
ing Ajax in their boasting   **128 reverend** (because old)   **133 grace**
sovereignty   **139 should** would   **140 being** since you are   **141 color**
complexion, character   **142 away** along

Will check him for 't. Your purposed low correction   145
Is such as basest and contemned'st wretches   146
For pilferings and most common trespasses
Are punished with. The King must take it ill
That he, so slightly valued in his messenger,
Should have him thus restrained.

CORNWALL   I'll answer that.   150

REGAN
My sister may receive it much more worse
To have her gentleman abused, assaulted,
For following her affairs. Put in his legs.
                        [*Kent is put in the stocks.*]
Come, my good lord, away.
                Exeunt [all but Gloucester and Kent].

GLOUCESTER
I am sorry for thee, friend. 'Tis the Duke's pleasure,
Whose disposition, all the world well knows,
Will not be rubbed nor stopped. I'll entreat for thee.   157

KENT
Pray, do not, sir. I have watched and traveled hard.   158
Some time I shall sleep out; the rest I'll whistle.
A good man's fortune may grow out at heels.   160
Give you good morrow!   161

GLOUCESTER
The Duke's to blame in this. 'Twill be ill taken.   *Exit.*

KENT
Good King, that must approve the common saw,   163
Thou out of heaven's benediction com'st
To the warm sun!   [*He takes out a letter.*]
Approach, thou beacon to this under globe,   166
That by thy comfortable beams I may   167

---

145 check rebuke, correct   **146 contemned'st** most despised
150 answer be answerable for   **157 rubbed** hindered, obstructed. (A
term from bowls.)   **158 watched** gone sleepless   **160 A . . . heels** i.e.,
even good men suffer decline in fortune at times   **161 Give you** i.e., God
give you   **163 approve** prove true.   **saw** proverb (i.e., "To run out of
God's blessing into the warm sun," meaning "to go from better to
worse")   **166 beacon . . . globe** i.e., the sun (?) (Some editors believe that
Kent means the moon, since it is night at ll. 31 and 176, but he probably
is saying that he hopes for daylight soon in order that he can read the
letter from Cordelia.)   **167 comfortable** useful, aiding

Peruse this letter. Nothing almost sees miracles   168
But misery. I know 'tis from Cordelia,   169
Who hath most fortunately been informed
Of my obscurèd course, and shall find time   171
From this enormous state, seeking to give   172
Losses their remedies. All weary and o'erwatched,   173
Take vantage, heavy eyes, not to behold   174
This shameful lodging.   175
Fortune, good night. Smile once more; turn thy
     wheel!   [*He sleeps.*]   176

2.3   *Enter Edgar.*

EDGAR   I heard myself proclaimed,
And by the happy hollow of a tree   2
Escaped the hunt. No port is free, no place   3
That guard and most unusual vigilance   4
Does not attend my taking. Whiles I may scape   5
I will preserve myself, and am bethought   6
To take the basest and most poorest shape
That ever penury, in contempt of man,   8
Brought near to beast. My face I'll grime with filth,
Blanket my loins, elf all my hairs in knots,   10
And with presented nakedness outface   11
The winds and persecutions of the sky.

168–169 Nothing . . . misery i.e., scarcely anything can make one appreciate miracles like being in a state of misery; miracles are most often
experienced by those who suffer misfortune   **171 obscurèd** disguised.
shall she shall   **171–173 and . . . remedies** (This seemingly incoherent
passage may be textually corrupt or may be meant to represent fragments from the letter Kent is reading.)   **172 From** i.e., to provide relief
from (?)   **enormous state** monstrous state of affairs, enormity
173 Losses reversals of fortune.   **o'erwatched** exhausted with staying
awake   **174 vantage** advantage (of sleep)   **175 lodging** i.e., the stocks
176 wheel (Since Kent is at the bottom of Fortune's wheel, any turning
will improve his situation.)

2.3. Location: Scene continues. Kent is dozing in the stocks.
2 happy luckily found   **3 port** (See 2.1.80 and note.)   **4 That** in which
5 attend watch, wait for   **6 bethought** resolved   **8 in . . . man** in order
to show how contemptible humankind is   **10 elf** tangle into elflocks
11 presented exposed to view, displayed

The country gives me proof and precedent   13
Of Bedlam beggars who with roaring voices   14
Strike in their numbed and mortified arms   15
Pins, wooden pricks, nails, sprigs of rosemary;   16
And with this horrible object, from low farms,   17
Poor pelting villages, sheepcotes, and mills,   18
Sometimes with lunatic bans, sometimes with prayers, 19
Enforce their charity. Poor Turlygod! Poor Tom!   20
That's something yet. Edgar I nothing am.   *Exit.* 21

2.4   *Enter Lear, Fool, and Gentleman.*

LEAR
'Tis strange that they should so depart from home
And not send back my messenger.
GENTLEMAN   As I learned,
The night before there was no purpose in them
Of this remove.
KENT   Hail to thee, noble master!   4
LEAR   Ha?
Mak'st thou this shame thy pastime?
KENT   No, my lord.
FOOL   Ha, ha, he wears cruel garters. Horses are tied by 7
the heads, dogs and bears by the neck, monkeys by the
loins, and men by the legs. When a man's overlusty at 9
legs, then he wears wooden netherstocks.   10
LEAR
What's he that hath so much thy place mistook
To set thee here?
KENT   It is both he and she: 12
Your son and daughter.

13 proof example   **14 Bedlam** (See note to 1.2.139.)   **15 Strike** stick.   **mortified** deadened   **16 wooden pricks** skewers   **17 object** spectacle.   **low** lowly   **18 pelting** paltry   **19 bans** curses   **20 Poor . . . Tom** (Edgar practices the begging role he is about to adopt. Beggars were known as poor Toms.)   **Turlygod** (Meaning unknown.)   **21 That's something yet** there's some kind of existence still for me as poor Tom.   **Edgar** i.e., as Edgar

2.4. Location: Scene continues before Gloucester's house. Kent still dozing in the stocks.
4 remove change of residence   **7 cruel** (In the quarto: *crewell*, a double meaning [1] unkind [2] crewel, a thin yarn of which garters were made.)   **9–10 overlusty at legs** given to running away   **10 netherstocks** stockings   **12 To** as to

LEAR   No.

KENT   Yes.

LEAR   No, I say.

KENT   I say yea.

LEAR   No, no, they would not.

KENT   Yes, they have.

LEAR   By Jupiter, I swear no.

KENT   By Juno, I swear ay.

LEAR   They durst not do 't!
They could not, would not do 't. 'Tis worse than murder
To do upon respect such violent outrage.   23
Resolve me with all modest haste which way   24
Thou mightst deserve, or they impose, this usage,
Coming from us.

KENT   My lord, when at their home   26
I did commend Your Highness' letters to them,   27
Ere I was risen from the place that showed   28
My duty kneeling, came there a reeking post,   29
Stewed in his haste, half breathless, panting forth   30
From Goneril his mistress salutations;
Delivered letters, spite of intermission,   32
Which presently they read; on whose contents   33
They summoned up their meiny, straight took horse,   34
Commanded me to follow and attend
The leisure of their answer, gave me cold looks;
And meeting here the other messenger,
Whose welcome, I perceived, had poisoned mine—
Being the very fellow which of late
Displayed so saucily against Your Highness—   40
Having more man than wit about me, drew.   41
He raised the house with loud and coward cries.

23 upon respect i.e., against my delegates (who deserve respect)
24 Resolve enlighten.   **modest** moderate   **26 their home** (Kent and
Oswald went first to Cornwall's palace after leaving Albany's palace.)
27 commend deliver   **28–29 from . . . kneeling** from the kneeling pos-
ture that showed my duty   **29 reeking** steaming (with heat of travel)
30 Stewed i.e., thoroughly heated, soaked   **32 spite of intermission**
in disregard of interrupting me; or, in spite of the interruptions caused
by his being out of breath   **33 presently** instantly.   **on** on the basis
of   **34 meiny** retinue of servants, household   **40 Displayed so saucily**
behaved so insolently   **41 man** manhood, courage.   **wit** discretion,
sense

Your son and daughter found this trespass worth
The shame which here it suffers.

FOOL Winter's not gone yet if the wild geese fly that 45
way.   46
    Fathers that wear rags
      Do make their children blind,   48
    But fathers that bear bags   49
      Shall see their children kind.
    Fortune, that arrant whore,
      Ne'er turns the key to the poor.   52
But, for all this, thou shalt have as many dolors for thy 53
daughters as thou canst tell in a year.   54

LEAR
O, how this mother swells up toward my heart!   55
Hysterica passio, down, thou climbing sorrow!   56
Thy element's below.—Where is this daughter?   57

KENT With the Earl, sir, here within.

LEAR Follow me not. Stay here.   *Exit.*

GENTLEMAN
Made you no more offense but what you speak of?

KENT None.
How chance the King comes with so small a number? 62

FOOL An thou hadst been set i' the stocks for that ques- 63
tion, thou'dst well deserved it.

KENT Why, Fool?

FOOL We'll set thee to school to an ant to teach thee 66
there's no laboring i' the winter. All that follow their 67
noses are led by their eyes but blind men, and there's 68
not a nose among twenty but can smell him that's 69
stinking. Let go thy hold when a great wheel runs 70
down a hill lest it break thy neck with following; but

45–46 Winter's . . . way i.e., the signs still point to continued and wors-
ening fortune; the wild geese are still flying south **48 blind** i.e., indifferent to their father's needs **49 bags** i.e., of gold **52 turns the key**
opens the door **53 dolors** griefs (with pun on *dollars*, English word
for an Austrian or Spanish coin). **for** on account of **54 tell** (1) relate
(2) count **55, 56 mother, Hysterica passio** i.e., hysteria, giving the sensation of choking or suffocating **57 element's** proper place is. (Hysteria
was thought to be produced by vapors ascending from the abdomen.)
62 chance chances it **63 An** if **66–67 We'll . . . winter** i.e., just as the
ant knows not to labor in the winter, the wise man knows not to labor
for one whose fortunes are fallen **67–70 All . . . stinking** i.e., one who is
out of favor can be easily detected (he smells of misfortune), and so is
easily avoided by timeservers

the great one that goes upward, let him draw thee after. When a wise man gives thee better counsel, give
me mine again. I would have none but knaves follow
it, since a fool gives it.

> That sir which serves and seeks for gain,
>   And follows but for form,
> Will pack when it begins to rain   78
>   And leave thee in the storm.
> But I will tarry; the fool will stay,
>   And let the wise man fly.
> The knave turns fool that runs away;   82
>   The fool no knave, pardie.   83

Enter Lear and Gloucester.

KENT   Where learned you this, Fool?
FOOL   Not i' the stocks, fool.

LEAR
Deny to speak with me? They are sick? They are weary?
They have traveled all the night? Mere fetches,   87
The images of revolt and flying off.   88
Fetch me a better answer.

GLOUCESTER   My dear lord,
You know the fiery quality of the Duke,
How unremovable and fixed he is
In his own course.

LEAR
Vengeance! Plague! Death! Confusion!   93
Fiery? What quality? Why, Gloucester, Gloucester,
I'd speak with the Duke of Cornwall and his wife.

GLOUCESTER
Well, my good lord, I have informed them so.

LEAR
Informed them? Dost thou understand me, man?

GLOUCESTER   Ay, my good lord.

LEAR
The King would speak with Cornwall. The dear father
Would with his daughter speak, commands, tends,
    service.   100

78 pack be off   **82 The knave . . . away** i.e., deserting one's master is
the greatest folly   **83 pardie** *par Dieu* (French), by God   **87 fetches**
pretexts, dodges   **88 images** signs.   **flying off** desertion   **93 Confusion**
destruction   **100 tends** attends, waits for

Are they informed of this? My breath and blood!
Fiery? The fiery Duke? Tell the hot Duke that—
No, but not yet. Maybe he is not well.
Infirmity doth still neglect all office   104
Whereto our health is bound; we are not ourselves   105
When nature, being oppressed, commands the mind
To suffer with the body. I'll forbear,
And am fallen out with my more headier will,   108
To take the indisposed and sickly fit   109
For the sound man. [*Looking at Kent.*] Death on my
     state! Wherefore   110
Should he sit here? This act persuades me
That this remotion of the Duke and her   112
Is practice only. Give me my servant forth.   113
Go tell the Duke and 's wife I'd speak with them,
Now, presently. Bid them come forth and hear me,   115
Or at their chamber door I'll beat the drum
Till it cry sleep to death.   117
GLOUCESTER   I would have all well betwixt you.   *Exit.*
LEAR
O me, my heart, my rising heart! But down!
FOOL   Cry to it, nuncle, as the cockney did to the eels   120
when she put 'em i' the paste alive. She knapped 'em   121
o' the coxcombs with a stick and cried, "Down, wan-   122
tons, down!" 'Twas her brother that, in pure kindness   123
to his horse, buttered his hay.   124

     Enter Cornwall, Regan, Gloucester, [and]
     servants.

---

104 still always   **104–105 all . . . bound** duties which in good health we
are bound to perform   **108–109 am . . . take** now disapprove of my
more impe :ious will in having rashly taken   **110 Death on my state**
may death come to my royal authority. (An oath with ironic appropriate-
ness.)   **112 remotion** removal, inaccessibility   **113 practice** deception.
forth out of the stocks   **115 presently** at once   **117 cry sleep to death**
i.e., put an end to sleep by the noise   **120 cockney** i.e., a Londoner,
ignorant of ways of cooking eels   **121 paste** pastry pie.   **knapped**
rapped   **122 coxcombs** heads   **122–123 wantons** playful creatures,
promiscuous things   **123–124 'Twas . . . hay** (Another city ignorance;
the act is well-intended, but horses do not like greasy hay. As with Lear,
good intentions are not enough.)   **brother** i.e., fellow creature, foolishly
tender-hearted in the same way

LEAR   Good morrow to you both.
CORNWALL   Hail to Your Grace!

                  Kent here set at liberty.

REGAN   I am glad to see Your Highness.
LEAR
Regan, I think you are. I know what reason
I have to think so. If thou shouldst not be glad,
I would divorce me from thy mother's tomb,   130
Sepulch'ring an adult'ress. [*To Kent.*] O, are you free?   131
Some other time for that.—Belovèd Regan,
Thy sister's naught. O Regan, she hath tied   133
Sharp-toothed unkindness, like a vulture, here.

            [*He lays his hand on his heart.*]

I can scarce speak to thee. Thou'lt not believe
With how depraved a quality—O Regan!   136
REGAN
I pray you, sir, take patience. I have hope   137
You less know how to value her desert   138
Than she to scant her duty.
LEAR   Say? How is that?   139
REGAN
I cannot think my sister in the least
Would fail her obligation. If, sir, perchance
She have restrained the riots of your followers,
'Tis on such ground and to such wholesome end
As clears her from all blame.
LEAR   My curses on her!
REGAN   O, sir, you are old;
Nature in you stands on the very verge   147
Of his confine. You should be ruled and led   148
By some discretion that discerns your state   149
Better than you yourself. Therefore, I pray you,
That to our sister you do make return.
Say you have wronged her.

---

130 divorce me from i.e., refuse to be buried beside   **131 Sepulch'ring**
i.e., since it would surely contain the dead body of   **133 naught** wicked
136 quality disposition   **137–139 I have . . . duty** i.e., I trust this is more
a matter of your undervaluing her merit than of her falling slack in her
duty to you   **147–148 Nature . . . confine** i.e., your life has almost com-
pleted its allotted scope   **149 discretion** discreet person. **discerns your
state** understands your dependent situation and aged condition

LEAR   Ask her forgiveness?
Do you but mark how this becomes the house: 153
                              [*He kneels.*]
"Dear daughter, I confess that I am old;
Age is unnecessary. On my knees I beg   155
That you'll vouchsafe me raiment, bed, and food."

REGAN
Good sir, no more. These are unsightly tricks.
Return you to my sister.

LEAR [*Rising*]   Never, Regan.
She hath abated me of half my train,   159
Looked black upon me, struck me with her tongue
Most serpentlike upon the very heart.
All the stored vengeances of heaven fall
On her ingrateful top! Strike her young bones,   163
You taking airs, with lameness!

CORNWALL   Fie, sir, fie!   164

LEAR
You nimble lightnings, dart your blinding flames
Into her scornful eyes! Infect her beauty,
You fen-sucked fogs drawn by the powerful sun   167
To fall and blister!   168

REGAN
O the blest gods! So will you wish on me
When the rash mood is on.

LEAR
No, Regan, thou shalt never have my curse.
Thy tender-hafted nature shall not give   172
Thee o'er to harshness. Her eyes are fierce, but thine
Do comfort and not burn. 'Tis not in thee
To grudge my pleasures, to cut off my train,
To bandy hasty words, to scant my sizes,   176
And, in conclusion, to oppose the bolt   177

153 becomes the house suits domestic decorum, is suited to the family
or household and its dutiful relationships   **155 Age is unnecessary** old
people are useless   **159 abated** deprived   **163 ingrateful top** ungrateful
head.   **her young bones** i.e., of her not-yet-born progeny (?)   **164 taking**
infectious   **167 fen-sucked** (It was supposed that the sun sucked up
poisons from fens or marshes.)   **168 To fall and blister** to fall upon her
and blister her beauty   **172 tender-hafted** set in a tender *haft*, i.e.,
handle or frame; moved by a tender feeling, gently disposed   **176 bandy**
volley, exchange.   **scant my sizes** diminish my allowances   **177 oppose
the bolt** lock the door

Against my coming in. Thou better know'st
The offices of nature, bond of childhood,   179
Effects of courtesy, dues of gratitude.   180
Thy half o' the kingdom hast thou not forgot,
Wherein I thee endowed.

REGAN   Good sir, to the purpose.   182

LEAR
Who put my man i' the stocks?   *Tucket within.*

CORNWALL   What trumpet's that?

REGAN
I know 't—my sister's. This approves her letter,   184
That she would soon be here.

          Enter steward [Oswald].

                              Is your lady come?

LEAR
This is a slave, whose easy-borrowed pride   186
Dwells in the fickle grace of her he follows.   187
Out, varlet, from my sight!

CORNWALL   What means Your Grace?   188

LEAR
Who stocked my servant? Regan, I have good hope
Thou didst not know on 't.

          Enter Goneril.

                              Who comes here? O heavens,
If you do love old men, if your sweet sway
Allow obedience, if you yourselves are old,   192
Make it your cause; send down, and take my part!
[*To Goneril.*] Art not ashamed to look upon this
    beard?   [*Goneril and Regan join hands.*]
O Regan, will you take her by the hand?

GONERIL
Why not by the hand, sir? How have I offended?
All's not offense that indiscretion finds   197
And dotage terms so.

179 **offices of nature** natural duties.   **bond of childhood** filial obligations due to parents   180 **Effects** actions, manifestations   182 **purpose**
point   184 **approves** confirms   186 **easy-borrowed** i.e., acquired with
little effort at deserving and with weak commitment   187 **grace** favor
188 **varlet** worthless fellow   192 **Allow** approve, sanction
197 **indiscretion finds** poor judgment deems to be so

LEAR   O sides, you are too tough!   198
  Will you yet hold?—How came my man i' the stocks?

CORNWALL
  I set him there, sir; but his own disorders
  Deserved much less advancement.

LEAR   You? Did you?   201

REGAN
  I pray you, Father, being weak, seem so.   202
  If till the expiration of your month
  You will return and sojourn with my sister,
  Dismissing half your train, come then to me.
  I am now from home, and out of that provision
  Which shall be needful for your entertainment.   207

LEAR
  Return to her? And fifty men dismissed?
  No! Rather I abjure all roofs, and choose
  To wage against the enmity o' th' air,   210
  To be a comrade with the wolf and owl—
  Necessity's sharp pinch. Return with her?
  Why, the hot-blooded France, that dowerless took   213
  Our youngest born—I could as well be brought
  To knee his throne and, squirelike, pension beg   215
  To keep base life afoot. Return with her?
  Persuade me rather to be slave and sumpter   217
  To this detested groom.   [*He points to Oswald.*]

GONERIL   At your choice, sir.

LEAR
  I prithee, daughter, do not make me mad.
  I will not trouble thee, my child. Farewell.
  We'll no more meet, no more see one another.
  But yet thou art my flesh, my blood, my daughter—
  Or rather a disease that's in my flesh,
  Which I must needs call mine. Thou art a boil,
  A plague-sore, or embossèd carbuncle   225
  In my corrupted blood. But I'll not chide thee;
  Let shame come when it will, I do not call it.   227

---

198 sides i.e., sides of the chest (stretched by the swelling heart)
201 much less advancement far less honor, i.e., far worse treatment
202 seem so i.e., don't act as if you were strong   **207 entertainment**
proper reception   **210 wage** wage war   **213 hot-blooded** choleric. (Cf.
1.2.23.)   **215 knee** fall on my knees before   **217 sumpter** packhorse;
hence, drudge   **225 embossèd** swollen, tumid   **227 call** summon

I do not bid the thunder-bearer shoot,   228
Nor tell tales of thee to high-judging Jove.   229
Mend when thou canst; be better at thy leisure.
I can be patient. I can stay with Regan,
I and my hundred knights.

REGAN   Not altogether so.
I looked not for you yet, nor am provided   234
For your fit welcome. Give ear, sir, to my sister;
For those that mingle reason with your passion   236
Must be content to think you old, and so—
But she knows what she does.

LEAR   Is this well spoken?

REGAN
I dare avouch it, sir. What, fifty followers?   239
Is it not well? What should you need of more?
Yea, or so many, sith that both charge and danger   241
Speak 'gainst so great a number? How in one house
Should many people under two commands
Hold amity? 'Tis hard, almost impossible.

GONERIL
Why might not you, my lord, receive attendance
From those that she calls servants, or from mine?

REGAN
Why not, my lord? If then they chanced to slack ye,   247
We could control them. If you will come to me—   248
For now I spy a danger—I entreat you
To bring but five-and-twenty. To no more
Will I give place or notice.   251

LEAR
I gave you all—

REGAN   And in good time you gave it.

LEAR
Made you my guardians, my depositaries,   253
But kept a reservation to be followed   254
With such a number. What, must I come to you
With five-and-twenty? Regan, said you so?

---

228 the thunder-bearer i.e., Jove   **229 high-judging** judging from on
high   **234 looked not for** did not expect   **236 mingle . . . passion** consider your passionate behavior reasonably   **239 avouch** vouch for
241 sith that since.   **charge** expense   **247 slack** neglect   **248 control**
correct   **251 notice** recognition, acknowledgment   **253 depositaries**
trustees   **254 kept a reservation** reserved a right

REGAN

   And speak 't again, my lord. No more with me.

LEAR

   Those wicked creatures yet do look well-favored   258
   When others are more wicked; not being the worst
   Stands in some rank of praise. [*To Goneril.*] I'll go
     with thee.   260
   Thy fifty yet doth double five-and-twenty,
   And thou art twice her love.

GONERIL   Hear me, my lord:

   What need you five-and-twenty, ten, or five,
   To follow in a house where twice so many   264
   Have a command to tend you?

REGAN   What need one?

LEAR

   O, reason not the need! Our basest beggars   266
   Are in the poorest thing superfluous.   267
   Allow not nature more than nature needs,   268
   Man's life is cheap as beast's. Thou art a lady;
   If only to go warm were gorgeous,   270
   Why, nature needs not what thou gorgeous wear'st,   271
   Which scarcely keeps thee warm. But, for true need—   272
   You heavens, give me that patience, patience I need!
   You see me here, you gods, a poor old man,
   As full of grief as age, wretched in both.
   If it be you that stirs these daughters' hearts
   Against their father, fool me not so much   277
   To bear it tamely; touch me with noble anger,   278
   And let not women's weapons, water drops,
   Stain my man's cheeks! No, you unnatural hags,
   I will have such revenges on you both
   That all the world shall—I will do such things—
   What they are yet I know not, but they shall be

---

258 well-favored attractive, fair of feature   **260 Stands . . . praise**
achieves, by necessity, some relative deserving of praise   **264 follow** be
your attendants   **266 reason not** do not dispassionately analyze.   **Our**
basest even our most wretched   **267 Are . . . superfluous** have some
wretched possession they can dispense with   **268 Allow not** if you do
not allow.   **needs** i.e., to survive   **270–272 If . . . warm** i.e., if fashions
in clothes were determined only by the need for warmth, this natural
standard wouldn't justify the rich robes you wear to be gorgeous—
which don't serve well for warmth in any case   **272 for** as for
277–278 fool . . . To do not make me so foolish as to

The terrors of the earth. You think I'll weep;
No, I'll not weep.   *Storm and tempest.*
I have full cause of weeping; but this heart
Shall break into a hundred thousand flaws   287
Or ere I'll weep. O Fool, I shall go mad!   288
      Exeunt [Lear, Gloucester, Kent, and Fool].

CORNWALL
Let us withdraw. 'Twill be a storm.

REGAN
This house is little. The old man and 's people
Cannot be well bestowed.   291

GONERIL
'Tis his own blame hath put himself from rest,   292
And must needs taste his folly.   293

REGAN
For his particular, I'll receive him gladly,   294
But not one follower.

GONERIL
So am I purposed. Where is my lord of Gloucester?

CORNWALL
Followed the old man forth.

     Enter Gloucester.

              He is returned.

GLOUCESTER
The King is in high rage.

CORNWALL   Whither is he going?

GLOUCESTER
He calls to horse, but will I know not whither.

CORNWALL
'Tis best to give him way. He leads himself.   300

GONERIL
My lord, entreat him by no means to stay.

GLOUCESTER
Alack, the night comes on, and the bleak winds
Do sorely ruffle. For many miles about   303
There's scarce a bush.

---

287 flaws fragments   **288 Or ere** before   **291 bestowed** lodged
292 blame fault.   **hath** that he has, or, that has.   **from rest** i.e., out of
the house; also, lacking peace of mind   **293 taste** experience   **294 For
his particular** as for him individually   **300 give . . . himself** give him his
own way. He is guided only by his own willfulness.   **303 ruffle** bluster

REGAN   O, sir, to willful men
   The injuries that they themselves procure
   Must be their schoolmasters. Shut up your doors.
   He is attended with a desperate train,
   And what they may incense him to, being apt   308
   To have his ear abused, wisdom bids fear.   309
CORNWALL
   Shut up your doors, my lord; 'tis a wild night.
   My Regan counsels well. Come out o' the storm.
                                        Exeunt.

❖

308–309 being . . . abused (he) being inclined to hearken to wild counsel

3.1   *Storm still. Enter Kent [disguised as Caius] and*
         a Gentleman, severally.

KENT   Who's there, besides foul weather?
GENTLEMAN
  One minded like the weather, most unquietly.
KENT   I know you. Where's the King?
GENTLEMAN
  Contending with the fretful elements;
  Bids the wind blow the earth into the sea
  Or swell the curlèd waters 'bove the main,   6
  That things might change or cease; tears his white hair,
  Which the impetuous blasts with eyeless rage
  Catch in their fury and make nothing of;   9
  Strives in his little world of man to outstorm   10
  The to-and-fro-conflicting wind and rain.
  This night, wherein the cub-drawn bear would couch, 12
  The lion and the belly-pinchèd wolf
  Keep their fur dry, unbonneted he runs
  And bids what will take all.
KENT   But who is with him?   15
GENTLEMAN
  None but the Fool, who labors to outjest   16
  His heart-struck injuries.
KENT   Sir, I do know you,
  And dare upon the warrant of my note   18
  Commend a dear thing to you. There is division,   19
  Although as yet the face of it is covered
  With mutual cunning, twixt Albany and Cornwall;
  Who have—as who have not, that their great stars   22
  Throned and set high?—servants, who seem no less, 23

3.1. Location: An open place in Gloucestershire.
s.d. severally at separate doors   **6 main** mainland   **9 make nothing of**
treat disrespectfully   **10 little world of man** i.e., the microcosm, which
is an epitome of the macrocosm or universe   **12 cub-drawn** famished,
with udders sucked dry (and hence ravenous).   **couch** lie close in its
den   **15 take all** (A cry of desperate defiance, said by a gambler in
staking his last.)   **16 outjest** exorcise or relieve by jesting   **18 upon . . .
note** on the strength of what I know (about you)   **19 Commend . . .
thing** entrust a precious undertaking   **22 that** whom.   **stars** destinies
23 no less i.e., no other than servants

Which are to France the spies and speculations   24
Intelligent of our state. What hath been seen,   25
Either in snuffs and packings of the Dukes,   26
Or the hard rein which both of them hath borne
Against the old kind King, or something deeper,
Whereof perchance these are but furnishings—   29
But true it is, from France there comes a power   30
Into this scattered kingdom, who already,   31
Wise in our negligence, have secret feet   32
In some of our best ports and are at point   33
To show their open banner. Now to you:
If on my credit you dare build so far   35
To make your speed to Dover, you shall find
Some that will thank you, making just report   37
Of how unnatural and bemadding sorrow
The King hath cause to plain.   39
I am a gentleman of blood and breeding,
And from some knowledge and assurance offer
This office to you.   42

GENTLEMAN
I will talk further with you.

KENT   No, do not.
For confirmation that I am much more
Than my outwall, open this purse and take   45
What it contains. [*He gives a purse and a ring.*] If
    you shall see Cordelia—
As fear not but you shall—show her this ring,
And she will tell you who that fellow is   48
That yet you do not know. Fie on this storm!
I will go seek the King.

GENTLEMAN
Give me your hand. Have you no more to say?

KENT
Few words, but, to effect, more than all yet: 52

---

24 speculations scouts, spies   **25 Intelligent of** supplying intelligence
pertinent to   **26 snuffs** quarrels.   **packings** intrigues   **29 furnishings**
outward shows   **30 power** army   **31 scattered** divided   **32 Wise in**
taking advantage of.   **feet** i.e., foothold   **33 at point** ready   **35 credit**
trustworthiness.   **so far** so far as   **37 making just report** for making an
accurate report   **39 plain** complain   **42 office** assignment   **45 outwall**
exterior appearance   **48 fellow** i.e., Kent   **52 to effect** in their consequences

That when we have found the King—in which your pain 53
That way, I'll this—he that first lights on him 54
Holla the other. *Exeunt* [*separately*].

✣

3.2 *Storm still. Enter Lear and Fool.*

LEAR
Blow, winds, and crack your cheeks! Rage, blow!
You cataracts and hurricanoes, spout 2
Till you have drenched our steeples, drowned the cocks! 3
You sulfurous and thought-executing fires, 4
Vaunt-couriers of oak-cleaving thunderbolts, 5
Singe my white head! And thou, all-shaking thunder,
Strike flat the thick rotundity o' the world!
Crack nature's molds, all germens spill at once 8
That makes ingrateful man!
FOOL　O nuncle, court holy water in a dry house is bet- 10
ter than this rainwater out o' door. Good nuncle, in,
ask thy daughters blessing. Here's a night pities 12
neither wise men nor fools.
LEAR
Rumble thy bellyful! Spit, fire! Spout, rain!
Nor rain, wind, thunder, fire, are my daughters.
I tax not you, you elements, with unkindness; 16
I never gave you kingdom, called you children.
You owe me no subscription. Then let fall 18
Your horrible pleasure. Here I stand your slave,
A poor, infirm, weak, and despised old man.
But yet I call you servile ministers, 21

53–54 in which . . . this in which task, you search in that direction while
I go this way

3.2. Location: An open place, as before.
2 hurricanoes waterspouts　**3 drenched** drowned.　**cocks** weather-
cocks　**4 thought-executing** acting with the quickness of thought.　**fires**
i.e., lightning　**5 Vaunt-couriers** forerunners　**8 nature's molds** the
molds in which nature makes men.　**germens** germs, seeds.　**spill**
destroy　**10 court holy water** flattery　**12 ask . . . blessing** (For Lear to
do so would be to acknowledge their authority.)　**16 tax** accuse.　**with**
of　**18 subscription** allegiance　**21 ministers** agents

That will with two pernicious daughters join
Your high-engendered battles 'gainst a head   23
So old and white as this. O, ho! 'Tis foul!
FOOL   He that has a house to put 's head in has a good
headpiece.   26
    The codpiece that will house   27
      Before the head has any,   28
    The head and he shall louse;   29
      So beggars marry many.   30
    The man that makes his toe   31
      What he his heart should make   32
    Shall of a corn cry woe,   33
      And turn his sleep to wake.   34
For there was never yet fair woman but she made   35
mouths in a glass.   36
LEAR
No, I will be the pattern of all patience;
I will say nothing.

Enter Kent, [disguised as Caius].

KENT   Who's there?
FOOL   Marry, here's grace and a codpiece; that's a wise   40
man and a fool.
KENT
Alas, sir, are you here? Things that love night
Love not such nights as these. The wrathful skies
Gallow the very wanderers of the dark   44

23 high-engendered battles battalions engendered in the heavens
26 headpiece (1) helmetlike covering for the head (2) head for common
sense   **27–34 The codpiece . . . wake** i.e., a man who houses his genitals
in a sexual embrace before he provides a roof for his head can expect
lice-infested penury; and one who elevates what is base above what is
noble (as Lear has done with his daughters) can expect misery and
wakeful tossing also. If he values the toe more than the heart, his
reward will be that the toe will cause him suffering.   **codpiece** covering for the genitals worn by men with their close-fitting hose; here
representing the genitals themselves   **35–36 made . . . glass** practiced
making attractive faces in a mirror   **40 Marry** (An oath, originally "by
the Virgin Mary.")   **grace** royal grace.   **codpiece** (Often prominent in
the Fool's costume.)   **44 Gallow** i.e., gally, frighten.   **wanderers of the
dark** wild beasts

And make them keep their caves. Since I was man,   45
Such sheets of fire, such bursts of horrid thunder,
Such groans of roaring wind and rain I never
Remember to have heard. Man's nature cannot carry   48
Th' affliction nor the fear.

LEAR   Let the great gods,   49
That keep this dreadful pother o'er our heads,   50
Find out their enemies now. Tremble, thou wretch,   51
That hast within thee undivulgèd crimes
Unwhipped of justice! Hide thee, thou bloody hand,   53
Thou perjured, and thou simular of virtue   54
That art incestuous! Caitiff, to pieces shake,   55
That under covert and convenient seeming   56
Has practiced on man's life! Close pent-up guilts,   57
Rive your concealing continents and cry   58
These dreadful summoners grace! I am a man   59
More sinned against than sinning.

KENT   Alack, bareheaded?
Gracious my lord, hard by here is a hovel;
Some friendship will it lend you 'gainst the tempest.
Repose you there while I to this hard house—
More harder than the stones whereof 'tis raised,
Which even but now, demanding after you,   65
Denied me to come in—return and force
Their scanted courtesy.

LEAR   My wits begin to turn.   67
Come on, my boy. How dost, my boy? Art cold?
I am cold myself.—Where is this straw, my fellow?
The art of our necessities is strange,
And can make vile things precious. Come, your hovel.—
Poor fool and knave, I have one part in my heart
That's sorry yet for thee.

---

45 keep occupy, remain inside   **48 carry** endure   **49 affliction** physical affliction   **50 pother** hubbub, turmoil   **51 Find . . . now** i.e., expose criminals (by their display of fear)   **53 of** by   **54 perjured** perjurer. **simular** pretender   **55 Caitiff** wretch   **56 seeming** hypocrisy   **57 practiced on** plotted against.   **Close** secret   **58 Rive** split.   **continents** covering, containers   **58–59 cry . . . grace** pray for mercy at the hands of the officers of divine justice. (A *summoner* was the police officer of an ecclesiastical court.)   **65 Which** i.e., the occupants of the house. **demanding** I inquiring   **67 scanted** stinted

FOOL [*Sings*]
> "He that has and a little tiny wit,   74
>   With heigh-ho, the wind and the rain,
> Must make content with his fortunes fit,
>   Though the rain it raineth every day."   77

LEAR
True, boy.—Come, bring us to this hovel.

> *Exit [with Kent].*

FOOL   This is a brave night to cool a courtesan. I'll speak   79
a prophecy ere I go:

> When priests are more in word than matter;   81
> When brewers mar their malt with water;   82
> When nobles are their tailors' tutors,   83
> No heretics burned but wenches' suitors,   84
> Then shall the realm of Albion   85
> Come to great confusion.

> When every case in law is right,   87
> No squire in debt, nor no poor knight;
> When slanders do not live in tongues,
> Nor cutpurses come not to throngs;
> When usurers tell their gold i' the field,   91
> And bawds and whores do churches build,
> Then comes the time, who lives to see 't,
> That going shall be used with feet.   94

> This prophecy Merlin shall make, for I live before his   95
> time.   *Exit.*

❖

74–77 (Derived from the popular song that Feste sings in *Twelfth Night*, 5.1.389ff.)   **79 This . . . courtesan** i.e., this wretched night might at least damp the fires of lust (?)   **brave** fine   **81 more . . . matter** better in speech than in substance or Gospel truth. (This and the next three lines satirize the present state of affairs.)   **82 mar** adulterate   **83 are . . . tutors** i.e., know more than their tailors about fashion   **84 No . . . suitors** i.e., when heresy is a matter not of religious faith but of perjured lovers (whose burning is not at the stake but in catching venereal disease)   **85 realm of Albion** kingdom of England. (The Fool is parodying a pseudo-Chaucerian prophetic verse.)   **87 right** just. (This and the next five lines offer a utopian vision of justice and charity that will never be realized in this corrupted world.)   **91 tell** count.   **i' the field** i.e., openly, without fear   **94 going . . . feet** walking will be done on foot   **95 Merlin** (A great wizard of the court of King Arthur, who came after Lear.)

3.3   *Enter Gloucester and Edmund [with lights].*

GLOUCESTER Alack, alack, Edmund, I like not this unnatural dealing. When I desired their leave that I might
pity him, they took from me the use of mine own ₃
house, charged me on pain of perpetual displeasure
neither to speak of him, entreat for him, or any way
sustain him.

EDMUND Most savage and unnatural!

GLOUCESTER Go to; say you nothing. There is division
between the Dukes, and a worse matter than that. I
have received a letter this night; 'tis dangerous to be
spoken; I have locked the letter in my closet. These in- ₁₁
juries the King now bears will be revenged home; ₁₂
there is part of a power already footed. We must in- ₁₃
cline to the King. I will look him and privily relieve ₁₄
him. Go you and maintain talk with the Duke, that
my charity be not of him perceived. If he ask for me, I ₁₆
am ill and gone to bed. If I die for 't, as no less is
threatened me, the King my old master must be relieved. There is strange things toward, Edmund. Pray ₁₉
you, be careful.   *Exit.*

EDMUND

This courtesy forbid thee shall the Duke   ₂₁
Instantly know, and of that letter too.
This seems a fair deserving, and must draw me   ₂₃
That which my father loses—no less than all.
The younger rises when the old doth fall.   *Exit.*

❖

3.4   *Enter Lear, Kent [disguised as Caius], and Fool.*

KENT

Here is the place, my lord. Good my lord, enter.

3.3. Location: Gloucester's house.
3 pity be merciful to, relieve **11 closet** private chamber **12 home**
thoroughly **13 power** armed force. **footed** landed **13–14 incline
to** side with **14 look** look for **16 of** by **19 toward** impending
21 courtesy forbid thee kindness (to Lear) which you were forbidden
to show **23 fair deserving** meritorious action

3.4. Location: An open place. Before a hovel.

The tyranny of the open night's too rough
For nature to endure.   *Storm still.*

LEAR   Let me alone.

KENT

Good my lord, enter here.

LEAR   Wilt break my heart?   4

KENT

I had rather break mine own. Good my lord, enter.

LEAR

Thou think'st 'tis much that this contentious storm
Invades us to the skin. So 'tis to thee,
But where the greater malady is fixed   8
The lesser is scarce felt. Thou'dst shun a bear,
But if thy flight lay toward the roaring sea
Thou'dst meet the bear i' the mouth. When the
   mind's free,   11
The body's delicate. This tempest in my mind   12
Doth from my senses take all feeling else
Save what beats there. Filial ingratitude!
Is it not as this mouth should tear this hand   15
For lifting food to 't? But I will punish home.   16
No, I will weep no more. In such a night
To shut me out? Pour on; I will endure.
In such a night as this? O Regan, Goneril,
Your old kind father, whose frank heart gave all—   20
O, that way madness lies; let me shun that!
No more of that.

KENT   Good my lord, enter here.

LEAR

Prithee, go in thyself; seek thine own ease.
This tempest will not give me leave to ponder   24
On things would hurt me more. But I'll go in.   25
[*To the Fool.*] In, boy; go first. You houseless poverty—
Nay, get thee in. I'll pray, and then I'll sleep.

                              Exit [*Fool into the hovel*].

---

4 break my heart i.e., cause me anguish by relieving my physical wants
and thus forcing me to confront again my *greater malady* (l. 8) **8 fixed**
lodged, implanted **11 i' the mouth** i.e., head-on. **free** free of anxiety
12 The body's delicate i.e., the body's importunate needs can assert
themselves **15 as** as if **16 home** fully **20 frank** liberal **24 will . . .
leave** i.e., keeps me too preoccupied **25 things would** things (such as
filial ingratitude) that would

Poor naked wretches, wheresoe'er you are,
That bide the pelting of this pitiless storm,   29
How shall your houseless heads and unfed sides,
Your looped and windowed raggedness, defend you   31
From seasons such as these? O, I have ta'en
Too little care of this! Take physic, pomp;   33
Expose thyself to feel what wretches feel,
That thou mayst shake the superflux to them   35
And show the heavens more just.

EDGAR [*Within*] Fathom and half, fathom and half!   37
Poor Tom!

Enter Fool [from the hovel].

FOOL   Come not in here, nuncle; here's a spirit. Help
me, help me!
KENT   Give me thy hand. Who's there?
FOOL   A spirit, a spirit! He says his name's poor Tom.
KENT
What art thou that dost grumble there i' the straw?
Come forth.

Enter Edgar [disguised as a madman].

EDGAR   Away! The foul fiend follows me! Through the   45
sharp hawthorn blows the cold wind. Hum! Go to thy   46
bed and warm thee.
LEAR   Didst thou give all to thy daughters? And art
thou come to this?
EDGAR   Who gives anything to poor Tom? Whom the
foul fiend hath led through fire and through flame,
through ford and whirlpool, o'er bog and quagmire;
that hath laid knives under his pillow and halters in   53
his pew, set ratsbane by his porridge, made him   54

29 bide endure   **31 looped and windowed** full of openings like windows
and loopholes   **33 Take physic, pomp** cure yourself, O distempered
great ones   **35 superflux** superfluity (with suggestion of *flux*, "bodily
discharge," introduced by *physic*, "purgative," in l. 33)   **37 Fathom and
half** (A sailor's cry while taking soundings, hence appropriate to a
deluge.)   **45 Away** keep away   **45–46 Through . . . wind** (Possibly a line
from a ballad.)   **53–54 knives, halters, ratsbane** (Tempting means to
commit suicide and hence be damned.)   **54 pew** gallery, place (?)
porridge soup

proud of heart, to ride on a bay trotting horse over 55
four-inched bridges to course his own shadow for a 56
traitor. Bless thy five wits! Tom's a-cold. O, do de, 57
do de, do de. Bless thee from whirlwinds, star-blast- 58
ing, and taking! Do poor Tom some charity, whom the 59
foul fiend vexes. There could I have him now—and 60
there—and there again—and there.   *Storm still.*

LEAR
Has his daughters brought him to this pass?   62
Couldst thou save nothing? Wouldst thou give 'em all?
FOOL   Nay, he reserved a blanket, else we had been all 64
shamed.
LEAR
Now, all the plagues that in the pendulous air   66
Hang fated o'er men's faults light on thy daughters!   67
KENT   He hath no daughters, sir.
LEAR
Death, traitor! Nothing could have subdued nature
To such a lowness but his unkind daughters.
Is it the fashion that discarded fathers
Should have thus little mercy on their flesh?   72
Judicious punishment! 'Twas this flesh begot   73
Those pelican daughters.   74
EDGAR   Pillicock sat on Pillicock Hill. Alow, alow, loo, 75
loo!
FOOL   This cold night will turn us all to fools and mad-
men.
EDGAR   Take heed o' the foul fiend. Obey thy parents;

55-56 over four-inched bridges i.e., taking mad risks on narrow bridges
with the devil's assistance   **56 course** chase.   **for** as   **57 five wits**
either the five senses, or common wit, imagination, fantasy, estimation,
and memory   **58-59 star-blasting** being blighted by influence of the
stars   **59 taking** pestilence; or witchcraft   **60 There** (Perhaps he slaps
at lice and other vermin as if they were devils.)   **62 pass** miserable
plight   **64 reserved a blanket** kept a wrap (for his nakedness)
66 pendulous suspended, overhanging   **67 fated** having the power of
fate   **72 have . . . flesh** i.e., punish themselves, as Edgar has done
(probably with pins and thorns stuck in his flesh)   **73 Judicious** appropriate to the crime   **74 pelican** greedy. (Young pelicans supposedly
smote their parents and fed on the blood of their mothers' breasts.)
75 Pillicock (From an old rhyme, suggested by the sound of *pelican.*
Pillicock in nursery rhyme seems to have been a euphemism for penis,
Pillicock Hill for the Mount of Venus.)

keep thy word's justice; swear not; commit not with 80
man's sworn spouse; set not thy sweet heart on proud
array. Tom's a-cold.

LEAR   What hast thou been?

EDGAR   A servingman, proud in heart and mind, that 84
curled my hair, wore gloves in my cap, served the lust 85
of my mistress' heart, and did the act of darkness with
her; swore as many oaths as I spake words, and broke
them in the sweet face of heaven. One that slept in the
contriving of lust and waked to do it. Wine loved I
deeply, dice dearly, and in woman out-paramoured 90
the Turk. False of heart, light of ear, bloody of hand; 91
hog in sloth, fox in stealth, wolf in greediness, dog in
madness, lion in prey. Let not the creaking of shoes 93
nor the rustling of silks betray thy poor heart to
woman. Keep thy foot out of brothels, thy hand out of
plackets, thy pen from lenders' books, and defy the 96
foul fiend. Still through the hawthorn blows the cold
wind; says suum, mun, nonny. Dolphin my boy, boy, 98
sessa! Let him trot by.   *Storm still.* 99

LEAR   Thou wert better in a grave than to answer with
thy uncovered body this extremity of the skies. Is man
no more than this? Consider him well. Thou ow'st the 102
worm no silk, the beast no hide, the sheep no wool,
the cat no perfume. Ha! Here's three on 's are sophis- 104
ticated. Thou art the thing itself; unaccommodated 105
man is no more but such a poor, bare, forked animal
as thou art. Off, off, you lendings! Come, unbutton
here.   [*Tearing off his clothes.*]

FOOL   Prithee, nuncle, be contented; 'tis a naughty night 109

---

80 justice integrity.   **commit not** i.e., do not commit adultery. (Edgar's
mad catechism contains fragments of the Ten Commandments.)
84 servingman either a "servant" in the language of courtly love or an
ambitious servant in a household   **85 gloves** i.e., my mistress's favors
90–91 out-paramoured the Turk outdid the Sultan in keeping mis-
tresses   **91 light of ear** foolishly credulous; frivolous   **93 prey** prey-
ing   **96 plackets** slits in skirts or petticoats.   **thy pen . . . books** i.e., do
not sign a contract for a loan   **98 suum . . . nonny** (Imitative of the
wind?)   **Dolphin my boy** (A slang phrase, or bit of song?)   **99 sessa** i.e.,
away, cease (?)   **102 ow'st** have borrowed from   **104 çat** civet cat
104–105 sophisticated clad in the trappings of civilized life; adulter-
ated   **105 unaccommodated** unfurnished with the trappings of civilization   **109 naughty** bad

to swim in. Now a little fire in a wild field were like 110
an old lecher's heart—a small spark, all the rest on 's 111
body cold.

 Enter Gloucester, with a torch.

Look, here comes a walking fire.

EDGAR This is the foul fiend Flibbertigibbet! He begins 114
at curfew and walks till the first cock; he gives the web 115
and the pin, squinnies the eye and makes the harelip, 116
mildews the white wheat, and hurts the poor creature 117
of earth.

 Swithold footed thrice the 'old; 119
 He met the nightmare and her ninefold; 120
  Bid her alight,
  And her troth plight,
 And aroint thee, witch, aroint thee! 123

KENT How fares Your Grace?

LEAR What's he?

KENT Who's there? What is 't you seek?

GLOUCESTER What are you there? Your names?

EDGAR Poor Tom, that eats the swimming frog, the
toad, the tadpole, the wall newt and the water; that in 129
the fury of his heart, when the foul fiend rages, eats
cow dung for salads, swallows the old rat and the
ditch-dog, drinks the green mantle of the standing 132
pool; who is whipped from tithing to tithing and 133
stock-punished and imprisoned; who hath had three 134
suits to his back, six shirts to his body, 135
 Horse to ride, and weapon to wear;
 But mice and rats and such small deer 137

110 **wild** barren, uncultivated   111 **on 's** of his   114 **Flibbertigibbet**
(A devil from Elizabethan folklore whose name appears in Samuel
Harsnett's *Declaration* of 1603 and elsewhere.)   115 **first cock** mid-
night   115–116 **web and the pin** cataract of the eye   116 **squinnies**
causes to squint   117 **white** ripening   119 **Swithold** Saint Withold, a
famous Anglo-Saxon exorcist, who here provides defense against the
nightmare, or demon thought to afflict sleepers, by commanding the
nightmare to *alight*, i.e., stop riding over the sleeper, and *plight* her
troth, i.e., vow true faith, promise to do no harm.   **footed . . . 'old** thrice
traversed the wold (tract of hilly upland)   120 **ninefold** nine offspring
(with possible pun on *fold, foal*)   123 **aroint thee** begone   129 **water** i.e.,
water newt   132 **ditch-dog** i.e., dead dog in a ditch.   **mantle** scum.
standing stagnant   133 **tithing to tithing** i.e., one ward or parish to
another   134 **stock-punished** placed in the stocks   134–135 **three suits**
(Like the menial servant at 2.2.15.)   137 **deer** animals

Have been Tom's food for seven long year.
Beware my follower. Peace, Smulkin! Peace, thou fiend! 139

GLOUCESTER
What, hath Your Grace no better company?

EDGAR The Prince of Darkness is a gentleman. Modo 141
he's called, and Mahu.   142

GLOUCESTER
Our flesh and blood, my lord, is grown so vile
That it doth hate what gets it.   144

EDGAR Poor Tom's a-cold.

GLOUCESTER
Go in with me. My duty cannot suffer   146
T' obey in all your daughters' hard commands.
Though their injunction be to bar my doors
And let this tyrannous night take hold upon you,
Yet have I ventured to come seek you out
And bring you where both fire and food is ready.

LEAR
First let me talk with this philosopher.
[To Edgar.] What is the cause of thunder?

KENT   Good my lord,
Take his offer. Go into the house.

LEAR
I'll talk a word with this same learnèd Theban.   155
[To Edgar.] What is your study?   156

EDGAR How to prevent the fiend, and to kill vermin.   157

LEAR Let me ask you one word in private.
                              [Lear and Edgar talk apart.]

KENT [To Gloucester]
Importune him once more to go, my lord.
His wits begin t' unsettle.

GLOUCESTER   Canst thou blame him?
                                        Storm still.
His daughters seek his death. Ah, that good Kent!
He said it would be thus, poor banished man.
Thou sayest the King grows mad; I'll tell thee, friend,
I am almost mad myself. I had a son,

139 follower familiar, attendant devil   **139, 141–142 Smulkin, Modo,
Mahu** (Shakespeare found these Elizabethan devils in Samuel
Harsnett's *Declaration*.)   **144 gets** begets   **146 suffer** permit me
155 Theban i.e., one deeply versed in "philosophy" or natural science
156 study special competence   **157 prevent** thwart

Now outlawed from my blood; he sought my life   165
But lately, very late. I loved him, friend,
No father his son dearer. True to tell thee,
The grief hath crazed my wits. What a night's this!—
I do beseech Your Grace—
LEAR   O, cry you mercy, sir.   170
[*To Edgar.*] Noble philosopher, your company.
EDGAR   Tom's a-cold.
GLOUCESTER [*To Edgar*]   In, fellow, there, into the hovel.
Keep thee warm.
LEAR [*Starting toward the hovel*]
Come, let's in all.
KENT   This way, my lord.
LEAR   With him!
I will keep still with my philosopher.
KENT [*To Gloucester*]
Good my lord, soothe him. Let him take the fellow.   177
GLOUCESTER [*To Kent*]   Take him you on.   178
KENT [*To Edgar*]
Sirrah, come on. Go along with us.
LEAR   Come, good Athenian.   180
GLOUCESTER   No words, no words! Hush.
EDGAR
Child Rowland to the dark tower came;   182
His word was still, "Fie, foh, and fum,   183
I smell the blood of a British man."   *Exeunt.*   184

❖

3.5   *Enter Cornwall and Edmund [with a letter].*

CORNWALL   I will have my revenge ere I depart his
house.
EDMUND   How, my lord, I may be censured, that nature   3

---

165 outlawed . . . blood exiled from kinship with me and legally outlawed   **170 cry you mercy** I beg your pardon   **177 soothe** humor
178 Take . . . on i.e., take Edgar along with you   **180 Athenian** i.e.,
philosopher   **182 Child Rowland,** etc. (Probably a fragment of a ballad
about the hero of the Charlemagne legends. A *child* is a candidate for
knighthood.)   **183 word** watchword.   **still** always   **183–184 Fie . . . man**
(This is essentially what the Giant says in "Jack, the Giant Killer.")

3.5. Location: Gloucester's house.
3 censured judged

thus gives way to loyalty, something fears me to 4
think of.

CORNWALL I now perceive it was not altogether your
brother's evil disposition made him seek his death, 7
but a provoking merit set awork by a reprovable 8
badness in himself. 9

EDMUND How malicious is my fortune that I must repent to be just! This is the letter he spoke of, which 11
approves him an intelligent party to the advantages 12
of France. O heavens! That this treason were not, or
not I the detector!

CORNWALL Go with me to the Duchess.

EDMUND If the matter of this paper be certain, you have
mighty business in hand.

CORNWALL True or false, it hath made thee Earl of
Gloucester. Seek out where thy father is, that he may
be ready for our apprehension. 20

EDMUND [*Aside*] If I find him comforting the King, it 21
will stuff his suspicion more fully.—I will persevere in 22
my course of loyalty, though the conflict be sore between that and my blood. 24

CORNWALL I will lay trust upon thee, and thou shalt
find a dearer father in my love.   *Exeunt.*

❖

3.6   *Enter Kent [disguised as Caius] and Gloucester.*

GLOUCESTER Here is better than the open air; take it
thankfully. I will piece out the comfort with what ad- 2
dition I can. I will not be long from you.

---

4 something fears somewhat frightens   **7 his** i.e., his father's   **8–9 a
provoking . . . himself** i.e., the badness of Gloucester which deserved
punishment, set awork by an evil propensity in Edgar himself   **11 to be
just** that I am righteous in my duty (to Cornwall)   **12 approves**
proves.   **an intelligent . . . advantages** a spy in the service   **20 apprehension** arrest   **21 him** i.e., Gloucester.   **comforting** offering aid and
comfort to, helping   **22 his** i.e., Cornwall's or, *his suspicion* may mean
"suspicion of him, Gloucester"   **24 blood** family loyalty, filial instincts

**3.6. Location: Within a building on Gloucester's estate, near or adjoin-
ing his house; or part of the house itself. See 3.4.146–154. Cushions are
provided, and stools.**
2 piece eke

KENT All the power of his wits have given way to his
impatience. The gods reward your kindness!   5

                           Exit [Gloucester].

    Enter Lear, Edgar [as poor Tom], and Fool.

EDGAR Frateretto calls me, and tells me Nero is an an- 6
gler in the lake of darkness. Pray, innocent, and be- 7
ware the foul fiend.

FOOL Prithee, nuncle, tell me whether a madman be a
gentleman or a yeoman?

LEAR A king, a king!

FOOL No, he's a yeoman that has a gentleman to his
son; for he's a mad yeoman that sees his son a gentleman before him.

LEAR

To have a thousand with red burning spits
Come hizzing in upon 'em—   16

EDGAR The foul fiend bites my back.

FOOL He's mad that trusts in the tameness of a wolf, a
horse's health, a boy's love, or a whore's oath.

LEAR

It shall be done; I will arraign them straight.
[*To Edgar.*] Come, sit thou here, most learnèd justicer. 21
[*To the Fool.*] Thou, sapient sir, sit here. Now, you
  she-foxes!

EDGAR Look where he stands and glares! Want'st thou 23
eyes at trial, madam?   24

[*Sings.*] "Come o'er the burn, Bessy, to me—"   25

FOOL [*Sings*]

        Her boat hath a leak,
        And she must not speak
      Why she dares not come over to thee.

---

5 impatience rage, inability to endure more **6 Frateretto** (Another of the
fiends from Harsnett.) **6–7 Nero is an angler** (See Chaucer's "Monk's
Tale," ll. 485–486; in Rabelais, 2.30, Nero is described as a fiddler and
Trajan an angler in the underworld.) **7 innocent** simpleton, fool (i.e., the
Fool) **16 hizzing** hissing **21 justicer** judge, justice **23 he** (Probably one
of Edgar's devils; or Lear.) **23–24 Want'st . . . trial** do you lack spectators
at your trial, or do you want to have them **25 Come . . . me** (First line of
a ballad by William Birche, 1558. A *burn* is a brook. The Fool makes a
ribald reply, in which the *leaky boat* suggests her easy virtue or perhaps
her menstrual period.)

EDGAR The foul fiend haunts poor Tom in the voice of
a nightingale. Hoppedance cries in Tom's belly for two 30
white herring. Croak not, black angel; I have no food 31
for thee.

KENT
How do you, sir? Stand you not so amazed. 33
Will you lie down and rest upon the cushions?

LEAR
I'll see their trial first. Bring in their evidence. 35
[*To Edgar.*] Thou robèd man of justice, take thy place; 36
[*To the Fool.*] And thou, his yokefellow of equity, 37
Bench by his side. [*To Kent.*] You are o' the commission; 38
Sit you too.   [*They sit.*]

EDGAR Let us deal justly.   [*He sings.*]
Sleepest or wakest thou, jolly shepherd?
Thy sheep be in the corn; 42
And for one blast of thy minikin mouth, 43
Thy sheep shall take no harm. 44
Purr the cat is gray. 45

LEAR Arraign her first; 'tis Goneril, I here take my oath
before this honorable assembly, kicked the poor King 47
her father.

FOOL Come hither, mistress. Is your name Goneril?

LEAR She cannot deny it.

FOOL Cry you mercy, I took you for a joint stool. 51

LEAR
And here's another, whose warped looks proclaim
What store her heart is made on. Stop her there! 53

---

30 Hoppedance (Harsnett mentions "Hoberdidance.") **31 white** un-
smoked (contrasted with *black angel*). **Croak** (Refers to the rumbling in
Edgar's stomach denoting hunger.) **33 amazed** bewildered **35 their
evidence** the witnesses against them **36 robèd man** i.e., Edgar, with his
blanket **37 yokefellow of equity** partner in the law **38 Bench** take
your place on the bench. **o' the commission** one commissioned to be a
justice **42 corn** grain field **43–44 And . . . harm** (This may mean that
if the shepherd recalls his sheep by piping to them before they consume
the grainfield, they will not be put in the pound.) **43 minikin** dainty,
pretty **45 Purr the cat** (A devil or familiar from Harsnett; see 3.4.114,
note. *Purr* may be the sound the familiar makes.) **47 kicked** who
kicked **51 joint stool** low stool made by a joiner, or maker of furniture
with joined parts. (Proverbially the phrase "I took . . . stool" meant "I
beg your pardon for failing to notice you." The reference is also presumably to a real stool onstage.) **53 store** material. **on** of

Arms, arms, sword, fire! Corruption in the place!   54
False justicer, why hast thou let her scape?
EDGAR   Bless thy five wits!
KENT
O, pity! Sir, where is the patience now
That you so oft have boasted to retain?
EDGAR [*Aside*]
My tears begin to take his part so much
They mar my counterfeiting.
LEAR   The little dogs and all,
Tray, Blanch, and Sweetheart, see, they bark at me.
EDGAR   Tom will throw his head at them. Avaunt, you   63
curs!
    Be thy mouth or black or white,
    Tooth that poisons if it bite,
    Mastiff, greyhound, mongrel grim,
    Hound or spaniel, brach or lym,   68
    Or bobtail tike or trundle-tail,   69
    Tom will make him weep and wail;
    For, with throwing thus my head,
    Dogs leapt the hatch, and all are fled.   72
Do de, de, de. Sessa! Come, march to wakes and fairs   73
and market towns. Poor Tom, thy horn is dry.   74
LEAR   Then let them anatomize Regan; see what breeds   75
about her heart. Is there any cause in nature that make
these hard hearts? [*To Edgar.*] You, sir, I entertain for   77
one of my hundred; only I do not like the fashion of
your garments. You will say they are Persian; but let   79
them be changed.
KENT
Now, good my lord, lie here and rest awhile.
LEAR [*Lying on cushions*]   Make no noise, make no
noise. Draw the curtains. So, so. We'll go to supper i'   83
the morning.   [*He sleeps.*]

---

54 Corruption in the place i.e., there is iniquity or bribery in this court
63 throw his head at i.e., threaten   **68 brach** hound bitch.   **lym** blood-
hound   **69 bobtail** short-tailed small dog, cur.   **trundle-tail** long-tailed
dog   **72 hatch** lower half of a divided door   **73 Sessa** i.e., away, cease (?)
wakes (Here, parish festivals.)   **74 horn** i.e., horn bottle used by beggars to beg for drinks   **75 anatomize** dissect   **77 entertain** take into
my service   **79 Persian** i.e., gorgeous intricate attire   **83 curtains** bed-
curtains. (They presumably exist only in Lear's mad imagination.)

FOOL   And I'll go to bed at noon.

Enter Gloucester.

GLOUCESTER
Come hither, friend. Where is the King my master?
KENT
Here, sir, but trouble him not. His wits are gone.
GLOUCESTER
Good friend, I prithee, take him in thy arms.
I have o'erheard a plot of death upon him.   89
There is a litter ready; lay him in 't
And drive toward Dover, friend, where thou shalt meet
Both welcome and protection. Take up thy master.
If thou shouldst dally half an hour, his life,
With thine and all that offer to defend him,
Stand in assurèd loss. Take up, take up,   95
And follow me, that will to some provision   96
Give thee quick conduct.
KENT   Oppressèd nature sleeps.   97
This rest might yet have balmed thy broken sinews,   98
Which, if convenience will not allow,   99
Stand in hard cure. [*To the Fool.*] Come, help to bear
thy master.   100
Thou must not stay behind.   [*They pick up Lear.*]
GLOUCESTER   Come, come, away!
                      Exeunt [all but Edgar].
EDGAR
When we our betters see bearing our woes,   102
We scarcely think our miseries our foes.   103
Who alone suffers suffers most i' the mind,   104
Leaving free things and happy shows behind;   105
But then the mind much sufferance doth o'erskip   106
When grief hath mates, and bearing fellowship.   107

---

89 upon against   **95 Stand . . . loss** will assuredly be lost   **96 provision**
supplies; or, means of providing for safety   **97 conduct** guidance
98 balmed cured, healed.   **sinews** nerves   **99 convenience** fortunate
circumstances   **100 Stand . . . cure** will be hard to cure   **102 our woes**
woes like ours   **103 our foes** i.e., hostile toward us alone (since we see how
human suffering afflicts even the great)   **104 Who . . . mind** i.e., he who
suffers alone suffers mental agonies greater than those who perceive they
have companions in misery   **105 free** carefree.   **shows** scenes   **106 sufferance** suffering   **107 bearing fellowship** tribulation (has) company

How light and portable my pain seems now,   108
When that which makes me bend makes the King bow—
He childed as I fathered. Tom, away!   110
Mark the high noises, and thyself bewray   111
When false opinion, whose wrong thoughts defile thee,
In thy just proof repeals and reconciles thee.   113
What will hap more tonight, safe scape the King!   114
Lurk, lurk.   [*Exit.*]

✤

3.7   *Enter Cornwall, Regan, Goneril, Bastard*
           [Edmund], and Servants.

CORNWALL [*To Goneril*]   Post speedily to my lord your hus- 1
band; show him this letter. [*He gives a letter.*] The army
of France is landed.—Seek out the traitor Gloucester.
                                   [*Exeunt some Servants.*]
REGAN   Hang him instantly.
GONERIL   Pluck out his eyes.
CORNWALL   Leave him to my displeasure. Edmund,
keep you our sister company. The revenges we are   7
bound to take upon your traitorous father are not fit   8
for your beholding. Advise the Duke, where you are   9
going, to a most festinate preparation; we are bound   10
to the like. Our posts shall be swift and intelligent be- 11
twixt us. Farewell, dear sister; farewell, my lord of   12
Gloucester.   13

      Enter steward [Oswald].

How now? Where's the King?

---

108 portable bearable, endurable   **110 He . . . fathered** i.e., he suffering
cruelty from his children as I from my father   **111 Mark . . . noises** i.e.,
observe what is being said about those in high places, or about great
events.   **bewray** reveal   **113 In . . . thee** upon your being proved innocent recalls you and restores you to favor   **114 What . . . King** whatever
else happens tonight, may the King escape safely

3.7. Location: Gloucester's house.
1 Post speedily hurry   **7 sister** i.e., sister-in-law, Goneril   **8 bound** intend-
ing; obliged   **9 the Duke** i.e., Albany   **10 festinate** hasty.   **are bound**
intend, are committed   **11 posts** messengers.   **intelligent** serviceable in
bearing information, knowledgeable   **12–13 my . . . Gloucester** i.e., Edmund, the recipient now of his father's forfeited estate and title. (Two lines
later, Oswald uses the same title to refer to Edmund's father.)

OSWALD
My lord of Gloucester hath conveyed him hence.
Some five- or six-and-thirty of his knights,   16
Hot questrists after him, met him at gate,   17
Who, with some other of the lord's dependents,·   18
Are gone with him toward Dover, where they boast
To have well-armèd friends.
CORNWALL Get horses for your mistress. [*Exit Oswald.*]
GONERIL Farewell, sweet lord, and sister.
CORNWALL
Edmund, farewell.   *Exeunt* [*Goneril and Edmund*].
          Go seek the traitor Gloucester.
Pinion him like a thief; bring him before us.
                 [*Exeunt Servants.*]
Though well we may not pass upon his life   25
Without the form of justice, yet our power
Shall do a court'sy to our wrath, which men   27
May blame but not control.

    Enter Gloucester, and Servants [*leading him*].

               Who's there? The traitor?
REGAN Ingrateful fox! 'Tis he.
CORNWALL Bind fast his corky arms.   30
GLOUCESTER
What means Your Graces? Good my friends, consider
You are my guests. Do me no foul play, friends.
CORNWALL
Bind him, I say.   [*Servants bind him.*]
REGAN   Hard, hard. O filthy traitor!
GLOUCESTER
Unmerciful lady as you are, I'm none.
CORNWALL
To this chair bind him.—Villain, thou shalt find—
       [*Regan plucks Gloucester's beard.*]
GLOUCESTER
By the kind gods, 'tis most ignobly done
To pluck me by the beard.

16–17 **his, him** i.e., Lear's, Lear 17 **questrists** searchers 18 **the lord's**
i.e., Gloucester's 25 **pass upon his life** pass the death sentence upon
him 27 **do a court'sy** i.e., bow before, yield precedence 30 **corky**
withered with age

REGAN
So white, and such a traitor?

GLOUCESTER   Naughty lady,   38
These hairs which thou dost ravish from my chin
Will quicken and accuse thee. I am your host.   40
With robbers' hands my hospitable favors   41
You should not ruffle thus. What will you do?   42

CORNWALL
Come, sir, what letters had you late from France?   43

REGAN
Be simple-answered, for we know the truth.   44

CORNWALL
And what confederacy have you with the traitors
Late footed in the kingdom?

REGAN   To whose hands   46
You have sent the lunatic King. Speak.

GLOUCESTER
I have a letter guessingly set down,   48
Which came from one that's of a neutral heart,
And not from one opposed.

CORNWALL   Cunning.

REGAN   And false.

CORNWALL   Where hast thou sent the King?

GLOUCESTER   To Dover.

REGAN
Wherefore to Dover? Wast thou not charged at peril—   55

CORNWALL
Wherefore to Dover? Let him answer that.

GLOUCESTER
I am tied to the stake, and I must stand the course.   57

REGAN   Wherefore to Dover?

GLOUCESTER
Because I would not see thy cruel nails
Pluck out his poor old eyes, nor thy fierce sister

---

38 white i.e., white-haired, venerable.   **Naughty** wicked   **40 quicken**
come to life   **41 my hospitable favors** the features of me, your host
42 ruffle tear or snatch at, treat with such violence   **43 late** lately
44 simple-answered straightforward in your answers   **46 footed**
landed   **48 guessingly set down** which was tentatively stated   **55 charged
at peril** commanded on peril of your life   **57 tied to the stake** i.e., like a
bear to be baited with dogs.   **the course** the dogs' attack

In his anointed flesh rash boarish fangs. 61
The sea, with such a storm as his bare head
In hell-black night endured, would have buoyed up 63
And quenched the stellèd fires; 64
Yet, poor old heart, he holp the heavens to rain. 65
If wolves had at thy gate howled that dern time, 66
Thou shouldst have said, "Good porter, turn the key." 67
All cruels else subscribe. But I shall see 68
The wingèd Vengeance overtake such children. 69

CORNWALL
See 't shalt thou never. Fellows, hold the chair.
Upon these eyes of thine I'll set my foot.

GLOUCESTER
He that will think to live till he be old, 72
Give me some help!
      [Servants hold the chair as Cornwall grinds
       out one of Gloucester's eyes with his boot.]
        O cruel! O you gods!

REGAN
One side will mock another. Th' other too.

CORNWALL
If you see Vengeance—

FIRST SERVANT   Hold your hand, my lord!
I have served you ever since I was a child;
But better service have I never done you
Than now to bid you hold.

REGAN   How now, you dog?

FIRST SERVANT *[To Regan]*
If you did wear a beard upon your chin,
I'd shake it on this quarrel.—What do you mean? 80

CORNWALL My villain?   *[He draws his sword.]* 81

---

61 anointed consecrated with holy oil. **rash** slash sideways
63–64 would . . . fires i.e., would have swelled high enough to quench
the stars. (The storm was monstrous in its scope and in its assault on
order.) **buoyed** lifted itself. **stellèd fires** stars **65 holp** helped
66 dern dire, dread **67 turn the key** i.e., let them in **68 All . . . subscribe** all other cruel creatures would show forgiveness except you; this
cruelty is unparalleled **69 The wingèd Vengeance** the swift vengeance
of the avenging angel of divine wrath **72 will think** hopes **80 I'd . . .
quarrel** i.e., I'd pull your beard in vehement defiance in this cause.
What do you mean i.e., what are you thinking of, what do you think
you're doing. (Said perhaps to Cornwall.) **81 villain** servant, bondman.
(Cornwall's question implies, "How dare you do such a thing?")

FIRST SERVANT [*Drawing*]
  Nay, then, come on, and take the chance of anger.   82
                    [*They fight. Cornwall is wounded.*]
REGAN [*To another Servant*]
  Give me thy sword. A peasant stand up thus?   83
                 [*She takes a sword and runs at him behind.*]
FIRST SERVANT
  O, I am slain! My lord, you have one eye left
  To see some mischief on him. O!   [*He dies.*] 85
CORNWALL
  Lest it see more, prevent it. Out, vile jelly!
                    [*He puts out Gloucester's other eye.*]
  Where is thy luster now?
GLOUCESTER
  All dark and comfortless. Where's my son Edmund?
  Edmund, enkindle all the sparks of nature   89
  To quit this horrid act.
REGAN   Out, treacherous villain!   90
  Thou call'st on him that hates thee. It was he
  That made the overture of thy treasons to us,   92
  Who is too good to pity thee.
GLOUCESTER
  O my follies! Then Edgar was abused.   94
  Kind gods, forgive me that, and prosper him!
REGAN
  Go thrust him out at gates and let him smell
  His way to Dover. *Exit* [*a Servant*] *with Gloucester.*
  How is 't, my lord? How look you?   97
CORNWALL
  I have received a hurt. Follow me, lady.—
  Turn out that eyeless villain. Throw this slave
  Upon the dunghill.—Regan, I bleed apace.
  Untimely comes this hurt. Give me your arm.
                 Exit [*Cornwall, supported by Regan*].

82 the chance of anger the risks of an angry encounter   **83 s.d. She . . .
behind** (This stage direction appears in the quarto.)   **85 mischief** injury
89 nature i.e., filial love   **90 quit** requite.   **Out** (An exclamation of anger
or impatience.)   **92 overture** disclosure   **94 abused** wronged   **97 How
look you** how is it with you

SECOND SERVANT
I'll never care what wickedness I do,
If this man come to good.

THIRD SERVANT   If she live long,
And in the end meet the old course of death,   104
Women will all turn monsters.

SECOND SERVANT
Let's follow the old Earl, and get the Bedlam
To lead him where he would. His roguish madness   107
Allows itself to anything.   108

THIRD SERVANT
Go thou. I'll fetch some flax and whites of eggs
To apply to his bleeding face. Now, heaven help him!   110
                           Exeunt [*separately*].

❖

104 old customary, natural   **107–108 His . . . anything** i.e., his being a madman and derelict allows him to do anything   **110 s.d. Exeunt** (At some point after ll. 99–100 the body of the slain First Servant must be removed.)

4.1   *Enter Edgar [as poor Tom].*

EDGAR
  Yet better thus, and known to be contemned,   1
  Than still contemned and flattered. To be worst,   2
  The lowest and most dejected thing of fortune,   3
  Stands still in esperance, lives not in fear.   4
  The lamentable change is from the best;   5
  The worst returns to laughter. Welcome, then,   6
  Thou unsubstantial air that I embrace!
  The wretch that thou hast blown unto the worst
  Owes nothing to thy blasts.

    Enter Gloucester, and an Old Man [leading him].

                      But who comes here?   9
  My father, poorly led? World, world, O world!
  But that thy strange mutations make us hate thee,   11
  Life would not yield to age.   12

OLD MAN
  O, my good lord, I have been your tenant
  And your father's tenant these fourscore years.

GLOUCESTER
  Away, get thee away! Good friend, begone.
  Thy comforts can do me no good at all;   16
  Thee they may hurt.

OLD MAN   You cannot see your way.

GLOUCESTER
  I have no way and therefore want no eyes;
  I stumbled when I saw. Full oft 'tis seen
  Our means secure us, and our mere defects   20
  Prove our commodities. O dear son Edgar,   21

4.1. Location: An open place.
1 Yet better thus i.e., it is better to be a beggar.   **known** know what it
is.   **contemned** despised   **2 contemned and flattered** despised behind
your back and flattered to your face   **3 dejected . . . of** debased or
humbled by   **4 esperance** hope.   **fear** i.e., of something worse happening   **5–6 The lamentable . . . laughter** i.e., any change from the best
is grievous, just as any change from the worst is bound to be for
the better   **9 Owes nothing** can pay no more, is free of obligation
11–12 But . . . age i.e., if it were not for your hateful inconstancy, we
would never be reconciled to old age and death   **16 comforts** kindnesses   **20 Our means secure us** our prosperity makes us overconfi-
dent.   **mere defects** sheer afflictions   **21 commodities** benefits

The food of thy abusèd father's wrath!   22
Might I but live to see thee in my touch,   23
I'd say I had eyes again!

OLD MAN   How now? Who's there?

EDGAR [*Aside*]
O gods! Who is 't can say, "I am at the worst"?
I am worse than e'er I was.

OLD MAN   'Tis poor mad Tom.

EDGAR [*Aside*]
And worse I may be yet. The worst is not   27
So long as we can say, "This is the worst."   28

OLD MAN
Fellow, where goest?

GLOUCESTER   Is it a beggar-man?

OLD MAN   Madman and beggar too.

GLOUCESTER
He has some reason, else he could not beg.   31
I' the last night's storm I such a fellow saw,
Which made me think a man a worm. My son
Came then into my mind, and yet my mind
Was then scarce friends with him. I have heard more
    since.
As flies to wanton boys are we to the gods;   36
They kill us for their sport.

EDGAR [*Aside*]   How should this be?   37
Bad is the trade that must play fool to sorrow,   38
Ang'ring itself and others.—Bless thee, master!   39

GLOUCESTER
Is that the naked fellow?

OLD MAN   Ay, my lord.

GLOUCESTER
Then, prithee, get thee gone. If for my sake
Thou wilt o'ertake us hence a milc or twain   42

---

22 The . . . wrath on whom thy deceived father's wrath fed, the object of
his anger   **23 in** i.e., by means of   **27–28 The worst . . . worst** so long as
we can speak and act and delude ourselves with false hopes, our fortunes can in fact grow worse   **31 reason** power of reason   **36 wanton**
playful   **37 How . . . be** i.e., how can he have suffered so much, changed
so much   **38 Bad . . . sorrow** i.e., it's a bad business to have to play
the fool to my sorrowing father   **39 Ang'ring** offending, distressing
42 o'ertake us catch up to us (after you have found clothing for Tom o'
Bedlam)

I' the way toward Dover, do it for ancient love,   43
And bring some covering for this naked soul,
Which I'll entreat to lead me.

OLD MAN   Alack, sir, he is mad.

GLOUCESTER
'Tis the time's plague, when madmen lead the blind.   46
Do as I bid thee, or rather do thy pleasure;
Above the rest, begone.   48

OLD MAN
I'll bring him the best 'parel that I have,
Come on 't what will.   *Exit*.

GLOUCESTER   Sirrah, naked fellow—   50

EDGAR
Poor Tom's a-cold. [*Aside*.] I cannot daub it further.   51

GLOUCESTER Come hither, fellow.

EDGAR [*Aside*]
And yet I must.—Bless thy sweet eyes, they bleed.

GLOUCESTER Know'st thou the way to Dover?

EDGAR Both stile and gate, horseway and footpath.
Poor Tom hath been scared out of his good wits. Bless
thee, good man's son, from the foul fiend! Five fiends
have been in poor Tom at once: of lust, as Obidicut; 58
Hobbididance, prince of dumbness; Mahu, of steal- 59
ing; Modo, of murder; Flibbertigibbet, of mopping 60
and mowing, who since possesses chambermaids and 61
waiting-women. So, bless thee, master!

GLOUCESTER [*Giving a purse*]
Here, take this purse, thou whom the heavens' plagues
Have humbled to all strokes. That I am wretched   64
Makes thee the happier. Heavens, deal so still!
Let the superfluous and lust-dieted man,   66
That slaves your ordinance, that will not see   67

43 ancient love i.e., the mutually trusting relationship of master and
tenant that Gloucester and the Old Man have long enjoyed   **46 'Tis the
times' plague** i.e., it well expresses the spreading sickness of our
present state   **48 the rest** all   **50 on 't** of it   **51 daub it further**
i.e., keep up this pretense   **58–60 Obidicut . . . Flibbertigibbet** (Fiends
borrowed, as before in 3.4.139–142, from Harsnett.)   **60–61 mopping
and mowing** making grimaces and mouths   **61 since** since that time
64 Have . . . strokes have brought so low as to be prepared to accept
every blow of Fortune   **66 superfluous** having a superfluity.   **lust-
dieted** feeding luxuriously   **67 slaves your ordinance** i.e., makes the
laws of heaven his slaves

Because he does not feel, feel your pow'r quickly!   68
So distribution should undo excess
And each man have enough. Dost thou know Dover?

EDGAR   Ay, master.

GLOUCESTER
There is a cliff, whose high and bending head   72
Looks fearfully in the confinèd deep.   73
Bring me but to the very brim of it
And I'll repair the misery thou dost bear
With something rich about me. From that place
I shall no leading need.

EDGAR   Give me thy arm.
Poor Tom shall lead thee.   *Exeunt.*

❖

4.2   *Enter Goneril [and] Bastard [Edmund].*

GONERIL
Welcome, my lord. I marvel our mild husband   1
Not met us on the way.

      [Enter] Steward [Oswald].

                 Now, where's your master?   2

OSWALD
Madam, within, but never man so changed.
I told him of the army that was landed;
He smiled at it. I told him you were coming;
His answer was "The worse." Of Gloucester's treachery
And of the loyal service of his son
When I informed him, then he called me sot   8
And told me I had turned the wrong side out.
What most he should dislike seems pleasant to him;
What like, offensive.

GONERIL *[To Edmund]* Then shall you go no further.

---

68 feel feel sympathy or fellow feeling; suffer   **72 bending** overhanging   **73 in . . . deep** i.e., into the sea below, which is confined by its shores

4.2. Location: Before the Duke of Albany's palace.
1 Welcome (Goneril, who has just arrived home from Gloucestershire escorted by Edmund, bids him brief welcome before he must return.)
2 Not met has not met   **8 sot** fool

It is the cowish terror of his spirit,   12
That dares not undertake. He'll not feel wrongs   13
Which tie him to an answer. Our wishes on the way   14
May prove effects. Back, Edmund, to my brother;   15
Hasten his musters and conduct his powers.   16
I must change names at home and give the distaff   17
Into my husband's hands. This trusty servant
Shall pass between us. Ere long you are like to hear,   19
If you dare venture in your own behalf,
A mistress's command. Wear this; spare speech.   21
                              [*She gives him a favor.*]
Decline your head. [*She kisses him.*] This kiss, if it
    durst speak,
Would stretch thy spirits up into the air.
Conceive, and fare thee well.   24

EDMUND
Yours in the ranks of death.   *Exit.*
GONERIL   My most dear Gloucester!
O, the difference of man and man!
To thee a woman's services are due;
My fool usurps my body.   28
OSWALD   Madam, here comes my lord.   [*Exit.*] 29

    Enter Albany.

GONERIL
I have been worth the whistling.
ALBANY   O Goneril,   30
You are not worth the dust which the rude wind

12 cowish cowardly   **13 undertake** venture   **13-14 He'll . . . answer** he
will ignore insults that, if he took notice, would oblige him to respond, to
fight   **14-15 Our . . . effects** i.e., the hopes we discussed on our journey
here (presumably concerning the supplanting of Albany by Edmund) may
come to pass   **15 brother** i.e., brother-in-law, Cornwall   **16 musters**
assembling of troops.   **powers** armed forces   **17 change names** i.e.,
exchange the roles of master and mistress of the household, and exchange
the insignia of man and woman: the sword and the *distaff*.   **distaff**
spinning staff, symbolizing the wife's role   **19 like** likely   **21 mistress's**
(with sexual double meaning)   **24 Conceive** understand, take my meaning
(with sexual double entendre, continuing from *stretch thy spirits* in the
previous line and continued in *death*, l. 25)   **28 My fool . . . body** i.e., my
husband claims possession of me but is unfitted to do so   **29 s.d. Exit**
(Oswald could exit later with Goneril, at l. 88.)   **30 worth the whistling**
i.e., worth the attentions of men. (Alludes to the proverb, "It is a poor dog
that is not worth the whistling.")

Blows in your face. I fear your disposition;   32
That nature which contemns its origin   33
Cannot be bordered certain in itself.   34
She that herself will sliver and disbranch   35
From her material sap perforce must wither   36
And come to deadly use.   37

GONERIL   No more. The text is foolish.   38

ALBANY
Wisdom and goodness to the vile seem vile;
Filths savor but themselves. What have you done?   40
Tigers, not daughters, what have you performed?
A father, and a gracious agèd man,
Whose reverence even the head-lugged bear would lick,   43
Most barbarous, most degenerate, have you madded.   44
Could my good brother suffer you to do it?   45
A man, a prince, by him so benefited?
If that the heavens do not their visible spirits   47
Send quickly down to tame these vile offenses,
It will come,
Humanity must perforce prey on itself,
Like monsters of the deep.

GONERIL   Milk-livered man,   51
That bear'st a cheek for blows, a head for wrongs,
Who hast not in thy brows an eye discerning   53
Thine honor from thy suffering, that not know'st   54
Fools do those villains pity who are punished   55
Ere they have done their mischief. Where's thy drum?   56
France spreads his banners in our noiseless land,   57

---

32 fear your disposition mistrust your nature   **33 contemns** despises
34 bordered certain safely restrained, kept within bounds   **35 sliver**
tear off   **36 material sap** nourishing substance, the stock from which
she grew   **37 to deadly use** to destruction, like firewood   **38 The text**
i.e., on which you have been preaching   **40 savor but themselves** i.e.,
hunger only for that which is filthy   **43 head-lugged** dragged by the
head (or by the ring in its nose) and infuriated   **44 madded** driven
mad   **45 brother** brother-in-law (Cornwall)   **47 visible** made visible
51 Milk-livered white-livered, cowardly   **53–54 discerning . . . suffering**
able to tell the difference between an insult to your honor and something you should tolerate   **55 Fools** i.e., only fools. (Goneril goes on to
say that only fools are so tenderhearted as to worry about injustices to
potential troublemakers, like Lear and Gloucester, instead of applaud-
ing measures taken to insure order.)   **56 thy drum** i.e., your military
preparations   **57 noiseless** peaceful, having none of the bustle of war

With plumèd helm thy state begins to threat,   58
Whilst thou, a moral fool, sits still and cries,   59
"Alack, why does he so?"
ALBANY   See thyself, devil!   60
Proper deformity shows not in the fiend   61
So horrid as in woman.
GONERIL   O vain fool!
ALBANY
Thou changèd and self-covered thing, for shame,   63
Bemonster not thy feature. Were 't my fitness   64
To let these hands obey my blood,   65
They are apt enough to dislocate and tear   66
Thy flesh and bones. Howe'er thou art a fiend,   67
A woman's shape doth shield thee.   68
GONERIL   Marry, your manhood! Mew!   69

Enter a Messenger.

ALBANY   What news?
MESSENGER
O, my good lord, the Duke of Cornwall's dead,
Slain by his servant, going to put out
The other eye of Gloucester.
ALBANY   Gloucester's eyes!
MESSENGER
A servant that he bred, thrilled with remorse,   74
Opposed against the act, bending his sword   75
To his great master, who, thereat enraged,   76
Flew on him and amongst them felled him dead,   77

58 thy state . . . threat i.e., France begins to threaten your kingdom
59 moral moralizing   **60 why does he so** i.e., why does the King of
France invade England   **61 Proper deformity** i.e., the deformity appropriate to the fiend. (Such deformity seems even uglier in a woman's
features than in a fiend's, since it is appropriate in a fiend's.)
63 changèd transformed.   **self-covered** having the true nature concealed   **64 Bemonster . . . feature** i.e., do not, however evil you are, take
on the outward form of a monster or fiend.   **my fitness** suitable for
me   **65 blood** passion   **66 apt** ready   **67 Howe'er . . . fiend** however
much you may be a fiend in reality   **68 shield** (Since I, as a gentleman,
cannot lay violent hands on a lady.)   **69 Mew** (An exclamation of dis-
gust, a derisive catcall: You speak of manhood in shielding me as a
woman. Some manhood!)   **74 bred** kept in his household.   **thrilled with
remorse** deeply moved with pity   **75 Opposed** opposed himself
75-76 bending . . . To directing his sword against   **77 amongst them**
together with the others (?) in their midst (?) out of their number (?)

But not without that harmful stroke which since
Hath plucked him after.
ALBANY   This shows you are above,   79
You justicers, that these our nether crimes   80
So speedily can venge! But, O poor Gloucester!
Lost he his other eye?
MESSENGER   Both, both, my lord.—
This letter, madam, craves a speedy answer;
'Tis from your sister.   [*He gives her a letter.*]
GONERIL [*Aside*]   One way I like this well;   84
But being widow, and my Gloucester with her,
May all the building in my fancy pluck   86
Upon my hateful life. Another way   87
The news is not so tart.—I'll read, and answer.   88
                                              [*Exit.*]

ALBANY
Where was his son when they did take his eyes?
MESSENGER
Come with my lady hither.
ALBANY   He is not here.
MESSENGER
No, my good lord. I met him back again.   91
ALBANY   Knows he the wickedness?
MESSENGER
Ay, my good lord. 'Twas he informed against him,
And quit the house on purpose that their punishment
Might have the freer course.
ALBANY   Gloucester, I live
To thank thee for the love thou show'dst the King
And to revenge thine eyes.—Come hither, friend.
Tell me what more thou know'st.   *Exeunt.*

❖

79 **after** along (to death)   80 **justicers** (heavenly) judges.   **nether** i.e.,
committed here below, on earth   84 **One way** i.e., because Edmund is
now Duke of Gloucester, and Cornwall, a dangerous rival for the throne,
is dead   86–87 **May . . . life** i.e., may pull down my imagined happiness
(of possessing the entire kingdom with Edmund) and make hateful my
life   88 **tart** bitter, sour   91 **back** going back

4.3   *Enter Kent and a Gentleman.*

KENT   Why the King of France is so suddenly gone back
know you no reason?

GENTLEMAN   Something he left imperfect in the state,   3
which since his coming forth is thought of, which im-   4
ports to the kingdom so much fear and danger that his   5
personal return was most required and necessary.

KENT
Who hath he left behind him general?

GENTLEMAN
The Marshal of France, Monsieur La Far.

KENT   Did your letters pierce the Queen to any demon-
stration of grief?

GENTLEMAN
Ay, sir. She took them, read them in my presence,
And now and then an ample tear trilled down   12
Her delicate cheek. It seemed she was a queen
Over her passion, who, most rebel-like,   14
Sought to be king o'er her.

KENT   O, then it moved her?

GENTLEMAN
Not to a rage. Patience and sorrow strove
Who should express her goodliest. You have seen   17
Sunshine and rain at once. Her smiles and tears
Were like a better way; those happy smilets   19
That played on her ripe lip seemed not to know
What guests were in her eyes, which parted thence   21 ·
As pearls from diamonds dropped. In brief,
Sorrow would be a rarity most beloved   23
If all could so become it.   24

KENT   Made she no verbal question?   25

GENTLEMAN
Faith, once or twice she heaved the name of "father"   26

4.3. Location: The French camp near Dover.
3 imperfect in the state unsettled in state affairs   **4–5 imports** por-
tends   **12 trilled** trickled   **14 passion, who** emotion, which   **17 Who
. . . goodliest** which of the two could make her appear more lovely
19 like a better way better than that, though similar   **21 which** i.e., the
guests or tears   **23 a rarity** i.e., a precious thing, like a jewel   **24 If . . .
it** i.e., if all persons were as attractive in sorrow as she   **25 verbal** i.e.,
as distinguished from her tears and looks   **26 heaved** breathed out
with difficulty

Pantingly forth, as if it pressed her heart;
Cried, "Sisters, sisters! Shame of ladies, sisters!
Kent! Father! Sisters! What, i' the storm, i' the night?
Let pity not be believed!" There she shook   30
The holy water from her heavenly eyes,
And, clamor-moistened, then away she started   32
To deal with grief alone.
KENT   It is the stars,
The stars above us, govern our conditions,   34
Else one self mate and make could not beget   35
Such different issues. You spoke not with her since? 36
GENTLEMAN No.
KENT
Was this before the King returned?
GENTLEMAN   No, since.   38
KENT
Well, sir, the poor distressèd Lear's i' the town,
Who sometimes in his better tune remembers   40
What we are come about, and by no means
Will yield to see his daughter.
GENTLEMAN   Why, good sir?
KENT
A sovereign shame so elbows him—his own unkindness 43
That stripped her from his benediction, turned her 44
To foreign casualties, gave her dear rights   45
To his dog-hearted daughters—these things sting
His mind so venomously that burning shame
Detains him from Cordelia.
GENTLEMAN Alack, poor gentleman!
KENT
Of Albany's and Cornwall's powers you heard not?   50
GENTLEMAN 'Tis so. They are afoot.   51
KENT
Well, sir, I'll bring you to our master Lear

---

30 believed i.e., believed to be extant　**32 clamor-moistened** i.e., her outcry of grief assuaged by tears.　**started** i.e., went　**34 conditions** characters　**35 Else . . . make** otherwise, one couple (husband and wife)　**36 issues** offspring　**38 the King** the King of France　**40 better tune** more composed state　**43 sovereign** overruling.　**elbows him** i.e., prods his memory, jostles him, thrusts him back　**44 turned her** turned her out　**45 foreign casualties** chances of fortune abroad　**50 powers** troops, armies　**51 afoot** on the march

And leave you to attend him. Some dear cause   53
Will in concealment wrap me up awhile.
When I am known aright, you shall not grieve   55
Lending me this acquaintance. I pray you, go   56
Along with me.   *Exeunt.*

❖

4.4   *Enter, with drum and colors, Cordelia, Doctor,*
         and soldiers.

CORDELIA
  Alack, 'tis he! Why, he was met even now
  As mad as the vexed sea, singing aloud,
  Crowned with rank fumiter and furrow weeds,   3
  With hardocks, hemlock, nettles, cuckooflowers,   4
  Darnel, and all the idle weeds that grow   5
  In our sustaining corn. A century send forth!   6
  Search every acre in the high-grown field
  And bring him to our eye. [*Exit a soldier or soldiers.*]
        What can man's wisdom   8
  In the restoring his bereavèd sense?
  He that helps him take all my outward worth.   10
DOCTOR   There is means, madam.
  Our foster nurse of nature is repose,
  The which he lacks. That to provoke in him   13
  Are many simples operative, whose power   14
  Will close the eye of anguish.
CORDELIA   All blest secrets,
  All you unpublished virtues of the earth,   16
  Spring with my tears! Be aidant and remediate   17
  In the good man's distress! Seek, seek for him,

53 dear cause important purpose   **55–56 grieve . . . acquaintance** regret
having made my acquaintance

4.4. Location: The French camp.
3 fumiter i.e., fumitory, a weed or herb   **4 hardocks** i.e., burdocks or
hoardocks, white-leaved (?) (Identity uncertain.)   **5 Darnel** (A weed of
the grass kind.)   **idle** worthless   **6 sustaining** giving sustenance.   **corn**
grain.   **century** troop of 100 men   **8 What . . . wisdom** i.e., what can
medical knowledge accomplish   **10 outward** material   **13 That to
provoke** to induce that   **14 simples** medicinal plants.   **operative** effective   **16 unpublished virtues** little-known benign herbs   **17 Spring**
grow.   **aidant and remediate** helpful and remedial

Lest his ungoverned rage dissolve the life   19
That wants the means to lead it.

    Enter Messenger.

MESSENGER   News, madam.   20
The British powers are marching hitherward.   21
CORDELIA
'Tis known before. Our preparation stands
In expectation of them. O dear Father,
It is thy business that I go about;
Therefore great France
My mourning and importuned tears hath pitied.   26
No blown ambition doth our arms incite,   27
But love, dear love, and our aged father's right.
Soon may I hear and see him!   *Exeunt.*

✤

4.5   *Enter Regan and steward [Oswald].*

REGAN   But are my brother's powers set forth?   1
OSWALD   Ay, madam.
REGAN   Himself in person there?
OSWALD   Madam, with much ado.   4
Your sister is the better soldier.
REGAN
Lord Edmund spake not with your lord at home?
OSWALD   No, madam.
REGAN
What might import my sister's letter to him?   8
OSWALD   I know not, lady.
REGAN
Faith, he is posted hence on serious matter.   10
It was great ignorance, Gloucester's eyes being out,   11
To let him live. Where he arrives he moves
All hearts against us. Edmund, I think, is gone,

19 **rage** frenzy   20 **wants** lacks.   **means** i.e., his reason   21 **powers**
armies   26 **importuned** importunate   27 **blown** puffed up with pride

4.5. **Location: Gloucester's house.**
1 **my brother's powers** i.e., Albany's forces   4 **with much ado** after
much fuss and persuasion   8 **import** bear as its purport, express   10 **is
posted** has hurried   11 **ignorance** error, folly

In pity of his misery, to dispatch
His nighted life; moreover to descry   15
The strength o' th' enemy.

OSWALD

I must needs after him, madam, with my letter.

REGAN

Our troops set forth tomorrow. Stay with us;
The ways are dangerous.

OSWALD   I may not, madam.
My lady charged my duty in this business.   20

REGAN

Why should she write to Edmund? Might not you
Transport her purposes by word? Belike   22
Something—I know not what. I'll love thee much;
Let me unseal the letter.

OSWALD   Madam, I had rather—

REGAN

I know your lady does not love her husband,
I am sure of that; and at her late being here   26
She gave strange oeillades and most speaking looks   27
To noble Edmund. I know you are of her bosom.   28

OSWALD   I, madam?

REGAN

I speak in understanding; y' are, I know 't.   30
Therefore I do advise you, take this note: 31
My lord is dead; Edmund and I have talked,   32
And more convenient is he for my hand   33
Than for your lady's. You may gather more.   34
If you do find him, pray you, give him this;   35
And when your mistress hears thus much from you, 36
I pray, desire her call her wisdom to her.   37
So, fare you well.
If you do chance to hear of that blind traitor,
Preferment falls on him that cuts him off.   40

15 nighted benighted, blinded   **20 charged** ordered strictly   **22 Belike**
it may be   **26 late** recently   **27 oeillades** amorous glances   **28 of her
bosom** in her confidence   **30 y' are** you are   **31 take this note** i.e.,
mark this advice   **32 have talked** have come to an understanding
33 convenient fitting   **34 gather more** i.e., infer what I am trying to
suggest   **35 this** i.e., this information, or possibly a letter (though only
one letter, Goneril's, is found on his dead body at 4.6.262)   **36 thus
much** what I have told you   **37 call . . . to her** recall her to her senses
40 Preferment advancement

OSWALD

  Would I could meet him, madam! I should show
  What party I do follow.

REGAN   Fare thee well.

                         Exeunt [separately].

❖

4.6   *Enter Gloucester, and Edgar [in peasant's*
      clothes, leading his father].

GLOUCESTER

  When shall I come to the top of that same hill?

EDGAR

  You do climb up it now. Look how we labor.

GLOUCESTER

  Methinks the ground is even.

EDGAR   Horrible steep.

  Hark, do you hear the sea?

GLOUCESTER   No, truly.

EDGAR

  Why, then, your other senses grow imperfect
  By your eyes' anguish.

GLOUCESTER   So may it be, indeed.

  Methinks thy voice is altered, and thou speak'st
  In better phrase and matter than thou didst.

EDGAR

  You're much deceived. In nothing am I changed
  But in my garments.

GLOUCESTER   Methinks you're better spoken.

EDGAR

  Come on, sir, here's the place. Stand still. How fearful
  And dizzy 'tis to cast one's eyes so low!
  The crows and choughs that wing the midway air   13
  Show scarce so gross as beetles. Halfway down   14
  Hangs one that gathers samphire—dreadful trade!   15
  Methinks he seems no bigger than his head.
  The fishermen that walk upon the beach
  Appear like mice, and yond tall anchoring bark

4.6. Location: Open place near Dover.
1 that same hill i.e., the cliff we talked about (4.1.72–74) **13 choughs**
jackdaws. **midway** halfway down **14 gross** large **15 samphire** (A
herb used in pickling.)

Diminished to her cock; her cock, a buoy   19
Almost too small for sight. The murmuring surge,
That on th' unnumbered idle pebble chafes,   21
Cannot be heard so high. I'll look no more,
Lest my brain turn, and the deficient sight   23
Topple down headlong.
GLOUCESTER   Set me where you stand.   24
EDGAR
  Give me your hand. You are now within a foot
  Of th' extreme verge. For all beneath the moon
  Would I not leap upright.
GLOUCESTER   Let go my hand.   27
  Here, friend, 's another purse; in it a jewel
  Well worth a poor man's taking. [*He gives a purse.*]
    Fairies and gods   29
  Prosper it with thee! Go thou further off.   30
  Bid me farewell, and let me hear thee going.
EDGAR [*Moving away*]
  Now fare ye well, good sir.
GLOUCESTER   With all my heart.
EDGAR [*Aside*]
  Why I do trifle thus with his despair
  Is done to cure it.
GLOUCESTER [*Kneeling*]   O you mighty gods!
  This world I do renounce, and in your sights
  Shake patiently my great affliction off.
  If I could bear it longer, and not fall
  To quarrel with your great opposeless wills,   38
  My snuff and loathèd part of nature should   39
  Burn itself out. If Edgar live, O, bless him!
  Now, fellow, fare thee well.   [*He falls forward.*]
EDGAR   Gone, sir. Farewell.—
  And yet I know not how conceit may rob   42

19 Diminished . . . cock reduced to the size of her cockboat, small ship's
boat   **21 unnumbered** innumerable.   **idle** randomly shifting.   **pebble**
pebbles   **23–24 the deficient sight Topple** my failing sight topple me
27 upright i.e., up and down, much less forward   **29–30 Fairies . . . thee**
i.e., may the fairies and gods who guard hidden treasure cause this to
multiply in your possession   **38 To quarrel with** into rebellion
against.   **opposeless** irresistible   **39 snuff** i.e., useless residue. (Literally, the smoking wick of a candle.)   **of nature** i.e., of my life
42 conceit imagination

The treasury of life, when life itself
Yields to the theft. Had he been where he thought,   44
By this had thought been past. Alive or dead?—
Ho, you, sir! Friend! Hear you, sir! Speak!—
Thus might he pass indeed; yet he revives.—   47
What are you, sir?

GLOUCESTER   Away, and let me die.   48

EDGAR
Hadst thou been aught but gossamer, feathers, air,
So many fathom down precipitating,
Thou'dst shivered like an egg; but thou dost breathe,
Hast heavy substance, bleed'st not, speak'st, art sound.   52
Ten masts at each make not the altitude   53
Which thou hast perpendicularly fell.
Thy life's a miracle. Speak yet again.

GLOUCESTER   But have I fallen or no?

EDGAR
From the dread summit of this chalky bourn.   57
Look up aheight; the shrill-gorged lark so far   58
Cannot be seen or heard. Do but look up.

GLOUCESTER   Alack, I have no eyes.
Is wretchedness deprived that benefit
To end itself by death? 'Twas yet some comfort
When misery could beguile the tyrant's rage   63
And frustrate his proud will.

EDGAR   Give me your arm.
                  [*He lifts him up.*]
Up—so. How is 't? Feel you your legs? You stand.

GLOUCESTER
Too well, too well.

EDGAR   This is above all strangeness.
Upon the crown o' the cliff what thing was that
Which parted from you?

GLOUCESTER   A poor unfortunate beggar.

EDGAR
As I stood here below, methought his eyes

---

44 Yields consents   **47 pass** die   **48 What** who. (Edgar now speaks in a new voice, differing from that of "poor Tom" and also from the "altered" voice he used at the start of this scene; see ll. 7–10.)   **52 heavy substance** the substance of the flesh   **53 at each** end to end   **57 bourn** limit, boundary (i.e., the edge of the sea)   **58 aheight** on high.   **shrill-gorged** shrill-throated   **63 beguile** outwit

Were two full moons; he had a thousand noses,
Horns whelked and waved like the enridgèd sea.   71
It was some fiend. Therefore, thou happy father,   72
Think that the clearest gods, who make them honors   73
Of men's impossibilities, have preserved thee.   74

GLOUCESTER
I do remember now. Henceforth I'll bear
Affliction till it do cry out itself   76
"Enough, enough," and die. That thing you speak of,   77
I took it for a man; often 'twould say
"The fiend, the fiend." He led me to that place.

EDGAR
Bear free and patient thoughts.

*Enter Lear [mad, fantastically dressed with wild
flowers].*

But who comes here?   80
The safer sense will ne'er accommodate   81
His master thus.   82

LEAR   No, they cannot touch me for coining. I am the   83
King himself.

EDGAR   O thou side-piercing sight!   85

LEAR   Nature's above art in that respect. There's your   86
press money. That fellow handles his bow like a crow-   87
keeper. Draw me a clothier's yard. Look, look, a   88
mouse! Peace, peace; this piece of toasted cheese will
do 't. There's my gauntlet; I'll prove it on a giant. Bring   90

---

71 whelked twisted, convoluted.   **enridgèd** furrowed (by the wind)
72 happy father lucky old man   **73 clearest** purest, most righteous
73–74 who . . . impossibilities who win our awe and reverence by doing
things impossible to men   **76–77 till . . . die** i.e., until affliction itself has
had enough, or until I die   **80 free** i.e., free from despair   **81–82 The safer
. . . thus** i.e., a person in his right senses would never dress himself in such
a fashion.   **His master** the owner of the *safer sense* or sane mind. (*His*
means "its.")   **83 touch** arrest, prosecute.   **coining** minting coins. (A royal
prerogative; the King wants money for his imaginary soldiers, ll. 86–87.)
85 side-piercing heartrending (with a suggestion also of Christ's suffering
on the cross)   **86 Nature's . . . respect** i.e., a born king is proof against any
counterfeiting; his coinage is superior to that of the counterfeiter (?)
87 press money enlistment bonus   **87–88 crowkeeper** laborer hired to
scare away the crows   **88 me** for me.   **clothier's yard** arrow the length of
a cloth yard   **90 do 't** i.e., capture the mouse, an imagined enemy.
gauntlet armored glove thrown down as a challenge.   **prove it on** maintain
it against

up the brown bills. O, well flown, bird! I' the clout, i' 91
the clout—hewgh! Give the word. 92

EDGAR   Sweet marjoram. 93

LEAR   Pass.

GLOUCESTER   I know that voice.

LEAR   Ha! Goneril with a white beard? They flattered
me like a dog and told me I had white hairs in my 97
beard ere the black ones were there. To say ay and 98
no to everything that I said ay and no to was 99
no good divinity. When the rain came to wet me 100
once and the wind to make me chatter, when the
thunder would not peace at my bidding, there I found 102
'em, there I smelt 'em out. Go to, they are not men o' 103
their words. They told me I was everything. 'Tis a lie;
I am not ague-proof.

GLOUCESTER
The trick of that voice I do well remember. 106
Is 't not the King?

LEAR   Ay, every inch a king.
When I do stare, see how the subject quakes.
I pardon that man's life. What was thy cause? 109
Adultery?
Thou shalt not die. Die for adultery? No.
The wren goes to 't, and the small gilded fly
Does lecher in my sight.
Let copulation thrive; for Gloucester's bastard son
Was kinder to his father than my daughters
Got 'tween the lawful sheets.
To 't, luxury, pell-mell, for I lack soldiers. 117
Behold yond simpering dame,
Whose face between her forks presages snow, 119

---

91 brown bills soldiers carrying pikes (painted brown), or the pikes
themselves.   **well flown, bird** (Lear uses the language of hawking to
describe the flight of an arrow.)   **clout** target, bull's-eye   **92 hewgh**
(The arrow's noise.)   **word** password   **93 Sweet marjoram** (A herb used
to cure madness.)   **97 like a dog** i.e., as a dog fawns   **97–98 had . . .
beard** i.e., had wisdom   **98–99 To . . . no** i.e., to agree flatteringly
with   **100 no good divinity** not good theology, contrary to biblical
teaching. (See 2 Cor. 1:18 and James 5:12.)   **102–103 found 'em** found
them out   **103 Go to** (An expression of impatience.)   **106 trick** peculiar
characteristic   **109 cause** offense   **117 luxury** lechery   **119 Whose . . .
snow** whose frosty countenance seems to suggest frigidity between
her legs

That minces virtue and does shake the head   120
To hear of pleasure's name;   121
The fitchew nor the soilèd horse goes to 't   122
With a more riotous appetite.
Down from the waist they are centaurs,   124
Though women all above.
But to the girdle do the gods inherit;   126
Beneath is all the fiends'.
There's hell, there's darkness, there is the sulfurous pit,
burning, scalding, stench, consumption. Fie, fie, fie!
Pah, pah! Give me an ounce of civet, good apothecary, 130
sweeten my imagination. There's money for thee.

GLOUCESTER   O, let me kiss that hand!

LEAR   Let me wipe it first; it smells of mortality.

GLOUCESTER
O ruined piece of nature! This great world   134
Shall so wear out to naught. Dost thou know me?   135

LEAR   I remember thine eyes well enough. Dost thou
squinny at me? No, do thy worst, blind Cupid; I'll not 137
love. Read thou this challenge. Mark but the penning
of it.

GLOUCESTER
Were all thy letters suns, I could not see.

EDGAR [*Aside*]
I would not take this from report. It is,   141
And my heart breaks at it.

LEAR   Read.

GLOUCESTER   What, with the case of eyes?   144

LEAR   Oho, are you there with me? No eyes in your 145
head, nor no money in your purse? Your eyes are in a
heavy case, your purse in a light, yet you see how this 147
world goes.

120 **minces** affects, mimics   121 **pleasure's name** i.e., any talk of sexual
pleasure   122 **fitchew** polecat.   **soilèd horse** horse turned out to grass,
well-fed and hence wanton   124 **centaurs** incontinent monsters, half man,
half horse   126 **But** only.   **girdle** waist.   **inherit** possess   130 **civet** musk
perfume   134 **piece** masterpiece.   **This great world** i.e., the macrocosm, of
which man, the masterpiece of nature, is the microcosm   135 **so** similarly   137 **squinny** squint   141 **take** believe, credit.   **It is** it is taking place,
incredibly enough   144 **case** mere sockets   145 **are . . . me** is that your
meaning, the point you are making, or your situation   147 **heavy case** sad
plight (with pun on *case* in l. 144)

GLOUCESTER   I see it feelingly.   149

LEAR   What, art mad? A man may see how this world
   goes with no eyes. Look with thine ears. See how
   yond justice rails upon yond simple thief. Hark in 152
   thine ear: change places and, handy-dandy, which is 153
   the justice, which is the thief? Thou hast seen a
   farmer's dog bark at a beggar?

GLOUCESTER   Ay, sir.

LEAR   And the creature run from the cur? There thou 157
   mightst behold the great image of authority: a dog's 158
   obeyed in office.   159
   Thou rascal beadle, hold thy bloody hand!   160
   Why dost thou lash that whore? Strip thine own back;
   Thou hotly lusts to use her in that kind   162
   For which thou whipp'st her. The usurer hangs the
     cozener.   163
   Through tattered clothes small vices do appear;
   Robes and furred gowns hide all. Plate sin with gold, 165
   And the strong lance of justice hurtless breaks;   166
   Arm it in rags, a pygmy's straw does pierce it.
   None does offend, none, I say, none. I'll able 'em.   168
   Take that of me, my friend, who have the power   169
   To seal th' accuser's lips. Get thee glass eyes,   170
   And like a scurvy politician seem
   To see the things thou dost not. Now, now, now, now!
   Pull off my boots. Harder, harder! So.

EDGAR [*Aside*]
   O, matter and impertinency mixed,   174
   Reason in madness!

---

149 feelingly (1) by touch (2) keenly, painfully   **152 simple** of humble
station   **153 handy-dandy** take your choice of hands (as in a well-known
child's game)   **157 creature** poor fellow   **158–159 a dog's . . . office** i.e.,
even currish power commands submission   **160 beadle** parish officer,
responsible for giving whippings   **162 kind** way   **163 The usurer** i.e., a
judge guilty of lending money at usurious rates.   **cozener** petty
cheater   **165 Plate** arm in plate armor   **166 hurtless breaks** splinters
harmlessly   **168 able** give warrant to   **169 that** i.e., a guarantee of
immunity   **170 glass eyes** (With glass eyes, possibly spectacles, Gloucester could pretend to see or understand what he does not comprehend,
like a vile *politician* governing through opportunism and trickery,
hiding his blindness behind his glass eyes.)   **174 matter and impertinency** sense and nonsense

LEAR
　If thou wilt weep my fortunes, take my eyes.
　I know thee well enough; thy name is Gloucester.
　Thou must be patient. We came crying hither.
　Thou know'st the first time that we smell the air
　We wawl and cry. I will preach to thee. Mark.
GLOUCESTER　Alack, alack the day!
LEAR
　When we are born, we cry that we are come
　To this great stage of fools.—This' a good block.　　183
　It were a delicate stratagem to shoe　　　　　　　　184
　A troop of horse with felt. I'll put 't in proof,　　185
　And when I have stolen upon these son-in-laws,
　Then, kill, kill, kill, kill, kill, kill!

　　　Enter a Gentleman [with attendants].

GENTLEMAN
　O, here he is. Lay hand upon him.—Sir,
　Your most dear daughter—
LEAR
　No rescue? What, a prisoner? I am even
　The natural fool of fortune. Use me well;　　　　　191
　You shall have ransom. Let me have surgeons;
　I am cut to the brains.
GENTLEMAN　　　　　　　　You shall have anything.　193
LEAR　No seconds? All myself?　　　　　　　　　　194
　Why, this would make a man a man of salt　　　　195
　To use his eyes for garden waterpots,
　Ay, and laying autumn's dust.
　I will die bravely, like a smug bridegroom. What?　198
　I will be jovial. Come, come, I am a king,
　Masters, know you that?
GENTLEMAN
　You are a royal one, and we obey you.

---

183 This' this is.　**block** felt hat (?) (Lear may refer to the weeds strewn
in his hair, which he removes as though doffing a hat before preaching a
sermon.)　**184 delicate** subtle　**185 in proof** to the test　**191 natural fool**
born plaything　**193 cut** wounded　**194 seconds** supporters　**195 of salt**
of salt tears　**198 bravely** (1) courageously (2) splendidly attired.　**smug**
trimly dressed. (*Bridegroom* continues the punning sexual suggestion of
die bravely, have sex successfully.)

LEAR   Then there's life in 't. Come, an you get it, you 202
shall get it by running. Sa, sa, sa, sa.   203
                    Exit [*running, followed by attendants*].

GENTLEMAN
A sight most pitiful in the meanest wretch,
Past speaking of in a king! Thou hast one daughter
Who redeems nature from the general curse   206
Which twain have brought her to.

EDGAR   Hail, gentle sir.   208

GENTLEMAN   Sir, speed you. What's your will?   209

EDGAR
Do you hear aught, sir, of a battle toward?   210

GENTLEMAN
Most sure and vulgar. Everyone hears that   211
Which can distinguish sound.

EDGAR   But, by your favor,   212
How near's the other army?

GENTLEMAN
Near and on speedy foot. The main descry   214
Stands on the hourly thought.   215

EDGAR   I thank you, sir; that's all.

GENTLEMAN
Though that the Queen on special cause is here,   217
Her army is moved on.

EDGAR   I thank you, sir.
                    Exit [*Gentleman*].

GLOUCESTER
You ever-gentle gods, take my breath from me;
Let not my worser spirit tempt me again   220
To die before you please!

EDGAR   Well pray you, father.

GLOUCESTER   Now, good sir, what are you?   223

---

202 life i.e., hope still.   **an** if   **203 Sa . . . sa** (A hunting cry.)
206 general curse universal damnation   **208 gentle** noble   **209 speed**
God speed   **210 toward** imminent   **211 vulgar** in everyone's mouth,
generally known   **212 Which** who   **214–215 The main . . . thought** the
full view of the main body is expected every hour   **217 on special cause**
for a special reason, i.e., to minister to Lear   **220 worser spirit** bad
angel, or ill thoughts   **223 what** who. (Again, Edgar alters his voice to
personate a new stranger assisting Gloucester. See l. 48, above, and
note.)

EDGAR
A most poor man, made tame to fortune's blows,   224
Who, by the art of known and feeling sorrows,   225
Am pregnant to good pity. Give me your hand.   226
I'll lead you to some biding.   [*He offers his arm.*]
GLOUCESTER   Hearty thanks.   227
The bounty and the benison of heaven   228
To boot, and boot!

    Enter steward [*Oswald*].

OSWALD   A proclaimed prize! Most happy!   229
                     [*He draws his sword.*]
That eyeless head of thine was first framed flesh   230
To raise my fortunes. Thou old unhappy traitor,
Briefly thyself remember. The sword is out   232
That must destroy thee.
GLOUCESTER   Now let thy friendly hand   233
Put strength enough to 't.   [*Edgar intervenes.*]
OSWALD   Wherefore, bold peasant,
Durst thou support a published traitor? Hence,   235
Lest that th' infection of his fortune take   236
Like hold on thee. Let go his arm.   237
EDGAR   'Chill not let go, zir, without vurther 'cagion.   238
OSWALD   Let go, slave, or thou diest!
EDGAR   Good gentleman, go your gait, and let poor volk   240
pass. An 'chud ha' bin zwaggered out of my life,   241
'twould not ha' bin zo long as 'tis by a vortnight. Nay,
come not near th' old man; keep out, 'che vor ye, or   243
Ise try whether your costard or my ballow be the   244
harder. 'Chill be plain with you.
OSWALD   Out, dunghill!

---

224 tame submissive   **225 known** personally experienced.   **feeling**
heartfelt, deep   **226 pregnant** prone   **227 biding** abiding place
228–229 The bounty . . . and boot i.e., in addition to my thanks, I wish
you the bounty and blessings of heaven   **229 proclaimed prize** one with
a price on his head.   **happy** fortunate   **230 framed flesh** born
232 thyself remember i.e., confess your sins   **233 friendly** i.e., welcome,
since I desire death   **235 published** proclaimed   **236 Lest that** lest
237 Like similar   **238 'Chill** I will. (Literally, a contraction of *Ich will.*
Edgar adopts Somerset dialect, a stage convention regularly used for
peasants.)   **vurther 'cagion** further occasion   **240 go your gait** go your
own way   **241 An 'chud** if I could.   **zwaggered** swaggered, bluffed
243 'che vor ye I warrant you   **244 Ise** I shall.   **costard** head. (Literally,
an apple.)   **ballow** cudgel

EDGAR   'Chill pick your teeth, zir. Come, no matter vor
 your foins. [*They fight. Edgar fells him with his cudgel.*]   248
OSWALD
 Slave, thou hast slain me. Villain, take my purse.   249
 If ever thou wilt thrive, bury my body
 And give the letters which thou find'st about me   251
 To Edmund, Earl of Gloucester. Seek him out
 Upon the English party. O, untimely death!   253
 Death!   [*He dies.*]
EDGAR
 I know thee well: a serviceable villain,   255
 As duteous to the vices of thy mistress
 As badness would desire.
GLOUCESTER   What, is he dead?
EDGAR   Sit you down, father. Rest you. [*Gloucester sits.*]
 Let's see these pockets; the letters that he speaks of
 May be my friends. He's dead; I am only sorry
 He had no other deathsman. Let us see.   262
                    [*He finds a letter, and opens it.*]
 Leave, gentle wax, and, manners, blame us not.   263
 To know our enemies' minds we rip their hearts;
 Their papers is more lawful.   (*Reads the letter.*)
 "Let our reciprocal vows be remembered. You have
 many opportunities to cut him off; if your will want   267
 not, time and place will be fruitfully offered. There is   268
 nothing done if he return the conqueror. Then am I   269
 the prisoner, and his bed my jail, from the loathed
 warmth whereof deliver me and supply the place for   271
 your labor.   272
      Your—wife, so I would say—
                    Affectionate servant,   Goneril."
 O indistinguished space of woman's will!   275
 A plot upon her virtuous husband's life,
 And the exchange my brother! Here in the sands

---

248 foins thrusts   **249 Villain** serf   **251 letters** letter.   **about me** upon
my person   **253 Upon** on.   **party** side   **255 serviceable** officious
262 deathsman executioner   **263 Leave** by your leave.   **wax** wax seal on
the letter   **267–268 want not** is not lacking   **268 fruitfully** plentifully and
with results   **268–269 There is nothing done** i.e., we will have accom-
plished nothing   **271–272 for your labor** (1) as recompense for your
efforts (2) as a place for your amorous labors   **275 indistinguished . . .
will** limitless and incalculable range of woman's appetite

Thee I'll rake up, the post unsanctified   278
Of murderous lechers; and in the mature time   279
With this ungracious paper strike the sight   280
Of the death-practiced Duke. For him 'tis well   281
That of thy death and business I can tell.

GLOUCESTER
The King is mad. How stiff is my vile sense,   283
That I stand up and have ingenious feeling   284
Of my huge sorrows! Better I were distract;   285
So should my thoughts be severed from my griefs,
And woes by wrong imaginations lose   287
The knowledge of themselves.   *Drum afar off.*

EDGAR   Give me your hand.
Far off, methinks, I hear the beaten drum.
Come, father, I'll bestow you with a friend.   *Exeunt.* 290

❖

4.7   *Enter Cordelia, Kent [dressed still in his*
       disguise costume, and Doctor].

CORDELIA
O thou good Kent, how shall I live and work
To match thy goodness? My life will be too short,
And every measure fail me.   3

KENT
To be acknowledged, madam, is o'erpaid.
All my reports go with the modest truth,   5
Nor more nor clipped, but so.

CORDELIA   Be better suited.   6

278 **rake up** cover up. **post unsanctified** unholy messenger 279 **in . . .
time** when the time is ripe 280 **ungracious** wicked. **strike** blast
281 **death-practiced** whose death is plotted 283 **stiff** obstinate. **sense**
consciousness, sane mental powers 284 **ingenious** conscious. (Gloucester laments that he remains sane and hence fully conscious of his troubles,
unlike Lear.) 285 **distract** distracted, crazy 287 **wrong imaginations**
delusions 290 **bestow** lodge. (At the scene's end, Edgar leads off Gloucester; presumably he also disposes of Oswald's body, which must be removed
from the stage or somehow concealed.)

4.7. Location: The French camp.
3 **every . . . me** i.e., every attempt to match your goodness will fall short
5 **All my reports go** i.e., let all reports (of my service as Caius to Lear)
conform 6 **Nor . . . clipped** i.e., neither more nor less. **suited** dressed

These weeds are memories of those worser hours;　　7
I prithee, put them off.

KENT　　　　　　　　　　　Pardon, dear madam;
Yet to be known shortens my made intent.　　9
My boon I make it that you know me not　　10
Till time and I think meet.　　11

CORDELIA
Then be 't so, my good lord. [*To the Doctor.*] How does
the King?

DOCTOR　　Madam, sleeps still.

CORDELIA　O you kind gods,
Cure this great breach in his abusèd nature!
Th' untuned and jarring senses, O, wind up　　16
Of this child-changèd father!　　17

DOCTOR　　So please Your Majesty
That we may wake the King? He hath slept long.

CORDELIA
Be governed by your knowledge, and proceed
I' the sway of your own will.—Is he arrayed?　　21

Enter Lear in a chair carried by servants,
[*attended by a Gentleman*].

GENTLEMAN
Ay, madam. In the heaviness of sleep
We put fresh garments on him.

DOCTOR
Be by, good madam, when we do awake him.
I doubt not of his temperance.

CORDELIA　　　　　　　　　Very well.　　[*Music.*] 25

DOCTOR
Please you, draw near.—Louder the music there!

CORDELIA [*Kissing him*]
O my dear Father! Restoration hang
Thy medicine on my lips, and let this kiss

---

7 weeds garments.　**memories** remembrances　**9 Yet . . . intent** i.e.,
to reveal my true identity now would alter my carefully made plan
10 My . . . it the reward I seek is.　**know** acknowledge　**11 meet** appropriate　**16 wind up** tune (as by winding the slackened string of an
instrument)　**17 child-changèd** changed (in mind) by children's cruelty
21 I' the sway under the direction　**25 temperance** self-control, calm
behavior

Repair those violent harms that my two sisters
Have in thy reverence made!

KENT   Kind and dear princess!

CORDELIA

Had you not been their father, these white flakes   31
Did challenge pity of them. Was this a face   32
To be opposed against the warring winds?
To stand against the deep dread-bolted thunder   34
In the most terrible and nimble stroke
Of quick cross lightning? To watch—poor perdu!—   36
With this thin helm? Mine enemy's dog,   37
Though he had bit me, should have stood that night
Against my fire; and wast thou fain, poor Father,   39
To hovel thee with swine and rogues forlorn   40
In short and musty straw? Alack, alack!   41
'Tis wonder that thy life and wits at once
Had not concluded all.—He wakes! Speak to him.   43

DOCTOR   Madam, do you; 'tis fittest.

CORDELIA

How does my royal lord? How fares Your Majesty?

LEAR

You do me wrong to take me out o' the grave.
Thou art a soul in bliss; but I am bound
Upon a wheel of fire, that mine own tears   48
Do scald like molten lead.

CORDELIA   Sir, do you know me?

LEAR

You are a spirit, I know. When did you die?

CORDELIA   Still, still, far wide!   51

DOCTOR

He's scarce awake. Let him alone awhile.

LEAR

Where have I been? Where am I? Fair daylight?

31 **Had you** even if you had. **flakes** locks of hair 32 **Did challenge**
would have demanded 34 **deep** bass-voiced. **dread-bolted** furnished
with the dreadful thunderstone 36 **cross** zigzag. **watch** stay awake
(like a sentry on duty). **perdu** soldier placed in a position of peculiar
danger 37 **helm** helmet, i.e., his scanty hair 39 **Against** before, in
front of. **fain** glad, constrained 40 **rogues forlorn** abandoned vaga-
bonds 41 **short** broken up and hence uncomfortable 43 **concluded
all** come to an end altogether 48 **wheel of fire** (A hellish torment
for the eternally damned.) **that** so that 51 **wide** wide of the mark,
wandering

I am mightily abused. I should ev'n die with pity   54
To see another thus. I know not what to say.   55
I will not swear these are my hands. Let's see;
I feel this pinprick. Would I were assured
Of my condition!
CORDELIA   O, look upon me, sir,
And hold your hand in benediction o'er me.
                        [*He attempts to kneel.*]
No, sir, you must not kneel.
LEAR   Pray, do not mock me.
I am a very foolish fond old man,   61
Fourscore and upward, not an hour more nor less;
And, to deal plainly,
I fear I am not in my perfect mind.
Methinks I should know you, and know this man,
Yet I am doubtful; for I am mainly ignorant   66
What place this is, and all the skill I have
Remembers not these garments, nor I know not
Where I did lodge last night. Do not laugh at me,
For, as I am a man, I think this lady
To be my child Cordelia.
CORDELIA [*Weeping*] And so I am, I am.
LEAR
Be your tears wet? Yes, faith. I pray, weep not.
If you have poison for me I will drink it.
I know you do not love me, for your sisters
Have, as I do remember, done me wrong.
You have some cause, they have not.
CORDELIA No cause, no cause.
LEAR Am I in France?
KENT In your own kingdom, sir.
LEAR Do not abuse me.   81
DOCTOR
Be comforted, good madam. The great rage,   82
You see, is killed in him, and yet it is danger
To make him even o'er the time he has lost.   84
Desire him to go in. Trouble him no more
Till further settling.   86

54 abused confused, deluded **55 thus** i.e., thus confused, bewildered
61 fond foolish **66 mainly** perfectly **81 abuse** deceive **82 rage**
frenzy **84 even o'er** fill in, go over in his mind **86 settling** composing
of his mind

CORDELIA Will 't please Your Highness walk?   87
LEAR You must bear with me.
Pray you now, forget and forgive.
I am old and foolish.
                    Exeunt [all but Kent and Gentleman].
GENTLEMAN Holds it true, sir, that the Duke of Corn- 91
wall was so slain?
KENT Most certain, sir.
GENTLEMAN Who is conductor of his people?   94
KENT As 'tis said, the bastard son of Gloucester.
GENTLEMAN They say Edgar, his banished son, is with
the Earl of Kent in Germany.
KENT Report is changeable. 'Tis time to look about; the 98
powers of the kingdom approach apace.   99
GENTLEMAN The arbitrament is like to be bloody. Fare 100
you well, sir.   [*Exit.*]
KENT
My point and period will be throughly wrought,   102
Or well or ill, as this day's battle's fought.   *Exit.* 103

✣

---

87 walk withdraw **91 Holds it true** is it still held to be true
94 conductor leader, general **98 look about** i.e., be wary **99 powers of
the kingdom** British armies (marching against the French invaders)
100 arbitrament decision by arms, decisive encounter **102 My . . .
wrought** i.e., the conclusion of my destiny (literally, the full stop at the
end of my life's sentence) will be thoroughly brought about **103 Or**
either. **as** according as

5.1   *Enter, with drum and colors, Edmund, Regan,*
         Gentlemen, and soldiers.

EDMUND [*To a Gentleman*]
  Know of the Duke if his last purpose hold,   1
  Or whether since he is advised by aught   2
  To change the course. He's full of alteration   3
  And self-reproving. Bring his constant pleasure.   4
                             [*Exit Gentleman.*]

REGAN
  Our sister's man is certainly miscarried.   5
EDMUND
  'Tis to be doubted, madam.
REGAN   Now, sweet lord,   6
  You know the goodness I intend upon you.   7
  Tell me, but truly—but then speak the truth—
  Do you not love my sister?
EDMUND   In honored love.   9
REGAN
  But have you never found my brother's way
  To the forfended place?   11
EDMUND   That thought abuses you.   12
REGAN
  I am doubtful that you have been conjunct   13
  And bosomed with her, as far as we call hers.   14
EDMUND   No, by mine honor, madam.
REGAN
  I never shall endure her. Dear my lord,
  Be not familiar with her.   17
EDMUND
  Fear me not.—She and the Duke her husband!   18

  Enter, with drum and colors, Albany, Goneril,
  [*and*] *soldiers.*

5.1. Location: The British camp near Dover.
1 Know inquire.   **last purpose hold** most recent intention (to fight)
remain firm   **2 since** since then.   **advised by aught** persuaded by any
consideration   **3 alteration** vacillation   **4 constant pleasure** settled
decision   **5 man** i.e., Oswald.   **miscarried** lost, perished   **6 doubted**
feared   **7 intend** intend to confer   **9 honored** honorable   **11 forfended**
forbidden (by the commandment against adultery)   **12 abuses** degrades,
wrongs   **13–14 I am . . . hers** I suspect that you have been coupled and
intimate with her in the fullest manner   **17 familiar** intimate   **18 Fear
me not** don't worry about me on that score

GONERIL [*Aside*]
   I had rather lose the battle than that sister
   Should loosen him and me.

ALBANY
   Our very loving sister, well bemet.   21
   Sir, this I heard: the King is come to his daughter,
   With others whom the rigor of our state   23
   Forced to cry out. Where I could not be honest,   24
   I never yet was valiant. For this business,   25
   It touches us as France invades our land,   26
   Not bolds the King, with others whom, I fear,   27
   Most just and heavy causes make oppose.   28

EDMUND   Sir, you speak nobly.

REGAN   Why is this reasoned?   30

GONERIL
   Combine together 'gainst the enemy;
   For these domestic and particular broils   32
   Are not the question here.

ALBANY   Let's then determine
   With th' ancient of war on our proceeding.   34

EDMUND
   I shall attend you presently at your tent.   35

REGAN   Sister, you'll go with us?

GONERIL   No.

REGAN
   'Tis most convenient. Pray, go with us.   38

GONERIL [*Aside*]
   Oho, I know the riddle.—I will go.   39

   [*As they are going out,*] *enter Edgar* [*disguised*].

EDGAR [*To Albany*]
   If e'er Your Grace had speech with man so poor,

21 **bemet** met   23 **rigor of our state** harshness of our rule   24 **Where** in
a case where.   **honest** honorable   25 **For** as for   26 **touches us as**
concerns us insofar as   27–28 **Not . . . oppose** not because France
encourages the King and others who, I fear, are driven into opposition
by just and weighty grievances.   **bolds** emboldens by offering encour-
agement and support   30 **reasoned** argued (i.e., why are we arguing
about reasons for fighting, instead of fighting)   32 **particular broils**
private quarrels   34 **ancient of war** veteran officers   35 **presently** at
once   38 **convenient** proper, befitting   39 **know the riddle** i.e., understand Regan's enigmatic demand that Goneril accompany her, which is
that Regan wants to keep Goneril from Edmund

Hear me one word.

ALBANY [*To the others*]   I'll overtake you.

Exeunt both the armies.

Speak.

EDGAR [*Giving a letter*]

Before you fight the battle, ope this letter.

If you have victory, let the trumpet sound   43

For him that brought it. Wretched though I seem,

I can produce a champion that will prove   45

What is avouchèd there. If you miscarry,   46

Your business of the world hath so an end,

And machination ceases. Fortune love you!   48

ALBANY   Stay till I have read the letter.

EDGAR   I was forbid it.

When time shall serve, let but the herald cry

And I'll appear again.   *Exit [Edgar].*

ALBANY

Why, fare thee well. I will o'erlook thy paper.   53

Enter Edmund.

EDMUND

The enemy's in view. Draw up your powers.

[*He offers Albany a paper.*]

Here is the guess of their true strength and forces   55

By diligent discovery, but your haste   56

Is now urged on you.

ALBANY   We will greet the time.   *Exit.*   57

EDMUND

To both these sisters have I sworn my love,

Each jealous of the other, as the stung   59

Are of the adder. Which of them shall I take?

Both? One? Or neither? Neither can be enjoyed

If both remain alive. To take the widow

Exasperates, makes mad her sister Goneril,

And hardly shall I carry out my side,   64

Her husband being alive. Now then, we'll use

His countenance for the battle, which being done,   66

---

43 sound sound a summons   **45 prove** i.e., in trial by combat
46 avouchèd maintained.   **miscarry** perish, come to destruction
48 machination plotting (against your life)   **53 o'erlook** peruse   **55 guess**
estimate   **56 discovery** reconnoitering   **57 greet the time** meet the occasion   **59 jealous** suspicious   **64 carry out my side** fulfill my ambition, and
satisfy her (Goneril)   **66 countenance** backing, authority of his name

Let her who would be rid of him devise
His speedy taking off. As for the mercy   68
Which he intends to Lear and to Cordelia,
The battle done and they within our power,
Shall never see his pardon, for my state   71
Stands on me to defend, not to debate.   72

                                 Exit.

✤

5.2   *Alarum within. Enter, with drum and colors,*
        Lear, Cordelia, and soldiers, over the stage; and
        exeunt.

     Enter Edgar and Gloucester.

EDGAR
   Here, father, take the shadow of this tree
   For your good host. Pray that the right may thrive.   2
   If ever I return to you again,
   I'll bring you comfort.
GLOUCESTER   Grace go with you, sir!   4
                          Exit [Edgar].

     Alarum and retreat within. Enter Edgar.

EDGAR
   Away, old man! Give me thy hand, away!
   King Lear hath lost, he and his daughter ta'en.
   Give me thy hand. Come on.
GLOUCESTER
   No further, sir. A man may rot even here.
EDGAR
   What, in ill thoughts again? Men must endure
   Their going hence, even as their coming hither;
   Ripeness is all. Come on.
GLOUCESTER   And that's true too.   11
                          Exeunt.

✤

68 taking off killing   **71 Shall** they shall   **71–72 my state . . . debate** my
position depends upon maintenance by force, not by talk

5.2. Location: The battlefield.
s.d. Alarum trumpet call to arms   **2 host** shelterer   **4 s.d. retreat**
trumpet signal for withdrawal   **11 Ripeness** i.e., fulfillment of one's
allotted years and readiness for death when it comes

5.3   *Enter, in conquest, with drum and colors,*
          Edmund; Lear and Cordelia, as prisoners;
          soldiers, Captain.

EDMUND
  Some officers take them away. Good guard,   1
  Until their greater pleasures first be known   2
  That are to censure them.
CORDELIA [*To Lear*]   We are not the first   3
  Who with best meaning have incurred the worst.   4
  For thee, oppressèd King, I am cast down;
  Myself could else outfrown false Fortune's frown.
  Shall we not see these daughters and these sisters?   7
LEAR
  No, no, no, no! Come, let's away to prison.
  We two alone will sing like birds i' the cage.
  When thou dost ask me blessing, I'll kneel down
  And ask of thee forgiveness. So we'll live,
  And pray, and sing, and tell old tales, and laugh
  At gilded butterflies, and hear poor rogues   13
  Talk of court news; and we'll talk with them too—
  Who loses and who wins; who's in, who's out—
  And take upon 's the mystery of things,   16
  As if we were God's spies; and we'll wear out,   17
  In a walled prison, packs and sects of great ones,   18
  That ebb and flow by the moon.
EDMUND   Take them away.   19
LEAR
  Upon such sacrifices, my Cordelia,
  The gods themselves throw incense. Have I caught thee?   21

5.3. Location: The British camp.
1 Good guard guard them well   **2 their greater pleasures** i.e., the
wishes of those in command   **3 censure** judge   **4 meaning** intentions
7 Shall . . . sisters i.e., aren't we even allowed to speak to Goneril and
Regan before they order to prison their own father and sister
13 gilded butterflies i.e., gaily dressed courtiers and other ephemeral
types, or perhaps actual butterflies   **16 take upon 's** assume the burden
of, or profess to understand   **17 God's spies** i.e., detached observers
surveying the deeds of mankind from an eternal vantage point.   **wear
out** outlast   **18–19 packs . . . moon** i.e., followers and cliques attached
to persons of high station, whose fortunes change erratically and constantly   **21 throw incense** participate as celebrants

He that parts us shall bring a brand from heaven   22
And fire us hence like foxes. Wipe thine eyes;   23
The goodyears shall devour them, flesh and fell,   24
Ere they shall make us weep. We'll see 'em starved first.
Come.   *Exit [with Cordelia, guarded].*

EDMUND   Come hither, Captain. Hark.
Take thou this note [*Giving a paper*]; go follow them
    to prison.
One step I have advanced thee; if thou dost
As this instructs thee, thou dost make thy way
To noble fortunes. Know thou this: that men
Are as the time is. To be tender-minded
Does not become a sword. Thy great employment   33
Will not bear question; either say thou'lt do 't   34
Or thrive by other means.

CAPTAIN   I'll do 't, my lord.

EDMUND
About it, and write "happy" when th' hast done.   36
Mark, I say, instantly, and carry it so   37
As I have set it down.

CAPTAIN
I cannot draw a cart, nor eat dried oats;
If it be man's work, I'll do 't.   *Exit Captain.*

> *Flourish. Enter Albany, Goneril, Regan, [another
> Captain, and] soldiers.*

ALBANY
Sir, you have showed today your valiant strain,
And fortune led you well. You have the captives
Who were the opposites of this day's strife;   43
I do require them of you, so to use them
As we shall find their merits and our safety
May equally determine.

EDMUND   Sir, I thought it fit

22–23 He . . . foxes i.e., anyone seeking to part us will have to employ a
heavenly firebrand to drive us out of our prison refuge as foxes are
driven out of their holes by fire and smoke. (Suggests that only death
will part them.)   **24 goodyears** (Apparently a word connoting evil or
conceivably the passage of time.)   **flesh and fell** flesh and skin, completely   **33 become a sword** i.e., suit a warrior   **34 bear question** admit
of discussion   **36 write "happy"** call yourself fortunate.   **th'** thou
37 carry it arrange it   **43 opposites** enemies

To send the old and miserable King
To some retention and appointed guard,   49
Whose age had charms in it, whose title more,   50
To pluck the common bosom on his side   51
And turn our impressed lances in our eyes   52
Which do command them. With him I sent the Queen,   53
My reason all the same; and they are ready
Tomorrow, or at further space, t' appear   55
Where you shall hold your session. At this time
We sweat and bleed; the friend hath lost his friend,
And the best quarrels in the heat are cursed   58
By those that feel their sharpness.   59
The question of Cordelia and her father
Requires a fitter place.

ALBANY   Sir, by your patience,
I hold you but a subject of this war,   62
Not as a brother.

REGAN   That's as we list to grace him.   63
Methinks our pleasure might have been demanded   64
Ere you had spoke so far. He led our powers,
Bore the commission of my place and person,
The which immediacy may well stand up   67
And call itself your brother.

GONERIL   Not so hot!
In his own grace he doth exalt himself
More than in your addition.

REGAN   In my rights,   70
By me invested, he compeers the best.   71

GONERIL
That were the most if he should husband you.   72

---

49 retention confinement   **50 Whose** i.e., the King's   **51 common bosom** affection of the multitude   **52 turn . . . eyes** i.e., turn against us the weapons of those very troops whom we impressed into service **53 Which** we who   **55 space** interval of time   **58–59 And . . . sharpness** i.e., and even the best of causes, at this moment when the passions of battle have not cooled, are viewed with hatred by those who have suffered the painful consequences. (Edmund pretends to worry that Lear and Cordelia would not receive a fair trial.)   **quarrels** causes. **sharpness** keenness, painful consequences   **62 subject of** subordinate in   **63 list** please   **64 pleasure** wish.   **demanded** asked about **67 immediacy** nearness of connection   **70 your addition** the titles you confer   **71 compeers** is equal with   **72 That . . . most** that investiture would be most complete

REGAN
  Jesters do oft prove prophets.

GONERIL   Holla, holla!   73
  That eye that told you so looked but asquint.   74

REGAN
  Lady, I am not well, else I should answer
  From a full-flowing stomach. [*To Edmund.*] General,   76
  Take thou my soldiers, prisoners, patrimony;   77
  Dispose of them, of me; the walls is thine.   78
  Witness the world that I create thee here
  My lord and master.

GONERIL   Mean you to enjoy him?

ALBANY
  The let-alone lies not in your good will.   81

EDMUND
  Nor in thine, lord.

ALBANY   Half-blooded fellow, yes.   82

REGAN [*To Edmund*]
  Let the drum strike and prove my title thine.   83

ALBANY
  Stay yet; hear reason. Edmund, I arrest thee
  On capital treason; and, in thy attaint   85
                          [*Pointing to Goneril*]
  This gilded serpent. For your claim, fair sister,
  I bar it in the interest of my wife;
  'Tis she is subcontracted to this lord,
  And I, her husband, contradict your banns.   89
  If you will marry, make your loves to me;
  My lady is bespoke.

GONERIL   An interlude!   91

ALBANY
  Thou art armed, Gloucester. Let the trumpet sound.

---

73 prove turn out to be   **74 asquint** (Jealousy proverbially makes the
eye look *asquint*, furtively, suspiciously.)   **76 full-flowing stomach** full
tide of angry rejoinder   **77 patrimony** inheritance   **78 the walls is thine**
i.e., the citadel of my heart and body surrenders completely to you
81 let-alone preventing, denying   **82 Half-blooded** only partly of noble
blood, bastard   **83 Let . . . strike** i.e., let there be a public announcement (?) a battle (?)   **85 in thy attaint** i.e., as partner in your corruption
and as one who has (unwittingly) provided the *attaint* or impeachment
against you   **89 banns** public announcement of a proposed marriage
91 An interlude a play; i.e., you are being melodramatic; or, what a farce
this is

If none appear to prove upon thy person
Thy heinous, manifest, and many treasons,
There is my pledge. [*He throws down a glove.*] I'll make
  it on thy heart,   95
Ere I taste bread, thou art in nothing less   96
Than I have here proclaimed thee.
REGAN   Sick, O, sick!
GONERIL [*Aside*]   If not, I'll ne'er trust medicine.   99
EDMUND [*Throwing down a glove*]
  There's my exchange. What in the world he is   100
  That names me traitor, villain-like he lies.
  Call by the trumpet. He that dares approach,
  On him, on you—who not?—I will maintain
  My truth and honor firmly.
ALBANY
  A herald, ho!
EDMUND   A herald, ho, a herald!

    Enter a Herald.

ALBANY
  Trust to thy single virtue; for thy soldiers,   106
  All levied in my name, have in my name
  Took their discharge.
REGAN   My sickness grows upon me.
ALBANY
  She is not well. Convey her to my tent.
                  [*Exit Regan, supported.*]
  Come hither, herald. Let the trumpet sound,
  And read out this.   [*He gives a paper.*]
CAPTAIN   Sound, trumpet!   *A trumpet sounds.*
HERALD (*Reads*) "If any man of quality or degree within 113
  the lists of the army will maintain upon Edmund, sup-
  posed Earl of Gloucester, that he is a manifold traitor,
  let him appear by the third sound of the trumpet. He
  is bold in his defense."
EDMUND Sound!   *First trumpet.*
HERALD Again!   *Second trumpet.*
HERALD Again!   *Third trumpet.*
            Trumpet answers within.

---

95 make prove   **96 in nothing less** in no respect less guilty
99 medicine i.e., poison   **100 What** whoever   **106 single virtue** unaided
prowess   **113 degree** rank

Enter Edgar, armed, [with a trumpeter before him].

ALBANY
Ask him his purposes, why he appears
Upon this call o' the trumpet.

HERALD   What are you?   122
Your name, your quality, and why you answer
This present summons?

EDGAR   Know my name is lost,
By treason's tooth bare-gnawn and canker-bit.   125
Yet am I noble as the adversary
I come to cope.

ALBANY   Which is that adversary?   127

EDGAR
What's he that speaks for Edmund, Earl of Gloucester?

EDMUND
Himself. What sayst thou to him?

EDGAR   Draw thy sword,
That, if my speech offend a noble heart,
Thy arm may do thee justice. Here is mine.
                        [*He draws his sword.*]
Behold, it is the privilege of mine honors,   132
My oath, and my profession. I protest,   133
Maugre thy strength, place, youth, and eminence,   134
Despite thy victor sword and fire-new fortune,   135
Thy valor, and thy heart, thou art a traitor—   136
False to thy gods, thy brother, and thy father,
Conspirant 'gainst this high-illustrious prince,
And from th' extremest upward of thy head   139
To the descent and dust below thy foot   140
A most toad-spotted traitor. Say thou no,   141
This sword, this arm, and my best spirits are bent   142
To prove upon thy heart, whereto I speak,
Thou liest.

EDMUND   In wisdom I should ask thy name.   144
But since thy outside looks so fair and warlike,

---

122 What who   **125 canker-bit** eaten as by the caterpillar   **127 cope**
encounter   **132 of mine honors** i.e., of my knighthood   **133 profession** i.e.,
knighthood   **134 Maugre** in spite of   **135 victor** victorious. **fire-new**
newly minted   **136 heart** courage   **139 upward** top   **140 descent** lowest
extreme   **141 toad-spotted** venomous, or having spots of infamy. **Say
thou** if you say   **142 bent** prepared   **144 wisdom** prudence

And that thy tongue some say of breeding breathes,　146
What safe and nicely I might well delay　147
By rule of knighthood, I disdain and spurn.　148
Back do I toss these treasons to thy head,　149
With the hell-hated lie o'erwhelm thy heart,　150
Which—for they yet glance by and scarcely bruise—　151
This sword of mine shall give them instant way,　152
Where they shall rest forever. Trumpets, speak!　153
　　　　　[*He draws.*] *Alarums. Fight.* [*Edmund falls.*]
ALBANY [*To Edgar*]
　Save him, save him!
GONERIL　　　　　　This is practice, Gloucester.　154
By th' law of war thou wast not bound to answer
An unknown opposite. Thou art not vanquished,
But cozened and beguiled.
ALBANY　　　　　　Shut your mouth, dame,　157
Or with this paper shall I stopple it.—Hold, sir.—　158
[*To Goneril.*] Thou worse than any name, read thine own
　evil.　　　　　　　　　[*He shows her the letter.*]
No tearing, lady; I perceive you know it.
GONERIL
Say if I do, the laws are mine, not thine.
Who can arraign me for 't?
ALBANY　　　　　　Most monstrous! O!
Know'st thou this paper?
GONERIL　　　　　　Ask me not what I know.
　　　　　　　　　　　　　　Exit.
ALBANY
Go after her. She's desperate; govern her.　164
　　　　　　　　　　　[*Exit a Soldier.*]

---

146 say smack, taste, indication　**147 safe and nicely** prudently and
punctiliously　**148 I . . . spurn** i.e., I disdain to insist on my right to
refuse combat with one of lower rank　**149 treasons . . . head** i.e.,
accusations of treason in your teeth　**150 hell-hated** hated as hell is
hated　**151 Which . . . bruise** i.e., which charges of treason—since they
merely glance off your armor and do no harm.　**for** since.　**yet** as yet
152 give . . . way i.e., provide them an immediate pathway to your
heart　**153 Where . . . forever** i.e., my victory in trial by combat will
prove forever that the charges of treason apply to you　**154 Save** spare.
(Albany wishes to spare Edmund's life so that he may confess and be
found guilty.)　**practice** trickery; or (said sardonically) astute manage-
ment　**157 cozened** tricked　**158 stopple** stop up.　**Hold, sir** (Perhaps
addressed to Edgar; see l. 154 and note.)　**164 govern** restrain

EDMUND
  What you have charged me with, that have I done,
  And more, much more. The time will bring it out.
  'Tis past, and so am I. But what art thou
  That hast this fortune on me? If thou'rt noble,   168
  I do forgive thee.
EDGAR   Let's exchange charity.   169
  I am no less in blood than thou art, Edmund;
  If more, the more th' hast wronged me.   171
  My name is Edgar, and thy father's son.
  The gods are just, and of our pleasant vices   173
  Make instruments to plague us.
  The dark and vicious place where thee he got   175
  Cost him his eyes.
EDMUND   Th' hast spoken right. 'Tis true.
  The wheel is come full circle; I am here.   177
ALBANY [*To Edgar*]
  Methought thy very gait did prophesy
  A royal nobleness. I must embrace thee.
                              [*They embrace.*]
  Let sorrow split my heart if ever I
  Did hate thee or thy father!
EDGAR Worthy prince, I know 't.
ALBANY Where have you hid yourself?
  How have you known the miseries of your father?
EDGAR
  By nursing them, my lord. List a brief tale,
  And when 'tis told, O, that my heart would burst!
  The bloody proclamation to escape   187
  That followed me so near—O, our lives' sweetness,
  That we the pain of death would hourly die
  Rather than die at once!—taught me to shift
  Into a madman's rags, t' assume a semblance
  That very dogs disdained; and in this habit
  Met I my father with his bleeding rings,   193
  Their precious stones new lost; became his guide,

168 fortune on victory over   **169 charity** forgiveness (for Edmund's
wickedness toward Edgar and Edgar's having slain Edmund)   **171 th'**
thou   **173 pleasant** pleasurable   **175 got** begot   **177 wheel** i.e., wheel of
fortune.   **here** i.e., at its bottom   **187 The . . . escape** in order to escape the
death-threatening proclamation   **193 rings** sockets

Led him, begged for him, saved him from despair;
Never—O fault!—revealed myself unto him   196
Until some half hour past, when I was armed.
Not sure, though hoping, of this good success,   198
I asked his blessing, and from first to last
Told him our pilgrimage. But his flawed heart—   200
Alack, too weak the conflict to support—
Twixt two extremes of passion, joy and grief,
Burst smilingly.

EDMUND   This speech of yours hath moved me,
And shall perchance do good. But speak you on;
You look as you had something more to say.

ALBANY
If there be more, more woeful, hold it in,
For I am almost ready to dissolve,   207
Hearing of this.

EDGAR   This would have seemed a period   208
To such as love not sorrow; but another,   209
To amplify too much, would make much more   210
And top extremity. Whilst I   211
Was big in clamor, came there in a man   212
Who, having seen me in my worst estate,
Shunned my abhorred society; but then, finding
Who 'twas that so endured, with his strong arms
He fastened on my neck and bellowed out
As he'd burst heaven, threw him on my father,   217
Told the most piteous tale of Lear and him
That ever ear received, which in recounting
His grief grew puissant, and the strings of life   220
Began to crack. Twice then the trumpets sounded,
And there I left him tranced.

ALBANY   But who was this?   222

EDGAR
Kent, sir, the banished Kent, who in disguise

---

196 fault mistake   **198 success** outcome   **200 flawed** cracked
207 dissolve i.e., in tears   **208 a period** the limit   **209 love not** are not in
love with   **209–211 but . . . extremity** i.e., another sorrowful circumstance,
adding to what is already too much, would increase it and exceed the
limit   **212 big in clamor** loud in my lamenting   **217 As** as if.   **threw . . .
father** threw himself on my father's body   **220 His** i.e., Kent's.   **puissant**
powerful.   **strings of life** heartstrings   **222 tranced** entranced, senseless

Followed his enemy king and did him service   224
Improper for a slave.

    Enter a Gentleman [with a bloody knife].

GENTLEMAN
  Help, help, O, help!
EDGAR   What kind of help?
ALBANY   Speak, man.
EDGAR
  What means this bloody knife?
GENTLEMAN   'Tis hot, it smokes.   227
  It came even from the heart of—O, she's dead!
ALBANY   Who dead? Speak, man.
GENTLEMAN
  Your lady, sir, your lady! And her sister
  By her is poisoned; she confesses it.
EDMUND
  I was contracted to them both. All three
  Now marry in an instant.
EDGAR   Here comes Kent.

    Enter Kent.

ALBANY
  Produce the bodies, be they alive or dead.
                     [Exit Gentleman.]
  This judgment of the heavens, that makes us tremble,
  Touches us not with pity.—O, is this he?
  [To Kent.] The time will not allow the compliment   237
  Which very manners urges.
KENT   I am come   238
  To bid my king and master aye good night.   239
  Is he not here?
ALBANY   Great thing of us forgot!
  Speak, Edmund, where's the King? And where's
    Cordelia?
        Goneril's and Regan's bodies [are] brought out.
  Seest thou this object, Kent?   242

224 his enemy king i.e., the king who had rejected and banished him
227 smokes steams **237 compliment** ceremony **238 very manners
urges** mere decency requires **239 aye good night** farewell forever. (Kent
believes he himself is near death, his heartstrings having begun to
crack.) **242 object** sight

KENT   Alack, why thus?

EDMUND   Yet Edmund was beloved.   244
  The one the other poisoned for my sake
  And after slew herself.   246

ALBANY   Even so. Cover their faces.

EDMUND
  I pant for life. Some good I mean to do,
  Despite of mine own nature. Quickly send—
  Be brief in it—to the castle, for my writ
  Is on the life of Lear and on Cordelia.
  Nay, send in time.

ALBANY   Run, run, O, run!

EDGAR
  To who, my lord? Who has the office? Send   253
  Thy token of reprieve.

EDMUND   Well thought on. Take my sword.
  Give it the Captain.

EDGAR   Haste thee, for thy life.
                  [*Exit one with Edmund's sword.*]

EDMUND
  He hath commission from thy wife and me
  To hang Cordelia in the prison and
  To lay the blame upon her own despair,
  That she fordid herself.   260

ALBANY
  The gods defend her! Bear him hence awhile.
                  [*Edmund is borne off.*]

  Enter Lear, with Cordelia in his arms; [*Captain*].

LEAR
  Howl, howl, howl! O, you are men of stones!
  Had I your tongues and eyes, I'd use them so
  That heaven's vault should crack. She's gone forever.
  I know when one is dead and when one lives;
  She's dead as earth. Lend me a looking glass;
  If that her breath will mist or stain the stone,   267
  Why, then she lives.

KENT   Is this the promised end?   268

---

244 Yet despite everything   **246 after** afterwards   **253 office** commission   **260 fordid** destroyed   **267 stone** crystal or polished stone of which the mirror is made   **268 promised end** i.e., Last Judgment

EDGAR
   Or image of that horror?
ALBANY   Fall and cease!   269
LEAR
   This feather stirs; she lives! If it be so,
   It is a chance which does redeem all sorrows
   That ever I have felt.
KENT [*Kneeling*]   O my good master!
LEAR
   Prithee, away.
EDGAR   'Tis noble Kent, your friend.
LEAR
   A plague upon you, murderers, traitors all!
   I might have saved her; now she's gone forever!
   Cordelia, Cordelia! Stay a little. Ha?
   What is 't thou sayst? Her voice was ever soft,
   Gentle, and low, an excellent thing in woman.
   I killed the slave that was a-hanging thee.
CAPTAIN
   'Tis true, my lords, he did.
LEAR   Did I not, fellow?
   I have seen the day, with my good biting falchion   281
   I would have made them skip. I am old now,
   And these same crosses spoil me.—Who are you?   283
   Mine eyes are not o' the best; I'll tell you straight.   284
KENT
   If Fortune brag of two she loved and hated,   285
   One of them we behold.
LEAR
   This is a dull sight. Are you not Kent?
KENT   The same,   287
   Your servant Kent. Where is your servant Caius?   288
LEAR
   He's a good fellow, I can tell you that;
   He'll strike, and quickly too. He's dead and rotten.

---

269 image representation.   **Fall and cease** i.e., let heavens fall and all
things cease   **281 falchion** light sword   **283 crosses spoil me** adversi-
ties take away my strength   **284 I'll ... straight** I'll recognize you in a
moment   **285 two** i.e., Lear, and a hypothetical individual whose misfortunes are without parallel.   **loved and hated** i.e., first raised and then
lowered   **287 This ... sight** i.e., my vision is clouding; or, this is a
dismal spectacle   **288 Caius** (Kent's disguise name)

KENT
  No, my good lord, I am the very man—
LEAR   I'll see that straight.   292
KENT
  That from your first of difference and decay   293
  Have followed your sad steps—
LEAR   You are welcome hither.
KENT
  Nor no man else. All's cheerless, dark, and deadly.   295
  Your eldest daughters have fordone themselves,   296
  And desperately are dead.
LEAR   Ay, so I think.   297
ALBANY
  He knows not what he says, and vain is it
  That we present us to him.
EDGAR   Very bootless.   299

  Enter a Messenger.

MESSENGER   Edmund is dead, my lord.
ALBANY   That's but a trifle here.
  You lords and noble friends, know our intent:
  What comfort to this great decay may come   303
  Shall be applied. For us, we will resign,
  During the life of this old majesty,
  To him our absolute power; [*To Edgar and Kent*] you,
    to your rights,
  With boot and such addition as your honors   307
  Have more than merited. All friends shall taste
  The wages of their virtue, and all foes
  The cup of their deservings.—O, see, see!
LEAR
  And my poor fool is hanged! No, no, no life?   311
  Why should a dog, a horse, a rat, have life,
  And thou no breath at all? Thou'lt come no more,

---

292 see that straight attend to that in a moment; or, comprehend that
soon   **293 first of difference** beginning of your change for the worse
295 Nor . . . else no, not I nor anyone else; or, I am *the very man* (l. 291),
him and no one else.   **deadly** deathlike   **296 fordone** destroyed
297 desperately in despair   **299 bootless** in vain   **303 What . . . come** i.e.,
whatever means of comforting this ruined king may present themselves
307 boot advantage, good measure.   **addition** titles, further distinctions
311 poor fool i.e., Cordelia. (*Fool* is here a term of endearment.)

Never, never, never, never, never!
Pray you, undo this button. Thank you, sir.
Do you see this? Look on her, look, her lips,
Look there, look there!   *He dies.*

EDGAR   He faints. My lord, my lord!
KENT
Break, heart, I prithee, break!
EDGAR   Look up, my lord.
KENT
Vex not his ghost. O, let him pass! He hates him   319
That would upon the rack of this tough world   320
Stretch him out longer.
EDGAR   He is gone indeed.
KENT
The wonder is he hath endured so long.
He but usurped his life.
ALBANY
Bear them from hence. Our present business
Is general woe. [*To Kent and Edgar.*] Friends of my
    soul, you twain
Rule in this realm, and the gored state sustain.
KENT
I have a journey, sir, shortly to go.   327
My master calls me; I must not say no.
EDGAR
The weight of this sad time we must obey;
Speak what we feel, not what we ought to say.
The oldest hath borne most; we that are young
Shall never see so much nor live so long.   332
                    Exeunt, with a dead march.

---

319 ghost departing spirit   **320 rack** torture rack (with suggestion, in
the Folio and quarto spelling *wracke,* of shipwreck, disaster)
327 journey i.e., to another world   **332 s.d. Exeunt** (Presumably the
dead bodies are borne out in procession.)

Date and Text

On November 26, 1607, Nathaniel Butter and John Busby entered on the Stationers' Register, the official record book of the London Company of Stationers (booksellers and printers), "A booke called. Master William Shakespeare his historye of Kinge Lear, as yt was played before the Kinges maiestie at Whitehall vppon Sainct Stephens night at Christmas Last, by his maiesties servantes playinge vsually at the Globe on the Banksyde." Next year appeared the following quarto:

> M. William Shak-speare: *HIS* True Chronicle Historie of the life and death of King Lear and his three Daughters. *With the vnfortunate life of* Edgar, *sonne* and heire to the Earle of Gloster, and his sullen and assumed humor of Tom of Bedlam: *As it was played before the Kings Maiestie at Whitehall vpon S.* Stephans *night in Christmas Hollidayes.* By his Maiesties seruants playing vsually at the Gloabe on the Bancke-side. london, Printed for *Nathaniel Butter,* and are to be sold at his shop in *Pauls* Church-yard at the signe of the Pide Bull neere St. *Austins* Gate. 1608.

This quarto is often called the "Pied Bull" quarto in reference to its place of sale. Twelve copies exist today, in ten different "states," because proofreading was being carried on while the sheets were being run off in the press; the copies variously combine corrected and uncorrected sheets. A second quarto, printed in 1619 by William Jaggard for Thomas Pavier with the fraudulent date of 1608, was based on a copy of the first quarto combining corrected and uncorrected sheets.

The First Folio text of 1623 may have been typeset from a promptbook cut for performance or from a transcript of such a manuscript, and the promptbook in its turn appears to have been based on Shakespeare's fair copy of his first draft. The Folio compositors also pretty certainly consulted a copy of the second quarto from time to time, or may have typeset directly from this quarto as annotated with reference to Shakespeare's fair copy. In writing the fair copy Shakespeare may have marked some 300 lines for deletion, but it is possible that he did so chiefly to shorten time of performance. He also seems to have added some 100 lines, an apparent contradiction in view of the need for cutting but possibly dictated by Shakespeare's developing sense of his play. It is also possible that the cuts were carried out by someone else in the preparation of the promptbook.

The first quarto, on the other hand, appears in some fashion to have descended from Shakespeare's unrevised and evidently very untidy foul or working papers. It is often corrupt. Still, in some matters—especially variants indifferent in meaning (such as *an/if* or *thine/thy*)—it may be closer to Shakespeare's preferences than the Folio, behind which are several stages of transmission.

This edition agrees with most recent students of the *Lear* text that the Folio represents a theatrical revision in which the cuts were devised for performance by Shakespeare's company, quite possibly made by Shakespeare himself as a member of that company. The case for artistic preference in the making of those cuts, on the other hand, is less certain and may have been overstated. Many of the cuts have the effect of shortening scenes, especially in the latter half of the play. Some scenes, like 3.6, show open gaps as a result of the cutting: Lear's "Then let them anatomize Regan" (l. 75) implies the trial of Goneril as it is dramatized in the first quarto but cut from the Folio. Other omissions as well read like expedients, although they can also be explained by a hypothesis of literary and theatrical rewriting; if Shakespeare himself undertook the cutting, he would presumably do so as expertly as possible. The fact that the Folio text gives no rewritten speeches may suggest that the large cuts were motivated by the need for shortening. This edition holds to the principle that it is unwise to omit the material cut from the Folio text, since we cannot be sure that Shakespeare would have shortened the text had there been no external constraints. At the same time, the added material in the Folio is clearly his and belongs in his conception of the play. The resulting text is a conflation, but one that avoids cutting material that Shakespeare may well have regretted having to excise.

The Stationers' Register entry for November 26, 1607, describes a performance at court on the previous St. Stephen's night, December 26, 1606. The title page of the first quarto confirms this performance on St. Stephen's night. Such a performance at court was not likely to have been the first, however. Shakespeare's repeated use of Samuel Harsnett's *Declaration of Egregious Popish Impostures*, registered on March 16, 1603, sets an early limit for composition of the play. Other circumstances point to the existence of the play by May of 1605. In that month, an old play called *The True Chronicle History of King Leir* was entered in the Stationers' Register as a "Tragecall historie," a phrase suggesting the influence of Shakespeare's play, since the old *King Leir* does not end tragically. Moreover, the title page of the old *King Leir*, issued in 1605, proclaims the text to be "as it hath bene diuers and sundry times lately acted." In view of the unlikelihood that such an old play (written before 1594) would be revived in 1605, scholars have suggested that the title page was the publisher's way of trying to capitalize on the recent popularity of Shakespeare's play. In this case, the likeliest date for the composition of Shakespeare's *King Lear* would be in the winter of 1604–1605. Shakespeare certainly used the old *King Leir* as a chief source, but he need not have waited for its publication in 1605 if, as seems perfectly plausible, his company owned the promptbook. On the other hand, Gloucester's mentioning of "These late eclipses in the sun and moon" (1.2.106) seems to refer to an eclipse of the moon in September and of the sun in October of 1605, and we are left wondering if Shakespeare was so foresighted as to have anticipated these events.

Textual Notes

These textual notes are not a historical collation, either of the early quartos and folios or of more recent editions; they are simply a record of departures in this edition from the copy text. The reading adopted in this edition appears in boldface, followed by the rejected reading from the copy text, i.e., the First Folio. Only major alterations in punctuation are noted. Changes in lineation are not indicated, nor are some minor and obvious typographical errors.

Abbreviations used:
F the First Folio
Q quarto
s.d. stage direction
s.p. speech prefix

Copy text: the First Folio, except for those 300 or so lines found only in the first quarto of 1608 [Q1]. Unless otherwise indicated, adopted readings are from the corrected state of Q1. A few readings are supplied from the second quarto of 1619 [Q2]. All readings subsequent to 1619 are marked as supplied by "eds."

1.1. 5 equalities qualities   **20–22 account . . . yet** [eds.] account, though . . . for: yet   **35 liege** Lord   **55 words** word   **66 issue** issues   **68 Speak** [Q1; not in F]   **74 possesses** professes   **85 interessed** [eds.] interest   **104** [Q1; not in F]   **110 mysteries** [eds.] miseries [F] mistresse [Q1]   **135 turns** turne   **156 as a** as   **157 nor** nere   **161 s.p. Lear** Kear   **162 s.p. Kent** Lent   **165 s.p. Cornwall** [eds.] Cor   **166 the** thy   **173 sentence** sentences   **191 s.p. Gloucester** Cor   **217 best object** obiect   **229 well** will   **252 respects of fortune** respect and Fortunes   **285 shame them** with shame   **286 s.d. Exeunt** [eds.] Exit   **293 hath not** hath   **306 hit** sit

1.2. 1 s.p. [and elsewhere] Edmund Bast   **21 top** [eds.] to'   **56 waked** wake   **97–99 Edmund. Nor . . . earth** [Q1; not in F]   **134 Fut, I** I   **136 Edgar** [Q1; not in F]   **137 and pat** [eds.] Pat [F] and out [Q1]   **147–155 as . . . come,** [Q1; not in F]   **182 s.d.** [at l. 181 in F]

1.3. 3 s.p. [and elsewhere] Oswald [eds.] Ste   **17–21** [Q1; not in F]   **26–27 I would . . . speak** [Q1; not in F]   **28 very** [Q1; not in F]

1.4. 1 well will   **43 s.d. Enter steward** [at l. 44 in F]   **50 daughter** Daughters   **76 s.d. Enter steward** [eds.; after l. 77 in F]   **96 s.p. Kent** Lear   **Fool** my boy   **138–153 Fool. That . . . snatching** [Q1; not in F]   **158 crown** Crownes   **175 fools** Foole   **195 nor crumb** not crum   **214 it had** it's had   **229–232** [Q1; not in F]   **255 O . . . come** [Q1; not in F]   **303 Yea . . . this** [Q1; not in F]   **343 You're** Your   **attasked** at task

1.5. s.d. Kent Kent, Gentleman   **51 s.d. Exit** Exeunt

2.1. 2 you your   **19 s.d.** [at l. 18 in F]   **39 stand 's** stand   **69 I should** should I   **70 ay, though** though   **78 I never got him** [Q1; not in F]   **78 s.d.** [at l. 77 in F]   **79 why** wher   **87 strange news** strangenesse   **125 thought** though

2.2. 22 clamorous clamours   **45 an** if   **52 What's** What is   **66 you'll** you
will   **78 Bring . . . their** Being . . . the   **79 Renege** Reuenge   **80 gale** gall
84 an if   **101 take 't** take it   **109 flickering** flicking   **124 dread** dead
127 their there   **132 respect** respects   **142 s.d.** [at l. 140 in F]   **144–148 His
. . . with** [Q1; not in F]   **146 contemned'st** [eds.] temnest [Q1]   **148 King**
King his Master, needs   **153** [Q1; not in F]   **154 Come . . . away** [assigned
in F to Cornwall   **good** [Q1; not in F]   **s.d. Exeunt** [eds.] Exit   **155 Duke's**
Duke

2.3. 18 sheepcotes Sheeps-Coates

2.4. 2 messenger Messengers   **9 man's** man   **18–19** [Q1; not in F]
30 panting painting   **33 whose** those   **56 Hysterica** [eds.] Historica   **62 the**
the the   **74 have** hause   **128 you** your   **130 mother's** Mother   **185 s.d.** [at
l. 183 in F]   **187 fickle** fickly   **190 s.d.** [at l. 188 in F]   **213 hot-blooded** hot-
bloodied   **297 s.d.** [after l. 295 in F]   **302 bleak** high

3.1. 7–15 tears . . . all [Q1; not in F]   **10 outstorm** [eds.] outscorne [Q1]
30–42 [Q1; not in F]

3.2. 3 drowned drown   **38 s.d.** [at l. 36 in F]   **85–86** [these lines follow l. 91
in F]

3.3. 17 for 't for it

3.4. 10 thy they   **12 This** the   **27 s.d.** [at l. 26 in F]   **31 looped** lop'd   **38 s.d.
Enter Fool** [F, at l. 36: "Enter Edgar, and Foole"]   **46 blows the cold wind**
blow the windes   **51 through fire** though Fire   **52 ford** Sword   **57, 58 Bless**
Blisse   **90 deeply** deerely   **99 sessa** [eds.] Sesey   **112 s.d.** [at l. 109 in F]
114 fiend [Q1; not in F]   **115 till the** at   **116 squinnies** [eds.] squints [F]
squemes [Q1]   **134 stock-punished** stockt, punish'd   **hath had** hath

3.5. 11 he which hee   **26 dearer** deere

3.6. 5 s.d. Exit [at l. 3 in F]   **17–55** [Q1; not in F]   **21 justicer** [eds.] Iustice
[Q1]   **22 Now** [Q2] No [Q1]   **25 burn** [eds.] broome [Q1]   **34 cushions** [eds.]
cushings [Q1]   **51 joint** [eds.] ioyne [Q1]   **53 on** [eds.] an [Q1]   **68 lym** [eds.]
Hym   **69 tike** tight   **trundle-tail** Troudle taile   **85 s.d.** [at l. 80 in F]
97–101 Oppressèd . . . behind [Q1; not in F]   **101 s.p. Gloucester** [not in F]
102–115 [Q1; not in F]

3.7. 10 festinate [eds.] festinate   **18 lord's dependents** Lords, dependants
23 s.d. Exeunt [Q1.] Exit   **61 rash** sticke   **66 dern** sterne   **75 s.p. First
Servant** Seru [also at ll. 79, 82, 84]   **83** [F provides a stage direction: "Killes
him"]   **102–110** [Q1; not in F]   **102 s.p. Second Servant** Seruant [and called
"1 Ser" at l. 106 in Q1]   **103, 109 s.p. Third Servant** 2 Seruant [Q1]
107 roguish [Q2; not in Q1]   **110 s.d. Exeunt** Exit

4.1. 41 Then . . . gone Get thee away   **57–62 Five . . . master** [Q1; not in F]
60 Flibbertigibbet [eds.] Stiberdigebit [Q]   **60–61 mopping and mowing**
[eds.] Mobing, & Mohing [Q]

4.2. s.d. Bastard Bastard, and Steward   **2 s.d. Steward** [Q1; placed at beginning in F]   **30 whistling** whistle   **32–51 I fear . . . deep** [Q1; not in F]   **33 its**
[eds.] ith [Q1]   **48 these** [eds.] this [Q1]   **54–60 that . . . so** [Q1; not
in F]   **58 to threat** thereat [Q1]   **61 shows** seemes   **63–69, 70** [Q1; not
in F]   **76 threat** threat   **80 justicers** [Q1 corrected] Iustices

4.3. 1–57 [scene omitted in F]   **11 sir** [eds.] say [Q1]   **16 strove** [eds.] streme
[Q1]   **20 seemed** [eds.] seeme [Q1]   **22 dropped. In** dropt in   **32 then** her,
then   **44 benediction, turned her** benediction turnd her,   **57 s.d. Exeunt**
[eds.] Exit [Q1]

4.4 [F reads "Scena Tertia"]   **s.d. Doctor** Gentlemen   **3 fumiter** [eds.]
femiter [Q1] Fenitar [F]   **6 century** Centery   **11 s.p. Doctor** Gent
18 distress desires   **28 right** Rite

4.5 [F reads "Scena Quarta"]   **23 Something** Some things   **27 oeillades**
[eds.] Eliads   **41 meet him** meet

4.6 [F reads "Scena Quinta"]   **17 walk** walk'd   **57 summit** Somnet
66–67 strangeness. / Upon . . . cliff what [eds.] strangenesse, / Vpon . . .
Cliffe. What   **71 enridgèd** enraged   **83 coining** crying   **97 white** the white
161 thine thy   **164 Through** Thorough   **small** great   **165 Plate sin** [eds.]
Place sinnes   **197 Ay . . . dust** [Q1; not in F]   **205 one a**   **218 s.d. Exit** [after
"moved on" in l. 218 in F]   **235 Durst** Dar'st   **238 'cagion** 'casion   **269 done
if . . . conqueror. Then** [eds.] done. If . . . Conqueror then   **275 indistinguished** indinguish'd   **288 s.d. Drum afar off** [after l. 286 in F]

4.7. 13 s.p. Doctor Gent [also at ll. 18, 44, 52, 82]   **24 s.p. Doctor** [Q1; not
in F]   **25 doubt not** doubt   **25–26 Cordelia. Very . . . there** [Q1; not in F]
33 warring iarring   **34–37 To stand . . . helm** [Q1; not in F]   **50 When**
where   **60 No, sir** [Q1; not in F]   **83–84 and . . . lost** [Q1; not in F]
91–103 [Q1; not in F]

5.1. 12–14 [Q1; not in F]   **18 me not** not   **19–20** [Q1; not in F]
24–29 Where . . . nobly [Q1; not in F]   **35** [Q1; not in F]   **41 s.d. Exeunt . . .
armies** [at l. 39 in F]   **48 love** loues

5.3. 39–40 [Q1; not in F]   **49 and appointed guard** [Q1 corrected; not in F]
56–61 At . . . place [Q1; not in F]   **57 We** [Q1 corrected] mee [Q1 uncor-
rected]   **59 sharpness** [Q1 corrected] sharpes [Q1 uncorrected]
72 s.p. Goneril Alb   **85 attaint** arrest   **86 sister** Sisters   **87 bar** [eds.] bare
100 he is hes   **105 Edmund. A herald, ho, a herald** [Q1; not in F]
106 s.p. Albany [not in F]   **112, 118** [Q1; not in F]   **132 the** my priuiledge,
The   **135 Despite** Despise   **151 scarcely** scarely   **153 s.d. Fight** [eds.]
Fights   **158 stopple** stop   **163 s.p. Goneril** Bast   **163 s.d. Exit** [at l. 162 after
"for 't" in F]   **208–225 This . . . slave** [Q1; not in F]   **217 him** [eds.] me
[Q1]   **241 s.d.** [at l. 234 in F; F reads "Gonerill"]   **262 you** your
280 s.p. Captain Gent   **282 them** him   **294 You are** [eds.] Your are [F] You'r
[Q1]   **299 s.d.** [after "to him" in l. 299 in F]

The above textual notes list all instances in which material not in F is included from Q1. To enable the reader to compare further the F and Q1 texts, a
list is here provided of material not in Q1 that is to be found in F. There are
some 100 lines in all.

1.1. 40–45 while . . . now   **49–50** Since . . . state   **64–65** and . . . rivers   **83–85** to
whose . . . interested   **88–89** LEAR Nothing? CORDELIA Nothing   **165** ALBANY, CORNWALL.
Dear sir, forbear.

1.2. 112–117 This . . . graves   **169–175** I pray . . . brother

1.4. 260 ALBANY Pray . . . patient   **273** Of . . . you   **321–333** This . . . unfitness

2.4. 6 KENT No, my lord   **21** KENT By Juno . . . ay   **45–54** FOOL Winter's . . . year
96–97 GLOUCESTER Well . . . man   **101–102** Are they . . . Fiery? The   **139–144** LEAR
Say . . . blame   **298–299** CORNWALL Whither . . . horse

3.1. 22–29 Who . . . furnishings

3.2. 79–96 FOOL This . . . time. Exit

3.4. 17–18 In . . . endure   **26–27** In . . . sleep   **37–38** Fathom . . . Tom

3.6. 12–14 FOOL No . . . him   **85** FOOL And . . . noon

4.1. 6–9 Welcome . . . blasts

4.2. 26 O, the . . . man

4.6. 165–170 Plate   lips

5.2. 11 GLOUCESTER. And . . . too

5.3. 78 Dispose . . . thine   **91** GONERIL. An interlude   **147** What . . . delay   **226** ALBANY
Speak, man   **316–317** Do you . . . look there

Shakespeare's Sources

The story of Lear goes back into ancient legend. The motif of two wicked sisters and a virtuous youngest sister reminds us of Cinderella. Lear himself appears to come from Celtic mythology. Geoffrey of Monmouth, a Welshman in close contact with Celtic legend, included a Lear or Leir as one of the pseudo-historical kings in his *Historia Regum Britanniae* (c. 1136). This fanciful mixture of history and legend traces a supposed line of descent from Brut, great-grandson of Aeneas of Troy, through Locrine, Bladud, Leir, Gorboduc, Ferrex and Porrex, Lud, Cymbeline, Bonduca, Vortigern, Arthur, to the historical kings of England. The Tudor monarchs made much of their purported claim to such an ancient dynasty, and in Shakespeare's day this mythology had a quasi-official status demanding a certain reverential suspension of disbelief.

King Leir, according to Geoffrey, is the father of three daughters, Gonorilla, Regan, and Cordeilla, among whom he intends to divide his kingdom. To determine who deserves most, he asks them who loves him most. The two eldest sisters protest undying devotion; but Cordeilla, perceiving how the others flatter and deceive him, renounces hyperbole and promises only to love him as a daughter should love a father. Furious, the King denies Cordeilla her third of the kingdom but permits her to marry Aganippus, King of the Franks, without dowry. Thereafter Leir bestows his two eldest daughters on the Dukes of Albania and Cornubia (Albany and Cornwall), together with half the island during his lifetime and the possession of the remainder after his death. In due course his two sons-in-law rebel against Leir and seize his power. Thereafter Maglaunus, Duke of Albania, agrees to maintain Leir with sixty retainers, but after two years of chafing at this arrangement Gonorilla insists that the number be reduced to thirty. Angrily the King goes to Henvin, Duke of Cornubia, where all goes well for a time; within a year, however, Regan demands that Leir reduce his retinue to five knights. When Gonorilla refuses to take him back with more than one retainer, Leir crosses into France and is generously received by Cordeilla and Aganippus. An invasion restores Leir to his throne. Three years later he and Aganippus die, after which Cordeilla rules successfully for five years until overthrown by the sons of Maglaunus and Henvin. In prison she commits suicide.

This story, as part of England's mythic genealogy, was repeated in various Tudor versions such as *The First Part of the Mirror for Magistrates* (1574), William Warner's *Albion's England* (1586), and Raphael Holinshed's *Chronicles* (second edition, 1587; see the first of the following selections). Warner refers to the King's sons-in-law as "the Prince of Albany" and "the Cornish prince"; Holinshed refers to them as "the Duke of Albania" and "the Duke of Cornwall," but reports that it is Cornwall who marries the eldest daughter Gonorilla. *The Mirror*, closer to Shakespeare in these details, speaks of "Gonerell" as married to "Albany" and of "Cordila" as married to "the King of France." Edmund Spenser's *The Faerie Queene* (2.10.27–32) reports that "Cordeill" or "Cordelia" ends her life by hanging herself. Other retellings appear in Gerard Legh's *Accidence of Armory* and William Camden's *Remains*. All of these accounts leave the story virtually unchanged.

Shakespeare's immediate source for *King Lear* was an old play called *The True Chronicle History of King Leir*. It was published in 1605 but plainly is much earlier in style. The Stationers' Register, the official record of the London Company of Stationers (booksellers and printers), for May 14, 1594, lists "A booke called the Tragecall historie of kinge Leir and his Three Daughters &c.," and a short time earlier Philip Henslowe's *Diary* records the performance of a "Kinge Leare" at the Rose Theatre on April 6 and 8, 1594. The actors were either the Queen's or the Earl of Sussex's men (two acting companies), though probably the Queen's. The play may have been written as early as 1588. George Peele, Robert Greene, Thomas Lodge, and Thomas Kyd have all been suggested as possible authors. Shakespeare probably knew the play before its publication in 1605.

This play of *Leir* ends happily, with the restoration of Leir to his throne. Essentially the play is a legendary history with a strong element of romance. (Some similarities and differences between the anonymous play and Shakespeare's *King Lear* can be seen in the second of the following selections, containing the first three scenes.) The two wicked sisters are warned of the King's plans for dividing his kingdom by an obsequious courtier named Skalliger (cf. Oswald). It is Skalliger, in fact, who proposes the idea of apportioning the kingdom in accord with the lovingness of the daughters' responses. Cordella receives the ineffectual support of an honest courtier, Perillus (cf. Kent), but is disinherited by her angry father. In subsequent scenes not included in this selection, Cordella, trusting herself to God's mercy and setting forth alone to live by her own labor, is found by the Gallian King and his bluff companion Mumford, who have come to England disguised as palmers to see if the English King's daughters are as beautiful as reported. The King hears Cordella's sad story, falls in love with her, and woos her (still wearing his disguise) in the name of the Gallian King. When she virtuously suggests the palmer woo for himself, he throws off his disguise and marries her forthwith.

Meanwhile the other sons-in-law, Cornwall and Cambria (cf. Albany), draw lots for their shares of the kingdom. Leir announces that he will sojourn with Cornwall and Gonorill first. Cornwall treats the King with genuine solicitude, but Gonorill, abetted by Skalliger, tauntingly drives her father away. The King acknowledges to his loyal companion Perillus that he has wronged Cordella. Regan, who rules her mild husband as she pleases, receives the King with seeming tenderness but secretly hires an assassin to end his life. (Gonorill is partner in this plot.) The suborned agent, frightened into remorse by a providentially sent thunderstorm, shows his intended victim the letter ordering the assassination.

The Gallian King and Cordella, who have previously sent ambassadors to Leir urging him to come to France, now decide to journey with Mumford into Britain disguised as countryfolk. Before they can do so, however, Leir and Perillus arrive in France, in mariners' garb, where they encounter Cordella and her party dressed as countryfolk. Cordella recognizes Leir's voice, and father and daughter are tearfully reunited. The Gallian King invades England and restores Leir to his throne.

Shakespeare has changed much in the narrative of his source. He discards not only the happy ending but the attempted assassination and the numerous romancelike uses of disguise (although Tom o' Bedlam, in an added plot, repeatedly uses disguise). Shakespeare eliminates the humorous Mumford and replaces Perillus with both Kent and the Fool. He turns Cornwall into a villain and Albany into a belated champion of justice. He creates the storm scene out of a mere suggestion of such an event, serving a very different purpose, in his source.

Most of all, he adds the parallel plot of Gloucester, Edgar, and Edmund. Here Shakespeare derived some of his material from Sir Philip Sidney's *Arcadia* (1590). In Book 2, chapter 10, of this greatest of all Elizabethan prose romances, presented in the third of the following selections, the two heroes Pyrocles and Musidorus encounter a son leading his blind old father. The old man tells his pitiful tale. He is the deposed King of Paphlagonia, father of a bastard son named Plexirtus who, he now bitterly realizes, turned the King against his true son Leonatus—the very son who is now his guide and guardian. The true son, having managed to escape his father's order of execution, has been forced to live poorly as a soldier, while the bastard son has proceeded to usurp his father's throne. In his wretchedness, the King has been succored by his forgiving true son and has been prevented from casting himself off the top of a hill. At the conclusion of this narrative, the villain Plexirtus arrives and attacks Leonatus; reinforcements arrive on both sides, but eventually Plexirtus is driven off, enabling the King to return to his court and bestow the crown on Leonatus. The old King thereupon dies, his heart having been stretched beyond the limits of endurance.

Other parts of the *Arcadia* may have given Shakespeare further suggestions; for example, the disguises adopted by Kent and Edgar are like those of Zelmane and Pyrocles in Sidney's prose work, and Albany's speeches about anarchy and the monstrosity that results from assaults on the rule of law recall one of Sidney's deepest concerns. Edmund is decidedly indebted to the allegorical Vice figure of the late medieval morality play tradition. For Tom o' Bedlam's mad language, Shakespeare consulted Samuel Harsnett's *Decla-*

ration of Egregious Popish Impostures, 1603. (See Kenneth
Muir's Arden edition of *King Lear*, pp. 253–256, for an ex-
tensive comparison.)

The First and Second Volumes
of Chronicles (1587 edition)
Compiled by Raphael Holinshed

VOLUME 1, THE HISTORY OF ENGLAND,
THE SECOND BOOK: LEIR, THE TENTH RULER

Leir, the son of Bladud, was admitted ruler over the Britons
in the year of the world 3105, at what time Joas reigned in
Judah. This Leir was a prince of right noble demeanor, governing his land and subjects in great wealth. He made the
town of Caerleir, now called Leicester, which standeth upon
the river of Soar. It is written that he had by his wife three
daughters, without other issue, whose names were
Gonorilla, Regan, and Cordeilla, which daughters he
greatly loved, but specially Cordeilla, the youngest, far
above the two elder. When this Leir therefore was come to
great years and began to wax unwieldy through age, he
thought to understand the affections of his daughters
towards him and prefer[1] her whom he best loved to the succession over the kingdom. Whereupon he first asked
Gonorilla, the eldest, how well she loved him; who, calling
her gods to record, protested that she loved him more than
her own life, which by right and reason should be most dear
unto her. With which answer the father, being well pleased,
turned to the second and demanded of her how well she
loved him; who answered, confirming her sayings with
great oaths, that she loved him more than tongue could express and far above all other creatures of the world.

Then called he his youngest daughter Cordeilla before
him and asked of her what account she made of him, unto
whom she made this answer as followeth: "Knowing the
great love and fatherly zeal that you have always borne
towards me, for the which I may not answer you otherwise

1 **prefer** advance

than[2] I think and as my conscience leadeth me, I protest unto you that I have loved you ever and will continually while I live love you as my natural father. And if you would more understand of the love that I bear you, ascertain[3] yourself that so much as you have, so much you are worth, and so much I love you and no more." The father, being nothing content with this answer, married his two eldest daughters, the one unto Henninus, the Duke of Cornwall, and the other unto Maglanus, the Duke of Albania, betwixt whom he willed and ordained that his land should be divided after his death, and the one half thereof immediately should be assigned to them in hand; but for the third daughter, Cordeilla, he reserved nothing.

Nevertheless it fortuned that one of the princes of Gallia (which now is called France), whose name was Aganippus, hearing of the beauty, womanhood, and good conditions of the said Cordeilla, desired to have her in marriage and sent over to her father requiring[4] that he might have her to wife; to whom answer was made that he might have his daughter, but as for any dower he could have none, for all was promised and assured to her other sisters already. Aganippus, notwithstanding this answer of denial to receive anything by way of dower with Cordeilla, took her to wife, only moved thereto (I say) for respect of her person and amiable virtues. This Aganippus was one of the twelve kings that ruled Gallia in those days, as in the British history it is recorded. But to proceed.

After that[5] Leir was fallen into age, the two dukes that had married his two eldest daughters, thinking it long ere the government of the land did come to their hands, arose against him in armor and reft[6] from him the governance of the land upon conditions to be continued for term of life, by the which he was put to his portion, that is, to live after a rate assigned to him for the maintenance of his estate, which in process of time was diminished as well by Maglanus as by Henninus. But the greatest grief that Leir took was to see the unkindness[7] of his daughters, which[8] seemed to think that all was too much which their father

2 than than as   3 ascertain assure   4 requiring requesting   5 After
that after   6 reft stripped, took   7 unkindness (with meaning also of
"unnaturalness")   8 which who

had, the same being never so little; insomuch that, going
from the one to the other, he was brought to that misery
that scarcely they would allow him one servant to wait
upon him.

In the end, such was the unkindness or (as I may say) the
unnaturalness which he found in his two daughters, notwithstanding their fair and pleasant words uttered in time
past, that, being constrained of necessity, he fled the land
and sailed into Gallia, there to seek some comfort of his
youngest daughter Cordeilla whom beforetime he hated.
The Lady Cordeilla, hearing that he was arrived in poor estate, she first sent to him privily[9] a certain sum of money to
apparel himself withal[10] and to retain a certain number of
servants that might attend upon him in honorable wise, as
appertained to the estate which he had borne. And then, so
accompanied,[11] she appointed him[12] to come to the court,
which he did, and was so joyfully, honorably, and lovingly
received, both by his son-in-law Aganippus and also by his
daughter Cordeilla, that his heart was greatly comforted,
for he was no less honored than if he had been king of the
whole country himself.

Now, when he had informed his son-in-law and his daughter in what sort he had been used by his other daughters,
Aganippus caused a mighty army to be put in a readiness,
and likewise a great navy of ships to be rigged, to pass over
into Britain with Leir, his father-in-law, to see him again
restored to his kingdom. It was accorded that Cordeilla
should also go with him to take possession of the land, the
which he promised to leave unto her as the rightful inheritor after his decease, notwithstanding any former grant
made to her sisters or to their husbands in any manner of
wise.

Hereupon, when this army and navy of ships were ready,
Leir and his daughter Cordeilla with her husband took the
sea and, arriving in Britain, fought with their enemies and
discomfited[13] them in battle, in the which Maglanus and
Henninus were slain. And then was Leir restored to his
kingdom, which he ruled after this by the space of two

9 privily secretly   **10 withal** with   **11 so accompanied** he being so
accompanied   **12 appointed him** arranged for him   **13 discomfited**
overthrew

years, and then died, forty years after he first began to reign. His body was buried at Leicester, in a vault under the channel of the river of Soar, beneath the town.

THE GUNARCHY[14] OF QUEEN CORDEILLA

Cordeilla, the youngest daughter of Leir, was admitted Queen and supreme Governess of Britain in the year of the world 3155, before the building of Rome 54,[15] Uzia then reigning in Judah and Jeroboam over Israel. This Cordeilla, after her father's decease, ruled the land of Britain right worthily during the space of five years, in which meantime her husband died; and then, about the end of those five years, her two nephews Margan and Cunedag, sons to her aforesaid sisters, disdaining to be under the government of a woman, levied war against her and destroyed a great part of the land, and finally took her prisoner and laid her fast in ward,[16] wherewith she took such grief, being a woman of a manly courage, and despairing to recover liberty, there she slew herself, when she had reigned (as before is mentioned) the term of five years.

The second edition of Raphael Holinshed's *Chronicles* was published in 1587. This selection is based on that edition, Volume 1, The History of England, folios 12–13.

---

14 Gunarchy government by a woman ruler   **15 3155, 54** (The beginning of Cordeilla's reign is reckoned to be 3155 years after God's creation of the world as recorded in Genesis and 54 years before the building of Rome, or c. 822–817 B.C. *Jeroboam* did actually reign over Israel c. 931.) **16 ward** prison

The True Chronicle History of King Leir and His Three Daughters

[*Dramatis Personae*

LEIR, *King of Brittany*
GONORILL,
RAGAN,   } *daughters of Leir*
CORDELLA,
KING OF GALLIA
KING OF CORNWALL
KING OF CAMBRIA
PERILLUS, *a nobleman*
MUMFORD, *a knight*
SKALLIGER, *a courtier*
A LORD
A MESSENGER
THE GALLIAN AMBASSADOR

Nobles, Mariners, Captains, Watchmen, Attendants, Soldiers,
    etc.

SCENE: *Brittany and Gallia*]

1.1   *Enter King Leir and Nobles.*

LEIR
    Thus to our grief the obsequies performed   1
    Of our too late deceased and dearest queen,   2
    Whose soul, I hope, possessed of heavenly joys
    Doth ride in triumph 'mongst the cherubins,
    Let us request your grave advice, my lords,
    For the disposing of our princely daughters,   6
    For whom our care is specially employed,
    As nature bindeth, to advance their states   8
    In royal marriage with some princely mates.

1.1. Location: The court of Britain.
1 performed having been performed   **2 our** i.e., my. (The royal plural.)   **too late** all too recently   **6 For** about   **8 bindeth** ties with obligations of family feeling.   **states** estates

For, wanting now their mother's good advice,   10
Under whose government they have received
A perfect pattern of a virtuous life,
Left as it were a ship without a stern   13
Or silly sheep without a pastor's care,   14
Although ourselves do dearly tender them,   15
Yet are we ignorant of their affairs.
For fathers best do know to govern sons,
But daughters' steps the mother's counsel turns.   18
A son we want for to succeed our crown,   19
And course of time hath cancellèd the date   20
Of further issue from our withered loins;   21
One foot already hangeth in the grave,
And age hath made deep furrows in my face.
The world of me, I of the world, am weary,
And I would fain resign these earthly cares   25
And think upon the welfare of my soul,
Which by no better means may be effected
Than by resigning up the crown from me
In equal dowry to my daughters three.

SKALLIGER

A worthy care, my liege, which well declares
The zeal you bare unto our quondam queen.   31
And since Your Grace hath licensed me to speak,
I censure thus: Your Majesty, knowing well   33
What several suitors your princely daughters have,   34
To make them each a jointure, more or less   35
As is their worth, to them that love profess.

LEIR

No more nor less, but even all alike
My zeal is fixed, all fashioned in one mold.
Wherefore unpartial shall my censure be?   39
Both old and young shall have alike for me.

A NOBLE

My gracious lord, I heartily do wish

---

10 wanting lacking   **13 stern** rudder and helm   **14 silly** innocent
15 tender cherish   **18 turns** directs   **19 want for to succeed** lack to
inherit   **20 date** season, period of time   **21 further issue** any more
children   **25 fain** gladly   **31 bare** bore.   **quondam** former   **33 censure**
pronounce judgment   **33–35 Your Majesty . . . To make** that Your
Majesty . . . make   **34 several** various   **35 jointure** dowry; property for
the joint use of husband and wife   **39 censure** judgment

That God had lent you an heir indubitate   42
Which might have set upon your royal throne
When fates should loose the prison of your life,   44
By whose succession all this doubt might cease,
And, as by you, by him we might have peace.
But after-wishes ever come too late,
And nothing can revoke the course of fate.
Wherefore, my liege, my censure deems it best
To match them with some of your neighbor kings
Bordering within the bounds of Albion,   51
By whose united friendship this our state
May be protected 'gainst all foreign hate.

LEIR

Herein, my lords, your wishes sort with mine,   54
And mine, I hope, do sort with heavenly powers.
For at this instant two near neighboring kings,
Of Cornwall and of Cambria, motion love   57
To my two daughters, Gonorill and Ragan.
My youngest daughter, fair Cordella, vows
No liking to a monarch unless love allows.
She is solicited by divers peers,
But none of them her partial fancy hears.   62
Yet if my policy may her beguile,   63
I'll match her to some king within this isle,
And so establish such a perfect peace
As fortune's force shall ne'er prevail to cease.   66

PERILLUS

Of us and ours, your gracious care, my lord,   67
Deserves an everlasting memory,   68
To be enrolled in chronicles of fame
By never-dying perpetuity.   70
Yet to become so provident a prince,
Lose not the title of a loving father.

---

42 indubitate undoubted, certain **44 When . . . life** i.e., when the Fates,
the three sisters of destiny, should set loose your soul from the prison
of your body **51 Albion** England **54 sort** accord **57 Cambria** i.e., the
mountainous area of Wales. (Shakespeare's equivalent character is the
Duke of Albany, in Scotland.) **motion** propose **62 partial fancy** incli-
nation in love **63 policy may her beguile** plan can win her over **66 As**
that. **to cease** i.e., to end this peace **67–68 Of . . . memory** your
gracious care of your kingdom, my lord, deserves from us and our
posterity an everlasting remembrance **70 By** i.e., in

Do not force love where fancy cannot dwell,   73
Lest streams, being stopped, above the banks do swell. 74
LEIR
I am resolved, and even now my mind
Doth meditate a sudden stratagem
To try which of my daughters loves me best,
Which, till I know, I cannot be in rest.
This granted, when they jointly shall contend   79
Each to exceed the other in their love,
Then at the vantage will I take Cordella: 81
Even as she doth protest she loves me best,
I'll say, "Then, daughter, grant me one request.
To show thou lovest me as thy sisters do,
Accept a husband, whom myself will woo."   85
This said, she cannot well deny my suit,
Although, poor soul, her senses will be mute.   87
Then will I triumph in my policy
And match her with a king of Brittany.
SKALLIGER [Aside]
I'll to them before and bewray your secrecy.   90
                    [Exeunt all but Perillus.]

PERILLUS
Thus fathers think their children to beguile,
And oftentimes themselves do first repent
When heavenly powers do frustrate their intent. Exit.

❖

1.2   *Enter Gonorill and Ragan.*

GONORILL
I marvel, Ragan, how you can endure
To see that proud pert peat, our youngest sister,   2
So slightly to account of us, her elders,   3

---

73 fancy love   **74 stopped** dammed up   **79 This granted** this having
been undertaken   **81 at the vantage** with this advantage or superior
position.   **take** (As in a game of chess.)   **85 woo** solicit for marriage
(with Cordella)   **87 her senses . . . mute** i.e., she will be stricken silent
90 I'll . . . secrecy i.e., I'll go first to Gonorill and Ragan and reveal your
confidential plan

1.2. Location: The court of Britain.
2 peat spoiled girl   **3 account of** esteem, value

As if we were no better than herself!
We cannot have a quaint device so soon,   5
Or new-made fashion of our choice invention,   6
But, if she like it, she will have the same,
Or study newer to exceed us both.   8
Besides, she is so nice and so demure,   9
So sober, courteous, modest, and precise,   10
That all the court hath work enough to do
To talk how she exceedeth me and you.

RAGAN
What should I do? Would it were in my power
To find a cure for this contagious ill!
Some desperate medicine must be soon applied
To dim the glory of her mounting fame;
Else, ere 't be long, she'll have both prick and praise,   17
And we must be set by for working days.   18
Do you not see what several choice of suitors   19
She daily hath, and of the best degree?
Say, amongst all, she hap to fancy one   21
And have a husband whenas we have none.   22
Why, then, by right to her we must give place,
Though it be ne'er so much to our disgrace.

GONORILL
By my virginity, rather than she shall have
A husband before me,
I'll marry one or other in his shirt!   27
And yet I have made half a grant already
Of my good will unto the King of Cornwall.

RAGAN   Swear not so deeply, sister. Here cometh my lord
Skalliger.
Something his hasty coming doth import.   32

    Enter Skalliger.

---

5 We . . . soon we no sooner have something (clothing, jewelry, etc.) that
is artistically or ingeniously devised   **6 of our choice invention** of our
own well-chosen devising   **8 study newer** i.e., apply her mind to divis-
ing newer fashions   **9 nice** fastidious, refined   **10 precise** scrupulous
17 prick and praise success and its acknowledgment   **18 set by . . . days**
i.e., treated as ordinary creatures for everyday use   **19 several** various
21 Say suppose.   **hap to fancy** happen to love   **22 whenas** when,
whereas   **27 in his shirt** i.e., half unready, in great haste   **32 import**
signify

SKALLIGER
    Sweet princesses, I am glad I met you here so luckily,
    Having good news which doth concern you both
    And craveth speedy expedition.   35
RAGAN
    For God's sake, tell us what it is, my lord.
    I am with child until you utter it.   37
SKALLIGER
    Madam, to save your longing, this it is:
    Your father in great secrecy today
    Told me he means to marry you out of hand   40
    Unto the noble Prince of Cambria;
    [To Gonorill] You, madam, to the King of Cornwall's
        Grace.
    Your younger sister he would fain bestow
    Upon the rich King of Hibernia,   44
    But that he doubts she hardly will consent,
    For hitherto she ne'er could fancy him.
    If she do yield, why then, between you three
    He will divide his kingdom for your dowries.
    But yet there is further mystery,
    Which, so you will conceal, I will disclose.   50
GONORILL
    Whate'er thou speak'st to us, kind Skalliger,
    Think that thou speak'st it only to thyself.
SKALLIGER
    He earnestly desireth for to know   53
    Which of you three do bear most love to him,
    And on your loves he so extremely dotes
    As never any did, I think, before.
    He presently doth mean to send for you   57
    To be resolved of this tormenting doubt;
    And look whose answer pleaseth him the best,   59
    They shall have most unto their marriages.
RAGAN
    O, that I had some pleasing mermaid's voice
    For to enchant his senseless senses with!   62

35 **expedition** speed   37 **with child** i.e., eager, yearning (to know)
40 **out of hand** at once   44 **Hibernia** Ireland   50 **so** provided   53 **for
to know** to know   57 **presently** immediately   59 **look whose answer**
whoever it is whose answer   62 **For to** to.   **senseless** incapable of
sensation (owing to old age)

SKALLIGER
　For he supposeth that Cordella will,
　Striving to go beyond you in her love,
　Promise to do whatever he desires.
　Then will he straight enjoin her for his sake　　　66
　The Hibernian King in marriage for to take.
　This is the sum of all I have to say,
　Which being done, I humbly take my leave,
　Not doubting but your wisdoms will foresee
　What course will best unto your good agree.　　　71
GONORILL
　Thanks, gentle Skalliger. Thy kindness, undeserved,
　Shall not be unrequited if we live.　　　*Exit Skalliger.*
RAGAN
　Now have we fit occasion offered us
　To be revenged upon her unperceived.
GONORILL
　Nay, our revenge we will inflict on her
　Shall be accounted piety in us.
　I will so flatter with my doting father　　　78
　As he was ne'er so flattered in his life.
　Nay, I will say that if it be his pleasure
　To match me to a beggar, I will yield,
　Forwhy I know whatever I do say　　　82
　He means to match me with the Cornwall King.
RAGAN
　I'll say the like, for I am well assured,
　What e'er I say to please the old man's mind,
　Who dotes as if he were a child again,
　I shall enjoy the noble Cambrian prince.
　Only to feed his humor will suffice　　　88
　To say I am content with anyone
　Whom he'll appoint me; this will please him more
　Than e'er Apollo's music pleasèd Jove.
GONORILL
　I smile to think in what a woeful plight

---

66 straight at once　**71 agree** serve　**78 flatter with** speak flatteringly
to, fawn upon　**82 Forwhy** because.　**whatever I do say** i.e., whatever I
say of a flattering kind, however I vary my outrageous flattery. (Compare Ragan in l. 85.)　**88 Only . . . suffice** it will suffice to feed his
whimsical mood

Cordella will be when we answer thus,
For she will rather die than give consent
To join in marriage with the Irish King.
So will our father think she loveth him not,
Because she will not grant to his desire,
Which we will aggravate in such bitter terms
That he will soon convert his love to hate.
For he, you know, is always in extremes.

RAGAN
Not all the world could lay a better plot.
I long till it be put in practice.   *'Exeunt.*

❖

1.3   *Enter Leir and Perillus.*

LEIR   Perillus, go seek my daughters.
  Will them immediately come and speak with me.
PERILLUS   I will, my gracious lord.   *Exit.*
LEIR
  O, what a combat feels my panting heart
  Twixt children's love and care of commonweal!
  How dear my daughters are unto my soul
  None knows but he that knows my thoughts and secret
    deeds.
  Ah, little do they know the dear regard
  Wherein I hold their future state to come!
  When they securely sleep on beds of down,
  These aged eyes do watch for their behalf.   11
  While they like wantons sport in youthful toys,   12
  This throbbing heart is pierced with dire annoys.   13
  As doth the sun exceed the smallest star,
  So much the father's love exceeds the child's.
  Yet my complaints are causeless, for the world
  Affords not children more conformable.   17
  And yet methinks my mind presageth still
  I know not what; and yet I fear some ill.

1.3. Location: The court of Britain.
11 watch for stay awake on   **12 While . . . toys** while they, like pampered children, frolic in idle youthful pastimes   **13 annoys** vexations
17 conformable tractable, submissive

Enter Perillus, with the three daughters.

Well, here my daughters come. I have found out
A present means to rid me of this doubt.

GONORILL

Our royal lord and father, in all duty
We come to know the tenor of your will,
Why you so hastily have sent for us.

LEIR

Dear Gonorill, kind Ragan, sweet Cordella,
Ye flourishing branches of a kingly stock
Sprung from a tree that once did flourish green,
Whose blossoms now are nipped with winter's frost,
And pale grim Death doth wait upon my steps
And summons me unto his next assizes.   30
Therefore, dear daughters, as ye tender the safety
Of him that was the cause of your first being,
Resolve a doubt which much molests my mind:
Which of you three to me would prove most kind,
Which loves me most, and which at my request
Will soonest yield unto their father's hest.   36

GONORILL

I hope, my gracious father makes no doubt
Of any of his daughters' love to him.
Yet for my part, to show my zeal to you,
Which cannot be in windy words rehearsed,   40
I prize my love to you at such a rate
I think my life inferior to my love.
Should you enjoin me for to tie a millstone
About my neck and leap into the sea,
At your command I willingly would do it.
Yea, for to do you good I would ascend
The highest turret in all Brittany
And from the top leap headlong to the ground.
Nay, more, should you appoint me for to marry   49
The meanest vassal in the spacious world,   50
Without reply I would accomplish it.
In brief, command whatever you desire,
And, if I fail, no favor I require.

---

30 assizes court session   **36 hest** behest   **40 rehearsed** recited, told
49 appoint me arrange for me   **50 meanest** most lowly born

LEIR

O, how thy words revive my dying soul!

CORDELLA [*Aside*]

O, how I do abhor this flattery!

LEIR

But what saith Ragan to her father's will?

RAGAN

O, that my simple utterance could suffice
To tell the true intention of my heart,
Which burns in zeal of duty to Your Grace
And never can be quenched but by desire   60
To show the same in outward forwardness!   61
O, that there were some other maid that durst
But make a challenge of her love with me!
I'd make her soon confess she never loved
Her father half so well as I do you.
Ay, then my deeds should prove in plainer case
How much my zeal aboundeth to Your Grace.
But for them all, let this one mean suffice   68
To ratify my love before your eyes:
I have right noble suitors to my love,
No worse than kings, and happily I love one;
Yet, would you have me make my choice anew,
I'd bridle fancy and be ruled by you.

LEIR

Did never Philomel sing so sweet a note.   74

CORDELLA [*Aside*]

Did never flatterer tell so false a tale.

LEIR

Speak now, Cordella. Make my joys at full
And drop down nectar from thy honey lips.

CORDELLA

I cannot paint my duty forth in words.
I hope my deeds shall make report for me.
But look what love the child doth owe the father,   80
The same to you I bear, my gracious lord.

60–61 And never . . . forwardness and can be quenched only by contin-
ual striving to display my ardent love in openly displayed zeal and
attentiveness **68 for them all** to stand for all my zealous deeds. **let
this one mean** let this humble and insufficient one **74 Philomel** the
nightingale **80 look what** whatever

GONORILL
Here is an answer answerless indeed.
Were you my daughter, I should scarcely brook it.   83

RAGAN
Dost thou not blush, proud peacock as thou art,
To make our father such a slight reply?

LEIR
Why how now, minion, are you grown so proud?
Doth our dear love make you thus peremptory?
What, is your love become so small to us
As that you scorn to tell us what it is?
Do you love us as every child doth love
Their father? True indeed, as some
Who by disobedience short their father's days,   92
And so would you. Some are so father-sick
That they make means to rid them from the world,
And so would you. Some are indifferent
Whether their aged parents live or die,
And so are you. But didst thou know, proud girl,
What care I had to foster thee to this,
Ah, then thou wouldst say as thy sisters do.
Our life is less than love we owe to you.   100

CORDELLA
Dear Father, do not so mistake my words
Nor my plain meaning be misconstrued.   102
My tongue was never used to flattery.

GONORILL
You were not best say I flatter. If you do,   104
My deeds shall show I flatter not with you.   105
I love my father better than thou canst.

CORDELLA
The praise were great, spoke from another's mouth;   107
But it should seem your neighbors dwell far off.   108

---

83 **brook** endure   92 **short** shorten   100 **Our life . . . to you** i.e., my very
life cannot equal the sum of the love I owe to you   102 **Nor** i.e., nor
let   104 **You were not best say** you had better not say. (Perhaps the text
should read, *You were best not say.*)   105 **I flatter not with you** I do not
flatter as you do   107 **The praise . . . mouth** that would be great praise
indeed if spoken by another (i.e., by one who could speak sincerely)
108 **But . . . far off** i.e., but it's obvious that you have no near competi-
tors in this business of flattery

RAGAN

    Nay, here is one that will confirm as much
    As she hath said, both for myself and her.
    I say thou dost not wish my father's good.

CORDELLA   Dear Father—

LEIR

    Peace, bastard imp, no issue of King Leir!
    I will not hear thee speak one tittle more.   114
    Call not me father, if thou love thy life,
    Nor these thy sisters once presume to name.   116
    Look for no help henceforth from me nor mine;
    Shift as thou wilt and trust unto thyself.   118
    My kingdom will I equally divide
    Twixt thy two sisters to their royal dower,   120
    And will bestow them worthy their deserts.   121
    This done, because thou shalt not have the hope   122
    To have a child's part in the time to come,
    I presently will dispossess myself   124
    And set up these upon my princely throne.

GONORILL

    I ever thought that pride would have a fall.

RAGAN

    Plain-dealing sister, your beauty is so sheen   127
    You need no dowry to make you be a queen.
                           Exeunt Leir, Gonorill, Ragan.

CORDELLA

    Now whither, poor forsaken, shall I go
    When mine own sisters triumph in my woe
    But unto Him which doth protect the just?
    In Him will poor Cordella put her trust.
    These hands shall labor for to get my spending,   133
    And so I'll live until my days have ending.   [*Exit*].

PERILLUS

    O, how I grieve to see my lord thus fond   135
    To dote so much upon vain flattering words!

---

109 here is one that i.e., I too am one who   **114 tittle** bit   **116 Nor . . . name** i.e., nor presume to claim a sisterly relationship to Gonorill and Ragan   **118 Shift** manage, get on   **120 to** as   **121 bestow them** i.e., settle them in marriages   **122 because** so that   **124 presently** at once   **127 sheen** fair, beautiful. (Cf. German *schön*.)   **133 for to get my spending** to earn my livelihood   **135 fond** foolish

Ah, if he but with good advice had weighed   137
The hidden tenor of her humble speech,
Reason to rage should not have given place
Nor poor Cordella suffer such disgrace.   *Exit.*

Text based on *The True Chronicle History of King Leir and His Three Daughters, Gonorill, Ragan, and Cordella. As it hath been divers and sundry times lately acted. London: Printed by Simon Stafford for John Wright. . . . 1605.*

In the following, the departure from the original text appears in boldface; the original reading is in roman.

1.1. 93 s.d. **Exit** Exeunt

Arcadia (1590)
By Sir Philip Sidney
BOOK 2, CHAPTER 10

The pitiful state and story of the Paphlagonian unkind[1] King and his kind son, first related by the son, then by the blind father.

It was in the kingdom of Galatia, the season being, as in the depth of winter, very cold, and as then suddenly grown to so extreme and foul a storm that never any winter, I think, brought forth a fouler child; so that the princes[2] were even compelled by the hail that the pride[3] of the wind blew into their faces to seek some shrouding place within.[4] A certain hollow rock offering it[5] unto them, they made it their shield

---

137 **advice** wisdom

1 **unkind** (With meaning also of "unnatural")   2 **the princes** i.e., Pyrocles and Mucidorus, son and nephew of the King of Macedon, gallant knights and close friends, whose shipwreck and subsequent adventures in Arcadia form the main plot of *Arcadia*. (The present story is a digression from the main narrative.)   3 **pride** imperiousness   4 **shrouding place within** shelter out of the storm   5 **it** itself

against the tempest's fury. And so, staying there till the violence thereof was past, they heard the speech of a couple[6] who, not perceiving them (being hid[7] within that rude canopy), held a strange and pitiful disputation, which made them step out,[8] yet in such sort as they might see unseen.

There they perceived an aged man and a young scarcely come to the age of a man, both poorly arrayed, extremely weather-beaten; the old man blind, the young man leading him. And yet through all those miseries, in both these[9] seemed to appear a kind of nobleness not suitable[10] to that affliction. But the first words they heard were these of the old man.

"Well, Leonatus," said he, "since I cannot persuade thee to lead me to that which should end my grief and thy trouble,[11] let me now entreat thee to leave me. Fear not; my misery cannot be greater than it is, and nothing doth become me[12] but misery. Fear not the danger of my blind steps. I cannot fall worse than I am. And do not, I pray thee, do not obstinately continue to infect thee[13] with my wretchedness. But fly, fly from this region only worthy of me."[14]

"Dear Father," answered he, "do not take away from me the only remnant of my happiness! While I have power to do you service, I am not wholly miserable."

"Ah, my son," said he, and with that he groaned as if sorrow strave to break his heart, "how evil fits it me[15] to have such a son, and how much doth thy kindness upbraid my wickedness!"

These doleful speeches and some others to like purpose, well showing they had not been born to the fortune they were in, moved the princes to go out unto them and ask the younger what[16] they were.

"Sirs," answered he with a good grace, and made the more agreeable by a certain noble kind of piteousness, "I see well you are strangers that know not our misery, so well

---

6 a couple i.e., two men   **7 being hid** i.e., the princes being hid   **8 them step out** i.e., the princes leave their shelter somewhat   **9 both these** both of them   **10 suitable** corresponding. (Their noble bearing seemed well above their wretched appearance.)   **11 to that which . . . trouble** i.e., to my suicide   **12 become me** suit me (in my present sad condition)   **13 thee** thyself   **14 only worthy of me** worthy only of (wretched) me   **15 how evil fits it me** i.e., how little do I deserve   **16 what** who

here known that no man dare know but that we must be miserable.[17] Indeed our state is such as though nothing is so needful unto us as pity, yet nothing is more dangerous unto us than to make ourselves so known as may stir pity. But your presence promiseth that cruelty shall not overrun hate.[18] And if it did,[19] in truth our state is sunk below the degree of fear.

"This old man whom I lead was lately rightful prince of this country of Paphlagonia, by the hard-hearted ungratefulness of a son of his deprived[20] not only of his kingdom (whereof no foreign forces were ever able to spoil[21] him) but of his sight, the riches which Nature grants to the poorest creatures. Whereby, and by other his[22] unnatural dealings, he hath been driven to such grief as even now he would have had me to have led him to the top of this rock, thence to cast himself headlong to death. And so would have made me, who received my life of him, to be the worker of his destruction. But, noble gentlemen," said he, "if either of you have a father and feel what dutiful affection is engraffed[23] in a son's heart, let me entreat you to convey this afflicted prince to some place of rest and security. Amongst your worthy acts it shall be none of the least that a king of such might and fame, and so unjustly oppressed, is in any sort by you relieved."

But before they could make him answer, his father began to speak. "Ah, my son," said he, "how evil an historian are you, that leave out the chief knot of all the discourse: my wickedness, my wickedness! And if thou dost it to spare my ears, the only sense now left me proper for knowledge,[24] assure thyself thou dost mistake me. And I take witness of that sun which you see"—with that he cast up his blind eyes as if he would hunt for light—"and wish myself in worse case than I do wish myself, which is as evil as may be, if I speak untruly: that nothing is so welcome to my thoughts as the publishing of my shame.

17 that no man . . . miserable i.e., that no one dare inquire about us (as fugitives from justice) other than to know we are wretched   **18 that cruelty . . . hate** i.e., that you will not cruelly turn against us in your hatred of what you must hear   **19 if it did** i.e., even if you did **20 by . . . deprived** i.e., who, by . . . was deprived   **21 spoil** despoil, plunder   **22 other his** his other, the ungrateful son's other **23 engraffed** engrafted   **24 proper for knowledge** suited to the acquiring of knowledge

"Therefore know you, gentlemen, to whom from my heart I wish that it may not prove ominous foretoken of misfortune to have met with such a miser[25] as I am, that whatsoever my son (O God, that truth binds me to reproach him with the name of my son!) hath said is true. But besides those truths this also is true: that, having had[26] in lawful marriage, of a mother fit to bear royal children, this son[27] (such one as partly you see and better shall know by my short declaration),[28] and so enjoyed the expectations in the world of him[29] till he was grown to justify their expectations, so as[30] I needed envy no father for the chief comfort of mortality to leave another oneself after me,[31] I was carried[32] by a bastard son of mine (if at least I be bound to believe[33] the words of that base woman my concubine, his mother) first to mislike, then to hate, lastly to destroy, to do my best to destroy, this son I think you think undeserving[34] destruction.

"What ways he used to bring me to it, if I should tell you, I should tediously trouble you with as much poisonous hypocrisy, desperate fraud, smooth malice, hidden ambition, and smiling envy as in any living person could be harbored. But I list it not.[35] No remembrance—no, of naughtiness[36]— delights me but mine own, and methinks the accusing his trains[37] might in some manner excuse my fault, which certainly I loathe to do. But the conclusion is that I gave order to some servants of mine, whom I thought as apt for such charities[38] as myself, to lead him out into a forest and there to kill him.

"But those thieves, better natured to my son than myself,

---

25 miser miserable, wretched person **26 had** begotten, sired **27 of a mother . . . son** this son, the child of a mother worthy to bear royal children **28 better . . . declaration** shall know better soon by my story **29 and so enjoyed . . . of him** i.e., and took such pleasure in people's high hopes for his success **30 was grown . . . so as** had grown up justifying everyone's expectations so fully that **31 for the chief . . . after me** i.e., as to the chief comfort a man has in the face of death, that of leaving an image of himself behind **32 carried** influenced, swayed **33 to believe** i.e., to believe that this bastard was mine and not some other man's **34 I think you think undeserving** whom I believe you must consider undeserving of **35 list it not** do not wish to do that **36 no, of naughtiness** no, not of any conceivable wickedness whatsoever **37 trains** treachery **38 charities** charitable, loving deeds. (Said with deep irony.)

spared his life, letting him go to learn to live poorly; which he did, giving himself to be[39] a private soldier in a country hereby.[40] But as he was ready to be greatly advanced for some noble pieces of service which he did, he heard news of me—who, drunk in my affection to that unlawful and unnatural son of mine, suffered[41] myself so to be governed by him that all favors and punishments passed by him, all offices and places of importance distributed to his favorites; so that, ere I was aware, I had left myself nothing but the name of a king. Which he shortly weary of too,[42] with many indignities (if anything may be called an indignity[43] which was laid upon me) threw me out of my seat[44] and put out my eyes; and then, proud in his tyranny, let me go, neither imprisoning nor killing me, but rather delighting to make me feel my misery. Misery indeed, if ever there were any! Full of wretchedness, fuller of disgrace, and fullest of guiltiness.

"And as he came to the crown by so unjust means, as unjustly he kept it, by force of stranger[45] soldiers in citadels, the nests of tyranny and murderers of liberty, disarming all his own countrymen, that no man durst show himself a well-willer of mine—to say the truth I think few of them being so, considering my cruel folly to my good son and foolish kindness to my unkind bastard. But if there were any who fell to pity of so great a fall and had yet any sparks of unstained duty left in them towards me, yet durst they not show it, scarcely with giving me alms at their doors—which yet was the only sustenance of my distressed life, nobody daring to show so much charity as to lend me a hand to guide my dark steps.

"Till this son of mine (God knows, worthy of a more virtuous and more fortunate father), forgetting my abominable wrongs, not recking[46] danger, and neglecting the present good way he was in doing himself good, came hither to do this kind office you see him perform towards me, to my un-

---

39 giving himself to be enlisting as   **40 hereby** nearby   **41 suffered** allowed   **42 Which he ... too** i.e., and he, the bastard, soon impatient with my having even that   **43 may ... an indignity** (The old King considers himself deserving of every punishment, so that no affliction laid on him can properly be called an *indignity* or undeserved blow.)   **44 seat** throne   **45 stranger** foreign (and mercenary)   **46 recking** heeding

speakable grief—not only because his kindness is a glass[47] even to my blind eyes of my naughtiness,[48] but that above all griefs it grieves me he should desperately adventure the loss of his soul-deserving life for mine, that yet owe more to fortune for my deserts,[49] as if he would carry mud in a chest[50] of crystal. For well I know, he that now reigneth, how much soever (and with good reason) he despiseth me, of all men despised,[51] yet he will not let slip any advantage to make away him whose just title, ennobled by courage and goodness,[52] may one day shake the seat of a never secure tyranny.

"And for this cause I craved of him to lead me to the top of this rock, indeed, I must confess, with meaning[53] to free him from so serpentine[54] a companion as I am. But he, finding what I purposed, only therein since[55] he was born showed himself disobedient unto me. And now, gentlemen, you have the true story, which I pray you publish to the world, that my mischievous[56] proceedings may be the glory of his filial piety, the only reward now left for so great a merit. And if it may be, let me obtain that of you which my son denies me.[57] For never was there more pity in saving any than in ending me,[58] both because therein my agonies shall end, and so shall you preserve this excellent young man who else willfully follows his own ruin."

The matter, in itself lamentable, lamentably expressed by the old prince (which[59] needed not take to himself[60] the gestures of pity, since his face could not put off[61] the marks thereof) greatly moved the two princes to compassion,

---

47 glass mirror   **48 naughtiness** wickedness   **49 that yet . . . deserts** I who must repay still more to fortune for my wicked deservings (and am likely therefore to poison my virtuous son's life with my evil fortune) **50 chest** coffer to contain valuables   **51 of all men despised** I who am despised by one and all   **52 ennobled . . . goodness** i.e., strengthened by the virtuous qualities of my son. (The bastard mercilessly kicked his blind father out of doors, contemptuously allowing him to live in wretchedness, but now that the father is joined by his son and legitimate heir to the crown he is a threat.)   **53 meaning** intention **54 serpentine** i.e., wicked   **55 only therein since** for the first time since **56 mischievous** wicked, poisonous   **57 obtain . . . me** obtain by your means that which my son denies me, i.e., the chance to kill myself **58 For . . . ending me** i.e., allowing me to die will be a more pitying and charitable act than the saving of someone else   **59 which** who   **60 take to himself** adopt, put on   **61 put off** efface, conceal

which could not stay in such hearts as theirs without seeking remedy. But by and by the occasion was presented. For Plexirtus (so was the bastard called) came thither with forty horse, only of purpose[62] to murder this brother; of whose coming he had soon advertisement,[63] and thought no eyes of sufficient credit[64] in such a matter but his own, and therefore came himself to be actor and spectator.

And as soon as he came, not regarding[65] the weak (as he thought) guard of but two men, commanded[66] some of his followers to set their hands to his[67] in the killing of Leonatus. But the young Prince, though not otherwise armed but with a sword, how falsely soever he was dealt with by others, would not betray himself;[68] but bravely drawing it[69] out, made the death of the first that assaulted him warn[70] his fellows to come more warily after him. But then Pyrocles and Musidorus were quickly become parties[71] (so just a defense deserving as much as old friendship) and so did behave them among that company (more injurious[72] than valiant) that many of them lost their lives for their wicked master.

Yet perhaps had the number of them at last prevailed if the King of Pontus (lately by them[73] made so) had not come unlooked-for to their succor. Who, having had a dream which had fixed his imagination vehemently upon some great danger presently[74] to follow those two Princes whom he most dearly loved, was come in all haste, following as well as he could their track with a hundred horses[75] in that country, which he thought (considering who then reigned) a fit place enough to make the stage[76] of any tragedy.

But then the match had been so ill made for Plexirtus that his ill-led life and worse-gotten honor should have tumbled together to destruction, had there not come in Tydeus and

---

62 horse, only of purpose horsemen, solely in order   **63 he had soon advertisement** i.e., Leonatus soon had warning, notice   **64 of sufficient credit** worthy to be believed   **65 not regarding** not having a proper respect or fear for   **66 commanded** he commanded   **67 set . . . to his** give him a helping hand   **68 betray himself** i.e., behave in cowardly fashion   **69 it** i.e., his sword   **70 warn** i.e., give warning to   **71 were . . . parties** quickly became participants   **72 injurious** intent on inflicting wrongful injury   **73 lately by them** i.e., recently by Musidorus and Pyrocles   **74 presently** immediately   **75 horses** horsemen   **76 stage** place where an action occurs

Telenor, with forty or fifty in their suit,[77] to the defense of
Plexirtus. These two were brothers of the noblest house
of that country, brought up from their infancy with
Plexirtus—men of such prowess as not to know fear in
themselves and yet to teach it others that should deal with
them. For they had often made their lives triumph over
most terrible dangers, never dismayed and ever fortunate,
and truly no more settled[78] in their valor than disposed to
goodness and justice, if either they had lighted on a better
friend or could have learned to make friendship a child and
not the father of virtue.[79] But bringing up rather than
choice[80] having first knit their minds unto him (indeed
crafty enough[81] either to hide his faults or never to show
them but when they might pay home),[82] they willingly held
out the course[83] rather to satisfy him than all the world, and
rather to be good friends than good men. So as[84] though
they did not like the evil he did, yet they liked him that did
the evil, and though not councilors of the offense, yet pro-
tectors of the offender.

Now they, having heard of this sudden going out[85] with so
small a company, in a country full of evil-wishing minds
toward him (though they knew not the cause), followed him,
till they found him in such case as they were to venture
their lives or else he to lose his; which they did with such
force of mind and body that truly I may justly say, Pyrocles
and Musidorus had never till then found any that could
make them so well repeat their hardest lesson in the feats of
arms. And briefly so they[86] did that, if they overcame not,
yet were they not overcome, but carried away that ungrateful master of theirs to a place of security howsoever the
princes labored to the contrary. But this matter being thus
far begun, it became not the constancy of[87] the princes so to

---

77 suit entourage   **78 settled** steadfast   **79 or could have learned . .**
virtue i.e., if they, Tydeus and Telenor, had not allowed their friendship
with Plexirtus to dominate over their otherwise virtuous impulses
80 But . . . choice i.e., but the circumstances in which they were reared
rather than their own deliberate choosing   **81 indeed crafty enough** he
(Plexirtus) indeed being crafty enough   **82 pay home** i.e., seem thoroughly to justify themselves by the results   **83 held out the course**
stuck to their determination   **84 So as** so that   **85 going out** excur-
sion   **86 they** i.e., Tydeus and Telenor   **87 it became . . . of** it was not
fitting to the knightly resolution and oaths of

leave it; but in all haste making forces both in Pontus and
Phrygia, they had in few days left him[88] but only that one
strong place where he was. For, fear having been the only
knot that had fastened his people unto him, that once un-
tied by a greater force, they all scattered from him like so
many birds whose cage had been broken.

In which season the blind King, having in the chief city of
his realm set the crown upon his son Leonatus' head, with
many tears both of joy and sorrow setting forth to the whole
people his own fault and his son's virtue, after he had
kissed him and forced his son to accept honor of him as of
his new-become subject, even in a moment died, as it should
seem his heart, broken with unkindness and affliction,
stretched so far beyond his[89] limits with this excess of comfort as it was able no longer to keep safe his royal spirits.
But the new king, having no less lovingly performed all duties to him dead than alive, pursued on[90] the siege of his
unnatural brother, as much for the revenge of his father as
for the establishing of his own quiet. In which siege truly I
cannot but acknowledge the prowess of those two brothers,[91] than whom the princes never found in all their travel
two men of greater ability to perform nor of abler skill for
conduct.

But Plexirtus, finding that, if nothing else, famine[92] would
at last bring him to destruction, thought better by humble-
ness to creep where by pride he could not march. For certainly so had nature formed him, and the exercise of craft
conformed him to all turnings of sleights,[93] that though no
man had less goodness in his soul than he, no man could
better find the places[94] whence arguments[95] might grow of
goodness to another; though no man felt less pity, no man
could tell better how to stir pity; no man more impudent to
deny where proofs were not manifest, no man more ready to
confess with a repenting manner of aggravating his own evil
where denial would but make the fault fouler. Now he took
this way that, having gotten a passport[96] for one that pre-

---

88 him i.e., Plexirtus   **89 his** its   **90 pursued on** pursued, carried on
91 two brothers i.e., Tydeus and Telenor   **92 famine** i.e., being starved
out in a siege   **93 turnings of sleights** fashioning of deceitful strata-
gems   **94 places** logical positions or topics   **95 arguments** proofs,
manifestations   **96 passport** i.e., pass through the enemy lines, from the
besieged city to the camp of Leonatus

tended he would put Plexirtus alive into his[97] hands, to
speak with the King his brother, he himself (though much
against the minds of the valiant brothers, who rather
wished to die in brave defense), with a rope about his neck,
barefooted, came to offer himself to the discretion of
Leonatus. Where what submission he used, how cunningly
in making greater the fault he made the faultiness the less,
how artificially he could set out the torments of his own conscience with the burdensome cumber he had found of his
ambitious desires, how finely—seeming to desire nothing but
death, as ashamed[98] to live—he begged life in the refusing
it,[99] I am not cunning enough to be able to express. But so
fell out of it that, though at first sight Leonatus saw him
with no other eye than as the murderer of his father, and
anger already began to paint revenge in many colors, ere
long he had not only gotten pity but pardon, and, if not an
excuse of the fault past, yet an opinion of future amend-
ment; while the poor villains[100] (chief ministers of his
wickedness, now betrayed by the author thereof) were delivered to many cruel sorts of death, he so handling it that it
rather seemed he had rather come into the defense of an
unremediable mischief already committed than that they
had done it at first by his consent.

―――――――――

Text based on *The Countess of Pembroke's Arcadia. Written by Sir Philip Sidney. London: Printed for William Ponsonbie, Anno Domini, 1590.* Book 2,
chapter 10.

97 his i.e., Leonatus's (Plexirtus obtains a passport ostensibly for one
who will turn Plexirtus over to Leonatus, and then uses the passport
himself to go to Leonatus and beg for mercy.) **98 as ashamed** as if he
were ashamed **99 in the refusing it** even as he seemed to be asking for
death **100 the poor villains** the poor wretches, i.e., his chief officers
and allies

Further Reading

Adelman, Janet. ed. *Twentieth Century Interpretations of "King Lear."* Englewood Cliffs, N.J.: Prentice-Hall, 1978. Adelman offers a useful anthology of modern criticism of the play, including commentary by C. L. Barber, L. C. Knights, Kenneth Muir, Phyllis Rackin, and her own valuable introductory essay, as well as interpretations, considered below, by Booth, Bradley, Cavell, Danby, Mack, and Rosenberg.

Alpers, Paul. "*King Lear* and the Theory of the 'Sight Pattern.'" In *In Defense of Reading: A Reader's Approach to Literary Criticism*, ed. Reuben A. Brower and Richard Poirier. New York: E. P. Dutton, 1962. Responding to the critical commonplace that the play's pattern of "sight imagery" traces a movement toward moral insight, Alpers argues that the recurring language of vision is used not metaphorically but literally to suggest human relationships and moral obligations. Eyes are important in *King Lear* because they permit recognition, because they weep, and because in their fragility they reveal the human vulnerability that is preyed upon in the play.

Booth, Stephen. "On the Greatness of *King Lear*." *"King Lear," "Macbeth," Indefinition, and Tragedy*. New Haven, Conn.: Yale Univ. Press, 1983. For Booth the play's "greatness" lies as much in its length onstage as in the depth and power of its artistic vision. *King Lear* forces an audience to experience the play in ways that reflect the characters' experience of events, as a shocking confrontation with cruelty in the face of the persistent promise—and failure—of order and resolution.

Bradley, A. C. "*King Lear*." *Shakespearean Tragedy*, 1904. Rpt., New York: St. Martin's Press, 1985. In a seminal essay, Bradley finds that the play confronts us with the rending image of the destruction of good by evil, a pattern true to the tragic facts of life but balanced by the assertion that adversity purges and purifies. Evil is powerful in the play but it is "*merely* destructive," Bradley says, as the play suggests that life is valuable and must be faced patiently.

Brooke, Nicholas. *Shakespeare: "King Lear."* London: Edward Arnold; Great Neck, N.Y.: Barron's Educational Series, 1963. Brooke's monograph contends that *King Lear* is our culture's bleakest literary experience, resisting all efforts to escape, contain, or compensate the tragic facts it presents. His act-by-act analysis traces the trajectory of Lear's emotional and moral development from arrogance through isolation, suffering, and reconciliation to final defeat.

Cavell, Stanley. "The Avoidance of Love: A Reading of *King Lear.*" *Must We Mean What We Say? A Book of Essays.* New York: Scribner's, 1969. Cavell's richly suggestive essay argues that the play's tragic action is motivated by characters' efforts to evade the threat of exposure and self-revelation. Lear's elaborate ritual in Act 1, Cornwall's blinding of Gloucester, Edgar's disguise and delay in abandoning it, and Lear's renunciation in Act 5 are each modulations of the play's characteristic action: the avoidance of recognition that is for Cavell the essence of the tragic experience.

Colie, Rosalie L., and F. T. Flahiff, eds. *Some Facets of "King Lear": Essays in Prismatic Criticism.* Toronto: Univ. of Toronto Press, 1974. This collection of twelve essays on *King Lear* is designed, as its title suggests, to respond to various aspects of a play that resists any single critical approach. Among the interesting contributions are Bridget Gellert Lyons's study of the subplot "as simplification" of the mystery of Lear's experience; Rosalie Colie's account of the contemporary social tensions articulated by the play; and Sheldon P. Zitner's analysis of language itself as one of *King Lear*'s central thematic concerns.

Danby, John F. *Shakespeare's Doctrine of Nature: A Study of "King Lear."* London: Faber and Faber, 1949. *King Lear*, according to Danby, dramatizes the conflict between opposing concepts of nature: one, articulated by Elizabethans such as Richard Hooker, assumes that nature is orderly, rational, and benign; the other, voiced in the play by Edmund, envisions nature as amoral, aggressive, and unrelated to any providential plan. Danby's intellectual history and his tracing of the theme of nature through the play and through Shakespeare's career discover behind

the play's tragic tension an ultimately Christian view of
the world and society.

Dollimore, Jonathan. "*King Lear* (c. 1605–6) and Essential-
ist Humanism." *Radical Tragedy: Religion, Ideology, and
Power in the Drama of Shakespeare and his Contempo-
raries*. Chicago: Univ. of Chicago Press, 1984. Arguing
against responses to *King Lear* that find the experience of
suffering redemptive, Dollimore believes the play's tragedy stems from the fact that human values (such as pity
or justice) are dependent upon material realities (such as
power and property). Only through his powerlessness
does Lear come to feel the deprivations of others, but,
Dollimore argues, pity born of powerlessness cannot redeem either Lear or his society.

Doran, Madeleine. " 'Give Me the Map There!': Command,
Question, and Assertion in *King Lear*." In *Shakespeare's
Art: Seven Essays*, ed. Milton Crane. Chicago: Univ. of Chicago Press, 1973. Rpt. in *Shakespeare's Dramatic Language*. Madison: Univ. of Wisconsin Press, 1976. Doran
examines the characteristic syntactic patterns of Lear's
speech and explores how the grammatical structures,
like other verbal resources, help create the universe of
the play. She identifies recurring patterns of command,
question, and assertion, and by tracing their modulation
shows how they articulate Lear's moral and emotional
growth to a full though tragic awareness of life's contin-
gencies.

Elton, William R. *"King Lear" and the Gods*. San Marino,
Calif.: Huntington Library, 1966. Challenging optimistic
Christian readings of *King Lear*, Elton explores both the
complex religious climate of Renaissance Europe and the
play's sources and structure. Elton finds in the play a
provocative ambiguity that permits spectators to discover in its grim spectacle either an example of the failure of pagan ethics or an image of the crisis of faith that
marked the late Renaissance.

Empson, William. "Fool in *Lear*." *Sewanee Review* 57
(1949): 177–214. Rpt. in *The Structure of Complex Words*.
New York: New Directions, 1951. In his characteristically
provocative manner, Empson explores the various mean-
ings of the word "fool" in the play. The ambiguities that
surround the word lead Empson to a sense of the play's

horror: Lear makes a fool of himself but in so doing reveals the folly of God and Nature. If there is an effective religious dimension of the play, Empson would locate it in Lear's relation to the tradition of the Holy Fool defined by Erasmus and Thomas More, though it is less for Lear's wisdom than for his endurance that we admire him.

Frye, Northrop. *Fools of Time: Studies in Shakespearean Tragedy*, pp. 103–121. Toronto: Univ. of Toronto Press, 1967. *King Lear*, according to Frye, articulates two versions of tragedy. Gloucester moves through terrible suffering to serenity as the violated moral order is validated and restored. Lear's experience is less explicable: his abdication isolates him from his social context, forcing a radical questioning of identity that ends in anguish and absurdity. The play's ultimate meaning, Frye finds, rests not in what characters learn but in what we learn by participating in their experience.

Goldberg, S. L. *An Essay on "King Lear."* London and New York: Cambridge Univ. Press, 1974. Tracing the developing logic of *King Lear*, Goldberg argues that the play's meaning resides in the unfolding of its poetry and action rather than in any moral or philosophical center. The play confronts both its characters and its audience with contradictory realities that resist any comprehensive and confident judgment of their meaning, affirming only the inescapable world of violence and an irreducible humanity that is vulnerable to it.

Goldman, Michael. "The Worst of *King Lear*." *Shakespeare and the Energies of Drama*. Princeton, N.J.: Princeton Univ. Press, 1972. Goldman explores the play's relentless intensification of suffering and degradation—the succession of savage shocks that demand from characters and audience efforts to make the horror bearable. Goldman shows the failure of these attempts to rationalize and contain the suffering, while he acknowledges their necessity: *King Lear* will not allow us to turn away from its pain, permitting us only the consolation of the discovery of the bond between ourselves and suffering humanity.

Hazlitt, William. "Lear." *Characters of Shakespear's Plays*, 1817. Rpt., London: Oxford Univ. Press, 1966. Hazlitt regards *King Lear* as "the best of all Shakespeare's plays" because of its powerful presentation of the passions that are its subject. *King Lear* balances its sense of the enormity of evil by exciting a desire for the goodness that has been destroyed; but, for Hazlitt, the play's achievement finally resists formulation: "To attempt to give a description of the play itself, of its effects upon the mind, is mere impertinence: yet we must say something."

Heilman, Robert B. *This Great Stage: Image and Structure in "King Lear,"* 1948. Rpt., Seattle: Univ. of Washington Press, 1963. In a book that was the first full-length New Critical study of a Shakespearean play, Heilman explores in detail the iterative language of sight, clothing, sex, and madness. In *King Lear*'s recurring patterns of imagery Heilman discovers its complex tragic awareness of both the reality of evil and the possibilities and value of goodness.

Johnson, Samuel. *"King Lear." Johnson on Shakespeare*, ed. Arthur Sherbo. *The Yale Edition of the Works of Samuel Johnson*, vol. 8. New Haven and London: Yale Univ. Press, 1969. Johnson's justly famous comments on the play defend the double plot as part of its "chief design" and respond to the question of its excessive cruelty. Johnson justifies the behavior of Regan and Goneril as "historical fact" but, approving Tate's revision (see below), he finds the death of Cordelia shocking: "I know not whether I ever endured to read again the last scenes of the play till I undertook to revise them as an editor."

Kott, Jan. "King Lear or Endgame." *Shakespeare Our Contemporary*, trans. Boleslaw Taborski. Garden City, N.Y.: Doubleday, 1964. Kott argues that the play is "grotesque" rather than tragic, since the tragic experience is located in an absurd universe where choice is irrelevant and defeat unavoidable. The play dramatizes the decay of the social order and offers no hope of healing or consolation. Only the Fool, in Kott's view, fully sees the absurdity of the world, and Lear comes finally to share his disillusioned vision.

Mack, Maynard. *"King Lear" in Our Time*. Berkeley and Los Angeles: Univ. of California Press, 1965. Mack, in a brief but influential study, considers *King Lear*'s stage history, its literary and imaginative sources, and its modernity. Mack's analysis reveals that *King Lear* resists the sentimentality either of Christian readings that would transfigure the play's suffering or of the nihilism that finds only imbecility in the play's world. For Mack, Lear's tragic experience agonizingly measures what human beings can both lose and win.

Reibetanz, John. *The "Lear" World: A Study of "King Lear" in Its Dramatic Context*. Toronto: Univ. of Toronto Press, 1977. Examining the relationship of *King Lear* to the dramatic traditions of Jacobean England, Reibetanz explores the dramaturgy of the play, especially how the play is designed to force spectators to confront and respond compassionately to the image of suffering. He discovers the play's unity not in narrative continuity but in emblematic and scenic juxtapositions that gradually reveal the emotional and moral issues of the play.

Rosenberg, Marvin. *The Masks of "King Lear."* Berkeley, Calif.: Univ. of California Press, 1972. Proceeding through the play scene by scene, Rosenberg combines critical analysis and theatrical history to explore the possibilities of meaning presented by the play. By surveying the interpretations of actors, directors, and critics, Rosenberg discovers that only in the theater is the full complexity of the play's design organized and experienced.

Tate, Nahum. *The History of King Lear* (1681), ed. James Black. Lincoln, Neb.: Univ. of Nebraska Press, 1975. Tate's Restoration adaptation of *King Lear* rejects Shakespeare's tragic denouement in favor of a happy ending in which Lear survives and Cordelia lives to marry Edgar. The play's commitment to poetic justice, as virtue is rewarded and vice punished, has been derided, but its theatrical success (keeping Shakespeare's original version off the stage until 1823) reveals something profound both about changes in taste and about the horrific power of Shakespeare's tragic design.

Taylor, Gary, and Michael Warren, eds. *The Division of the Kingdoms: Shakespeare's Two Versions of "King Lear."* Oxford: Clarendon Press; New York: Oxford Univ. Press, 1983. The essays here are devoted to the thesis that the text of *King Lear* in the First Folio of 1623 represents Shakespeare's revision of an earlier design rather than an imperfect version that must be corrected and supplemented by readings from the 1608 quarto. Contributors examine both the bibliographic and critical evidence for the theory that the two texts of *King Lear* are each unified and coherent versions of the play.

Memorable Lines

Nothing will come of nothing. (LEAR 1.1.90)

Fairest Cordelia, that art most rich being poor,
Most choice, forsaken, and most loved, despised . . .
(FRANCE 1.1.254–255)

Thou, Nature, art my goddess. (EDMUND 1.2.1)

Now, gods, stand up for bastards! (EDMUND 1.2.22)

Have more than thou showest,
Speak less than thou knowest,
Lend less than thou owest. (FOOL 1.4.116–118)

Ingratitude, thou marble-hearted fiend . . . (LEAR 1.4.257)

Hear, Nature, hear! Dear goddess, hear!
Suspend thy purpose if thou didst intend
To make this creature fruitful! (LEAR 1.4.274–276)

How sharper than a serpent's tooth it is
To have a thankless child! (LEAR 1.4.287–288)

You see me here, you gods, a poor old man,
As full of grief as age, wretched in both. (LEAR 2.4.274–275)

Blow, winds, and crack your cheeks! Rage, blow!
(LEAR 3.2.1)

Here I stand your slave,
A poor, infirm, weak, and despised old man.
(LEAR 3.2.19–20)

Let the great gods,
That keep this dreadful pother o'er our heads,
Find out their enemies now. (LEAR 3.2.49–51)

                        I am a man
More sinned against than sinning.   (LEAR   3.2.59–60)

The art of our necessities is strange,
And can make vile things precious.   (LEAR   3.2.70–71)

Poor naked wretches, wheresoe'er you are,
That bide the pelting of this pitiless storm,
How shall your houseless heads and unfed sides,
Your looped and windowed raggedness, defend you
From seasons such as these?   (LEAR   3.4.28–32)

                        O, I have ta'en
Too little care of this! Take physic, pomp;
Expose thyself to feel what wretches feel. (LEAR   3.4.32–34)

Is man no more than this?   (LEAR   3.4.101–102)

Unaccommodated man is no more but such a poor, bare,
forked animal as thou art.   (LEAR   3.4.105–107)

'tis a naughty night to swim in.   (FOOL   3.4.109–110)

Child Rowland to the dark tower came.   (EDGAR   3.4.182)

I am tied to the stake, and I must stand the course.
                              (GLOUCESTER   3.7.57)

The lamentable change is from the best;
The worst returns to laughter.   (EDGAR   4.1.5–6)

                   World, world, O world!
But that thy strange mutations make us hate thee,
Life would not yield to age.   (EDGAR   4.1.10–12)

                   Full oft 'tis seen
Our means secure us, and our mere defects
Prove our commodities.   (GLOUCESTER   4.1.19–21)

The worst is not
So long as we can say, "This is the worst."

(EDGAR   4.1.27–28)

As flies to wanton boys are we to the gods;
They kill us for their sport.   (GLOUCESTER   4.1.36–37)

If that the heavens do not their visible spirits
Send quickly down to tame these vile offenses,
It will come,
Humanity must perforce prey on itself,
Like monsters of the deep.   (ALBANY   4.2.47–51)

This shows you are above,
You justicers, that these our nether crimes
So speedily can venge!   (ALBANY   4.2.79–81)

Ay, every inch a king.   (LEAR   4.6.107)

But to the girdle do the gods inherit;
Beneath is all the fiends'.   (LEAR   4.6.126–127)

There thou mightst behold the great image of authority: a
dog's obeyed in office.   (LEAR   4.6.157–159)

When we are born, we cry that we are come
To this great stage of fools.   (LEAR   4.6.182–183)

I am bound
Upon a wheel of fire.   (LEAR   4.7.47–48)

I fear I am not in my perfect mind.   (LEAR   4.7.64)

Men must endure
Their going hence, even as their coming hither;
Ripeness is all.   (EDGAR   5.2.9–11)

and hear poor rogues
Talk of court news; and we'll talk with them too—
Who loses and who wins; who's in, who's out . . .

(LEAR   5.3.13–15)

The gods are just, and of our pleasant vices
Make instruments to plague us.   (EDGAR   5.3.173–174)

The wheel is come full circle.   (EDMUND   5.3.177)

Howl, howl, howl! O, you are men of stones!   (LEAR   5.3.262)

KENT   Is this the promised end?
EDGAR   Or image of that horror?   (5.3.268–269)

                    Her voice was ever soft,
Gentle, and low, an excellent thing in woman.
                              (LEAR   5.3.277–278)

If Fortune brag of two she loved and hated,
One of them we behold.   (KENT   5.3.285–286)

The wonder is he hath endured so long.   (KENT   5.3.322)

Contributors

DAVID BEVINGTON, Phyllis Fay Horton Professor of Humanities at the University of Chicago, is editor of *The Complete Works of Shakespeare* (Scott, Foresman, 1980) and of *Medieval Drama* (Houghton Mifflin, 1975). His latest critical study is *Action Is Eloquence: Shakespeare's Language of Gesture* (Harvard University Press, 1984).

DAVID SCOTT KASTAN, Professor of English and Comparative Literature at Columbia University, is the author of *Shakespeare and the Shapes of Time* (University Press of New England, 1982).

JAMES HAMMERSMITH, Associate Professor of English at Auburn University, has published essays on various facets of Renaissance drama, including literary criticism, textual criticism, and printing history.

ROBERT KEAN TURNER, Professor of English at the University of Wisconsin–Milwaukee, is a general editor of the New Variorum Shakespeare (Modern Language Association of America) and a contributing editor to *The Dramatic Works in the Beaumont and Fletcher Canon* (Cambridge University Press, 1966–).

JAMES SHAPIRO, who coedited the bibliographies with David Scott Kastan, is Assistant Professor of English at Columbia University.

♣

JOSEPH PAPP, one of the most important forces in theater today, is the founder and producer of the New York Shakespeare Festival, America's largest and most prolific theatrical institution. Since 1954 Mr. Papp has produced or directed all but one of Shakespeare's plays—in Central Park, in schools, off and on Broadway, and at the Festival's permanent home, The Public Theater. He has also produced such award-winning plays and musical works as *Hair, A Chorus Line, Plenty,* and *The Mystery of Edwin Drood,* among many others.

THE COMPLETE WORKS IN 29 VOLUMES
Edited, with introductions by David Bevington
•Forewords by Joseph Papp

☑	ANTONY AND CLEOPATRA	21289-3 $2.95	☐	TWELFTH NIGHT	21308-3 $2.75	
☐	AS YOU LIKE IT	21290-7 $2.50	☐	FOUR COMEDIES	21281-8 $4.95	
☐	THE COMEDY OF ERRORS	21291-5 $2.95		*(The Taming of the Shrew, A Midsummer Night's Dream, The Merchant of Venice, and Twelfth Night)*		
☑	HAMLET	21292-3 $2.95	☐	THREE EARLY COMEDIES	21282-6 $4.95	
☐	HENRY IV, PART ONE	21293-1 $2.50		*(Love's Labor's Lost, The Two Gentlemen of Verona, and The Merry Wives of Windsor)*		
☐	HENRY IV, PART TWO	21294-X $2.95				
☐	HENRY V	21295-8 $3.50	☐	FOUR TRAGEDIES	21283-4 $4.95	
☐	JULIUS CAESAR	21296-6 $1.95		*(Hamlet, Othello, King Lear, and Macbeth)*		
☑	KING LEAR	21297-4 $2.95	☐	THREE CLASSICAL TRAGEDIES	21284-2 $4.95	
☑	MACBETH	21298-2 $2.95		*(Titus Andronicus, Timon of Athens, and Coriolanus)*		
☐	THE MERCHANT OF VENICE	21299-0 $2.25				
☑	A MIDSUMMER NIGHT'S DREAM	21300-8 $2.95	☐	HENRY VI, PARTS ONE, TWO, and THREE	21285-0 $4.95	
☐	MUCH ADO ABOUT NOTHING	21301-6 $2.95	☐	KING JOHN and HENRY VIII	21286-9 $4.95	
☑	OTHELLO	21302-4 $3.50	☐	MEASURE FOR MEASURE, ALL'S WELL THAT ENDS WELL, and TROILUS AND CRESSIDA		
☑	RICHARD II	21303-2 $2.50			21287-7 $4.95	
☐	RICHARD III	21304-0 $2.75				
☑	ROMEO AND JULIET	21305-9 $2.95	☐	THE LATE ROMANCES	21288-5 $4.95	
☑	THE TAMING OF THE SHREW	21306-7 $2.50		*(Pericles, Cymbeline, The Winter's Tale, and The Tempest)*		
☑	THE TEMPEST	21307-5 $2.25	☐	THE POEMS	21309-1 $4.95	

Bantam Books, Dept. SH2, 2451 South Wolf Road, Des Plaines, IL 60018

Please send me the items I have checked above. I am enclosing $_____
(please add $2.50 to cover postage and handling). Send check or money
order, no cash or C.O.D.s please.

Mr/Ms _____

Address _____

City/State _____ Zip _____

SH2–3/92

Please allow four to six weeks for delivery.
Prices and availability subject to change without notice.